09.2858 #7-

*Patterns of
Repetition in
Trollope*

Patterns of Repetition in Trollope

Elizabeth R. Epperly

The Catholic University of America Press
Washington, D.C.

Copyright © 1989
The Catholic University of America Press
All rights reserved
Printed in the United States of America

LIBRARY OF CONGRESS CATALOGING-IN-PUBLICATION DATA
Epperly, Elizabeth R.
  Patterns of repetition in Trollope / Elizabeth R. Epperly.
    p. cm.
  Bibliography: p.
  Includes index.
  1. Trollope, Anthony, 1815–1882—Style. 2. Repetition in literature. 3. Allusions. I. Title.
  PR5688.S8E66 1989
  823'.8—dc 19   88-38588
  ISBN 0-8132-0704-5

For Muriel Houston,
friend and colleague

Contents

Acknowledgments	ix
Notes on References	x
Introduction: Anthony Trollope's Allusions and Repetitions	1
1. *Barchester Towers*	14
2. *The Last Chronicle of Barset*	46
3. *He Knew He Was Right*	82
4. *Phineas Redux*	111
5. *The Prime Minister*	142
6. *The Way We Live Now*	170
Conclusion	206
Notes	209
Works Cited	221
Index	229

Acknowledgments

My thanks to these libraries and their librarians: the Bodleian Library, Oxford University; the British Library; the Folger Shakespeare Library, Washington, D.C.; the London Library; Queen Elizabeth II Library, Memorial University of Newfoundland; Robertson Library, University of Prince Edward Island; Sterling Library, University of London.

My special thanks to my graduate students in English 6064 (Trollope, Meredith, and Hardy) at Memorial University of Newfoundland for many stimulating discussions.

My gratitude also goes to the Social Sciences and Humanities Research Council of Canada for funding and for time to complete parts of this study.

My personal thanks to Frances M. Frazer for introducing me to Trollope's writing and for inspiring me to pursue my interest in it; to N. John Hall for his invaluable scholarship and for many delightful conversations about Trollope; to David J. McGonagle, Director of The Catholic University of America Press, for his patient guidance; to Susan Thornton, copy editor for the manuscript, for her cheerful, meticulous comments (any errors that remain are mine).

Notes on References

I have followed, when possible, the Oxford Crown and World's Classics Editions. The quotations are identified in the text by chapter numbers for the novels and *An Autobiography*. Trollope's letters (following N. John Hall's two-volume 1983 edition) are cited as *Letters*. For contemporary reviews I have relied on Donald Smalley's collection, citing the original reference, "Smalley," and the page number of his *Anthony Trollope: The Critical Heritage*.

*Patterns of
Repetition in
Trollope*

Introduction: Anthony Trollope's Allusions and Repetitions

In forty-seven novels, scores of short stories, half a dozen travel histories, three biographies, volumes of essays, and hundreds of letters, Anthony Trollope strove for readability, clarity, and shrewd accuracy. He trained himself, as his *Autobiography* explains, to write rapidly and precisely, and he tested his own sentences with an ear tuned to the cadences of the best of English and Latin literature, which he read and annotated throughout his life. Literary criticism in recent years has acknowledged readily Trollope's skill and artistry (though Trollope's reputation as a whole will probably continue to wax and wane as the critical fashions themselves change). One of the major organizing principles of writing that has been largely ignored, despite the growing volume of criticism, is directly related to both the rapidity and the clarity of his writing and to his sensitive perceptions of literature and language. Trollope became a master of repetition.

Perhaps from his reading and certainly from his creation of scores of characters and stories, Trollope learned to use repetitions ingeniously; through repetition he shared with his readers an accessible and sophisticated shorthand. By repeating literary allusions, clichés, speech tags, intra- (as well as inter-) textual echoes, and thematic parallels, the narrator and characters invite the reader's (participating) evaluations of ironic interplay between emotions and ideas.

Trollope's apparently simple method proved marvelously flexible: a novel is shaped through certain organizing (repeated) themes or ideas; aspects of these themes or principles are espoused by different characters; most characters are identified by or associated with certain expressions or quality of expression; the narrator sometimes creates patterns of expressions that are then echoed by the characters or sometimes the narrator echoes what the characters themselves have said; some characters echo expressions or quality of expressions used by other characters (thus underscoring ironically similar or dissimilar circumstances or thinking); the narrator comments on the characters, often blurring the distinctions between his own commentary and the characters' thoughts, by imitating or echoing the characters' own allusions or associative phrases or internal rhythms. The resulting repetitions between characters and between characters and narrator suggest powerful interconnections between apparently dissimilar situations, characters (and voices), or themes. Repetition is the key to Trollope's polyphonous unity; the repeated allusions, clichés, and tags are the markers within as well as the substance of large, resonant texts.

When we trace them, we find that simple repetitions are complex echoes. As J. Hillis Miller says, "Any novel is a complex tissue of repetitions and of repetitions within repetitions."[1] Trollope's repetitions involve many clichés and tags and numerous common literary allusions; their very familiarity makes them charming and potent. The choices of allusions and stock expressions are as deliberate and considered as is the style of which they create so important a part. Trollope's apparently effortless, supposedly featureless style is really a delightful paradox: he orchestrates an intricate simplicity. Eschewing elaborate metaphor or complex syntactical variations, he forms straightforward sentences charged with highly distinctive, ingenious repetitions of the familiar and ordinary. To mistake Trollope's repetitions or allusions for hasty notations or even for spontaneous overflow of feelings is to miss the masterly understatement of his control. Trollope's apparent ease was the product of years of rigorous training; the resulting portraits and parallels reveal—repeatedly—a conscious artistry.

Let us look at the quality of allusions and expressions Trollope chose and the way he involved his readers with them. Trollope could have learned the art of allusion, if not of repetition generally, from any number of great Victorians—Charlotte Brontë, Dickens, Thackeray, George Eliot[2]—or from a long history of early English or European novelists.³ He was himself an indefatigable reader and had a well-stocked memory. He spent long hours daily, even in his late career, reading classical and modern literature. Studies of his library suggest the scope of his reading,⁴ as do his early projects of A History of World Literature and A History of English Prose Fiction,⁵ his commonplace book,⁶ his record of reading aloud to his family,⁷ and his lively annotations of more than two hundred and seventy Elizabethan and Jacobean plays.⁸

Clearly Trollope had much to draw on by way of source and example⁹ to create the many literary allusions in his own forty-seven novels. And yet we find that despite Trollope's classical learning and despite his varied (and probably deep) reading, the literary allusions in his novels usually are easy to recognize and are from familiar sources. John W. Clark devotes a chapter to cataloguing Trollope's allusions, quotations, and echoes, showing that Trollope alludes most to Shakespeare and the Bible even though he does also use less well known works from writers such as Wither and Sir Henry Taylor.¹⁰ Even Trollope's use of Latin proverbs and literature would not have been obscure to an audience reared in the public school system or familiar with parliamentary practice.¹¹ Trollope evidently wanted his works to be accessible to a wide audience, feeling of his allusions, what Carmela Perri says of allusion in general: the fully activated ones involve purposeful "recognizing, remembering, realizing, connecting."¹²

But all readers will not respond in the same way to literary allusions no matter how easy they may be to identify. (I am using the term *literary allusion* to include covert and overt references, quotations, and recognizable echoes, following Ziva Ben-Porat's definition: "The literary allusion is a device for the simultaneous activation of two texts."¹³) Some readers will not recognize the allusions, but, as Michael Wheeler explains, ". . . allusions in Victorian novels can at once have important functions, noticed by those who recognise them, and yet ignored if they are not recognised, because they themselves are dependent for their effects upon their relationship to the main thematic or plot line of the novel, which can be followed without paying attention to the allusions."[14] Others will identify the allusions merely as literary or as extraneous to the novel; some will make surface identifications only—recognizing the referent text but stopping short of further comparisons; some will explore the full parallels and ironies of the literary allusion to create multiple intertextual patterns that enrich both the referent and alluding texts.[15]

Some of Trollope's central allusions promote the creation of rich intertextual patterns. For example, Louis Trevelyan's identifications with Othello and Lear make his jealousy and madness almost tragic in *He Knew He Was Right*. The power of Shakespeare invigorates the story of Trevelyan, but even these important Shakespearean allusions must find their complete significance in the novel's larger patterns and repetitions; Trevelyan's tragedy must be understood to unfold against the melodrama and farce of several minor characters. Our understanding of Trevelyan is thus shaped by the interweaving and repetition of numerous patterns. We learn most about Trollope's characters from a cumulative involvement with allusions, clichés, and tags[16] rather than from the isolated impact of single allusions (though some of them are splendid). The progression of details is elemental to Trollope's style (even in a work so densely allusive as *Barchester Towers*). He may use the melancholy music of a flute to symbolize Sir Thomas Underwood's failure with his biography of Bacon (*Ralph the Heir*) or suggest the serious frolicsomeness of Lady George's character (*Is He Popenjoy?*) through her reading of *Aurora Leigh* and her games of bagatelle, but we understand these characters because of pages of details and repetitions of details, not solely because of Bacon or Mrs. Browning, effective though use of them may be.

The recurring patterns support what William West describes as Trollope's pervasive tone: "If his style is even, untroubled for the most part by either metaphor or passion, and, being even, implicitly reassuring, it is also, more importantly, always warm, humane, kindly. It is difficult to discuss what one means by a sympathetic tone in specific terms, because it is impossible

Introduction 5

to cite any single passage to represent it. But the longer one listens to Trollope tell his story, the more reassured one is by the tone. The sympathy of the author for his characters accumulates like a subliminal aura of warmth and light."[17] This subliminal accumulation determines the reader's gradual and progressive involvement with the characters and the parallels the novels reveal.

There are so many inter- and intratextual patterns at play in the accumulation of details in Trollope's novels that the interpreter of Trollope is embarrassed by riches. When we have in mind Roland Barthes's definition of intertext, we can appreciate even more fully the position of Trollope's allusions and repetitions in the already elaborate coding of any novel:

> Every text is an intertext; other texts are present in it, at variable levels, in more or less recognizable forms: the texts of the previous culture and those of the surrounding culture; every text is a new fabric woven out of bygone quotations. Scraps of code, formulas, rhythmic patterns, fragments of social idioms, etc. are absorbed into the text and redistributed in it, for there is always language prior to the text and language around it. A prerequisite for any text, intertextuality cannot be reduced to a problem of sources and influences; it is a general field of anonymous formulas whose origin is seldom identifiable, of unconscious or automatic quotations given without quotation marks.[18]

Trollope's allusions and repeated tags, clichés, and metaphors are clear, welcome markers in the necessarily unpredictable patterns[19] of intertextuality.

Often Trollope repeats one expression or allusion or image to compare the activities of many characters on many levels. Even in his one overembellished novel, *The Three Clerks*, the flower imagery, Biblical undertones, and classical ornamentation are all subordinated to the narrator's and characters' uses of *excelsior*. The novel is a lengthy exploration of the way each of the three young clerks interprets his own goal, usually identified by the word *excelsior*. The work has some worth because of the way the stories illuminate each other within this framework. The key word *excelsior*, even when crowded by a jumble of literary allusions, still has the power to unify the numerous

6   Introduction

parts of what Sadleir mistakenly called a "formless and flaccid"[20] whole.

Even an astute critic like Ruth apRoberts dismisses the repetitions thus:

> Many of his images are repeated so often, and are so commonplace anyway—I would add—that they simply do not function as images; the world is one's oyster, the beautiful woman is the candle that singes the moth's wings, people row in the same boat, and so on. I might further add that this is a way Chaucer also had, in his stories—to draw on the common stock of conventional figures of speech. Such images are hardly what we are used to call poetic, as all they do is maintain an air of comfortable ordinariness between teller and reader.[21]

Juliet McMaster suggests, on the other hand, that these worn images are revitalized by repetition in various parts of a novel. She shows that in *The Small House at Allington* the image of the dying moth is reproduced to comment on each of the major characters' fatal attraction to the desirable and unattainable.[22] The expressions, allusions, or images lose their triteness in the way Trollope introduces them into the narrative. A repeated image or expression becomes powerful first because it defines a situation or conflict, and second because the expression or image itself becomes emblematic of various situations and conflicts. Trollope did not create patterns of intense imagery as did George Eliot or Dickens, but gradually and insistently infused new life into worn expressions. (Thus Trollope chooses to emblematize and the expressions then serve as rich "allusion markers" in the text.[23])

The significant repetitions, occurring within a few pages or over an entire novel, may come from the narrator, one or more characters, the narrator and a character, or a combination of the narrator and character in what appears to be internal monologue. In the chapters that follow I illustrate all of these types, but here let us look at two examples. First, in *Phineas Finn* the same cliché[24]—"reaching for the top brick of the chimney"—is used twice within two pages, once by a character and once by the narrator-author, to comment on the similarities of four characters' predicaments. Lady Laura accuses Phineas of immaturity and fickleness when he insists on pursuing Violet Effingham: "'There are moments in which we try to give a child any brick on the chimney top for which it may whimper'" (LVI). It is ironic that Lady Laura taunts Phineas thus since it is her own love for him that makes her resent his hopeless love for Violet. The very next chapter following their interview is entitled "The Top Brick of the Chimney," this time referring to the old Duke of Omnium's "passion" for Madame Max Goesler. The irony of the expression for Madame Max is that she bears a love for Phineas that is, at this time, as hopeless as the duke's for her, or Phineas's for Violet, or Lady Laura's for Phineas. The cliché is revitalized by Trollope's ironic repetition; the commonness of the expression understates the characters' pain, and yet that commonness also sustains the "subliminal aura of warmth and light" by uniting the characters' interpretations of themselves with the narrator's collective assessment of them. Trollope does not dismiss their difficulties in a comforting formula, but he does allow to the reader a kindly and ironic view of their joint misery when he associates them equally with a stock expression. The power and significance of repetition here come from the fact that we experience it from two different perspectives—the characters' and the narrator's. In the dialogue "the top brick of the chimney" is used as an accusation; by the narrator it is used as an emblem of four characters' similar struggles. The reader relates to it by adopting the narrator's broader view of human frailties and machinations.

Second, let us look at an example of the combined use of commentary, allusion, and cliché in what amounts to a confusion between the narrator's voice and a character's internal monologue.[25] In *Phineas Finn* Trollope uses an expression from dialogue to initiate the narrator's collective pronouncement on the characters; in his other good novels he also uses allusions and clichés to give continuity to the narrator's and characters' analyses. Often it is difficult to tell who is thinking or speaking—the narrator or the character. The following passage gives Lady Mason's reaction to her confession of fraud in *Orley Farm*:

8   Introduction

And then she went, and as she slowly made her way across the hall she felt that all of evil, all of punishment that she had ever anticipated, had now fallen upon her. There are periods in the lives of some of us—I trust but of few—when, with the silent inner voice of suffering, we call on the mountains to fall and crush us, and on the earth to gape open and take us in. When, with an agony of intensity, we wish that our mothers had been barren. In those moments the poorest and most desolate are objects to us of envy, for their sufferings can be as nothing to our own. Lady Mason, as she crept silently across the hall, saw a servant girl pass down towards the entrance to the kitchen, and would have given all, all that she had in the world, to have changed places with that girl. But no change was possible for her. Neither would the mountains crush her, nor would the earth take her in. There was her burden, and she must bear it to the end. There was the bed which she had made for herself, and she must lie upon it. No escape was possible to her. She had herself mixed the cup, and she must now drink of it to the dregs (XLV).

Here we find a repeated allusion to Marlowe coupled with three clichés. The combination encourages close assessment of Lady Mason's depth. Bradford Booth identifies "we call on the mountains to fall and crush us, and on the earth to gape open and take us in" with these lines from Marlowe's *Faustus*:

> Mountaines and hilles, come, come and fall on me,
> And hide me from heavy wrath of God.
> No, no.
> Then wil I headlong runne into the earth:
> Earth gape. Ono, it wil not harbour me.[26]

The first part of the paragraph approaches the intensity of Faustus's impassioned speech, but the tone changes as the point of view shifts between the narrator and Lady Mason. The philosophical (though perhaps ironic) dignity of the statement "In these moments the poorest and most desolate are objects to us of envy, for their suffering can be as nothing to our own" is humbled by its immediate translation to (what appears to be) Lady Mason's thoughts. The "poorest and most desolate" becomes a prosaic servant girl. The appeal to universal suffering is reduced to the clichés of "bearing one's burden to the end," "making one's bed and lying on it," and "mixing a cup and drinking it to the dregs." The clichés may not be Lady Mason's literal thoughts, but the sense and quality of them approximate what we are encouraged to believe is her kind of reflection. We judge her as an ordinary woman because her thoughts can be defined in such simple, homely expressions, and yet we appreciate her singularity because of the subtle strength of the oblique allusion to Marlowe. Where, precisely, is the narrator transcribing and where is he interpreting? Clearly the reader feels the need to investigate Lady Mason's thoughts more closely.

Because the reader senses that the voices of the narrator and the character are combined in the internal monologues, one can relate to a character's impassioned eloquence the same way one does to the narrator's alternations of sympathy and irony. The effectiveness of the allusions then depends not on individual impact but on the implications of their collective association with the character and situation. And whether or not the reader knows the references to Marlowe in the passage from *Orley Farm*, one will probably see that Lady Mason now feels the full impact of her two acts of self-destruction: forging the will and confessing to Sir Peregrine. Her abasement is complete.

If one does recognize the allusion to *Faustus*, one will see how richly ironic is Trollope's comparison of the sin and suffering of the two characters: society would see that Lady Mason sold her integrity for the wealth and comfort of Orley Farm, just as Faustus sold his soul for the riches of knowledge and power. But the reader must also see that Lady Mason did not sell herself for her own gain—she sacrificed peace of mind and freedom of spirit for her son, Lucius, that he might grow up with dignity. The comparison of the two cases, as is so often true with Trollope, removes moral absolutes: is Lady Mason so wrong to have protected her only child from her cruel husband by altering his will? Other possible intertextual patterns similarly enrich the story of Lady Mason's double trial (compare, for instance, Faustus's vision of Helen with Lady Mason's temptation to marry Sir Peregrine Orme).

Most of Trollope's allusions are easier to identify than this one to Marlowe, but they operate in the same way, and the reader is given the same freedom (true of all allusions) of surface or deep reading. But Trollope's allusions and the accompanying clichés or tags do reward further thought. How can we fully appreciate Mr. Crawley's pathos and humor if we do not know or bother to read "Samson Agonistes" or *Seven Against Thebes*? How can we know the depth of Phineas's pain or the extent of his foolishness if we cannot understand his and the narrator's reactions to Mrs. Browning's "A Musical Instrument"? Can we really know Lizzie Eustace's duplicity without contemplating her ignorant distortions of Byron and Shelley and her kinship with Becky Sharp?

On the surface, without interpreting the significance of the individual allusions and repetitions, we can handily categorize Crawley as a misunderstood scholar, and Phineas's thoughts as extreme and nearly poetic, and Lizzie Eustace's entanglements as misguided romanticism or wilful deceit. But recognizing and responding to the various patterns of language, we try to assess Crawley in the light of tragedy, and Phineas in the position of transformed poet, and Lizzie in relation to Conrad's faithfulness or to life's Vanity Fair. This second level of interpretation is what gives irony and depth to Thackeray's use of Iachimo in *Vanity Fair*, George Eliot's reference to *The Lyrical Ballads* in *Adam Bede*, Tolstoy's allusion to *The Lives of the Saints* in *War and Peace*, Charlotte Brontë's inclusion of *Rasselas* in *Jane Eyre*, Hardy's persistent use of Shelley,[27] or Virginia Woolf's repetition of lines from *Cymbeline* in *Mrs. Dalloway*.[28] Trollope's technique differs from these novelists' in the way he invites his readers to respond to the intertextuality of his works. His narrative pace, familiar expressions, casual language, repetitions of ideas and phrases, and overall pervasion of "warmth and light" together seem to relieve the reader of the responsibility of assimilating and analyzing the complexities his works actually reveal.

The effortlessness of reading and understanding the novels is only partly an illusion, for ironically, complete involvement with Trollope's tone and pace lessens the difficulties of analysis. Whether or not we wrestle with their implications, the classics

Introduction   11

are a fixed part of Crawley, as "A Musical Instrument" is with Phineas, or Byron, Shelley, or Thackeray are with Lizzie Eustace. As E. E. Kellett says aptly in his early study of allusions: ". . . the best allusions will be those which lie beneath the surface: those that do not give the reader the sense that his author is always quoting, or that he depends upon others, but which whisper to him, almost inaudibly, that the allusions are the natural overflow of a rich and well-stored mind. . . ."[29]

Trollope used allusions, clichés, and familiar tags throughout his writing career. John W. Clark introduces his lengthy, useful chapter on "Trollope's Reading" as follows:

> A striking feature of Trollope's style is the multitude of literary allusions, quotations, and echoes, of which there are, I think, proportionately (and perhaps, considering his output, absolutely) more in his novels than in those of Dickens or Thackeray or Meredith. Unquestionably Trollope read a great deal, he remembered (*verbatim* as well as in substance) much of what he had read, and he seems to have been spontaneously reminded of his reading as he wrote his novels and often as it were irresistibly driven to reflect his reading in his writing.[30]

In the following chapters, I challenge Clark's characterization "spontaneously reminded of his reading." For Trollope to have repeated so many allusions and clichés and to have made the studies of character successful and the stories interesting he could not have simply "spontaneously" reflected his reading in his writing. The fact that a careful scholar can call a prominent feature of Trollope's style "spontaneous" suggests that Trollope's methods are still often underestimated or misunderstood.

In the following pages I will explain the importance of the narrator's and characters' repeated allusions, clichés, and tags in six of Trollope's major novels: *Barchester Towers, The Last Chronicle of Barset, He Knew He Was Right, Phineas Redux, The Prime Minister,* and *The Way We Live Now.* These novels are representative of Trollope's scope and abilities and suggest the different stages of his writing career. In them is the best of his clerical, political, and social commentary. In all six the patterns in expression and situation outline and emphasize theme, while both the patterns and themes are embodied in the characters themselves. It is interesting to see how these patterns develop within a series of novels in which the same characters reappear. The six Barsetshire novels find expression through Septimus Harding and Josiah Crawley. Harding manifests the quiet faith of the established church, and Crawley, whose painful intellectualism suggests the darker side of Barsetshire life, acts as a foil for him. The two minds together present Trollope's rational humanitarianism. In the political novels Phineas Finn and Plantagenet Palliser complement (and later parallel) each other. Phineas's buoyancy and Palliser's moroseness together reveal Trollope's belief in sensitive, honest politicians. In each of Trollope's novels, and therefore in the independent novels I use in this study to represent the work apart from the series, this interplay of opposites is sharply defined. The whole of *He Knew He Was Right* depends on the quality of contrast between tragedy and comedy; *The Way We Live Now* depends on a complex tension between comedy and satire. The repeated patterns of language offer keys to the narratives.

I have grouped these novels together, out of their chronological order, for two reasons: first so that those from the series could be studied together, and second so that the two independent novels would be seen as extensions and refinements of the two series. Much of the atmosphere of *He Knew He Was Right* is in keeping with the rural calm of the Barsetshire novels; *The Way We Live Now* seems a distortion of the London viewed in the political works. The characters in the two separate novels share some of the attributes of the prominent characters in the series. Josiah Crawley and Louis Trevelyan resemble one another; Lopez and Melmotte are unmistakably similar.

A study such as this, necessarily limited to six good and representative works, naturally invites similar scrutiny of other fine Trollope novels. I hope other readers will join me in examining the books in the spirit David Lodge describes in his second edition of *The Language of Fiction*: ". . . what seems to me now to be the task of the novel critic is not to reduce everything to questions of style or rhetoric, but to unravel the relationship of the rhetorical code to all the other codes in the novel."[31] Trollope's repetitions offer one fruitful way to decode his protean perceptions of character, society, and art.

1
Barchester Towers

Anthony Trollope completed his writing apprenticeship with his fourth novel, *The Warden*, in 1855. His first three novels (*The Macdermots of Ballycloran* [1847], *The Kellys and the O'Kellys* [1848], *La Vendée* [1850]), a series of letters to the *Examiner*,[1] and a play called *The Noble Jilt*[2] made little impression (perhaps rightly[3]) on the reading public, and so the mild success of *The Warden* was a pleasant surprise. With a fifth novel, *Barchester Towers* (1857), he came fully into his own, and the exuberance of its style suggests his enthusiasm.

If we marked in red ink the allusions, clichés, tags, and general repetitions found in *Barchester Towers*, our copy would resemble the red-letter prayer-book Mrs. Proudie thought iniquitous. There are more tags and references, more extensive use of literature and repetitions in this novel than in any of Trollope's other works. Capitalizing on the style and voice of the moderately successful *The Warden*, Trollope creates in *Barchester Towers* a comic, echoing medley made from cliché and proverb and from Shakespeare, the Bible, Scott, Thackeray, Cooper, Byron, Thomas Tusser, Milton, Sterne, Goldsmith, Henry Taylor, Goethe, Dickens, Fielding, and the classics.

Like its predecessor *The Warden* and all the good novels to follow, *Barchester Towers* is more apparently concerned with character development than social issues, even though there are distinct lessons to be learned about life in general from the important characters' reactions to the society around and to individual moral dilemmas. In fact, the clerical disputes seem excuses to follow the careers of characters Trollope had so happily created in *The Warden*. Trollope had not taken a stand on the Whiston Matter[4] when he described Hiram's Hospital in *The Warden*,[5] and he was certainly uninterested in reviving the religious controversies of the Oxford Movement in *Barchester*

Towers.⁶ Instead, the clerical controversies are but one part of a highly complex comedy; *Barchester Towers*, as Robert Daniel says, is in the tradition of English comedy,⁷ and Trollope's narrator deflates most of the philosophical issues in an exuberant exhibition of stagecraft and mock-heroic (or merely exaggerated) embellishments.

The structure of the novel is itself playful. The characters are initially introduced as partisans in a war for clerical supremacy; the battle imagery and the mock-heroic quality of the narrator's frequent asides suggest that the entire novel will be made up of campaigns and stratagems. Then the love intrigues add another dimension to the controversy, and suggest, particularly in the Ullathorne Sports chapters, that the novel is more a protracted melodrama than a comic *Iliad*. The main characters, still identified by their Oxford labels, become more involved in Eleanor's love than in the Barchester War. And then we find that neither the war nor the romance nor the melodrama as a whole is the object of the narrator's focus.

When the love story disentangles itself and the battles over the wardenship cease, it is obvious that the core of the novel is not found in the struggle for power nor in the romance, but in the quiet ascendancy of Septimus Harding and in his response to the questions that perplex him.⁸ The whole of *Barchester Towers* operates on a kind of joyous irony. Since nothing is quite what it seems to be, we can enjoy first this and then that in the narrator's humor, as we effortlessly sort out what is of lasting and what is of passing importance in the (Barchester) world. Harding, practically alone amid so many self-absorbed or self-deluding characters, is troubled by the fundamental questions of life: What is good? What am I meant to do? What should change? What should remain the same? In the form of Slope and the arguments of the rubbish cart, Harding faces the mid-Victorian questions posed by Benthamism, by later utilitarianism, and by the Oxford Movement itself. Harding, the most apparently vulnerable and noncombative of the Barchester clergymen, finds answers—in his own humble faith—to the harrying questions that the novel's numerous comic devices expose and exploit. Thus nothing can be what it seems to be at first; we are led to suppose, along with the people of Barchester, that the real controversy will be over who will be bishop, but war fizzles out. We are led to feel that romance may be the focus of sympathetic attention, but Eleanor and Arabin are frequently foolish or irritatingly clumsy. We think, perhaps, the novel is really about the good old days and our need to preserve them, but Harding sees and knows that the Deanery—a traditional stronghold of the traditional church—should go to a younger, more energetic man, and even Monica Thorne dimly perceives the need to adapt to the times. At every turn the narrator uses comic scene and ironic allusion to share with the reader a healthy perception of the difference between enduring and apparent truths. After all the hoopla of expected battle and projected love intrigue, we welcome Septimus Harding's quietly insistent affirmation of life as the moral center of the narrator's comic whorl.

The narrator is the most vocal character in and is the director of the *Barchester Towers* comedy. To appreciate the novel's ironies, and Harding's singular position among them, one must explore the narrator's voice and control. The narrator is responsible not only for creating many of the patterns of allusions, clichés, and tags but also for repeating them—sometimes slightly altered—with different characters and in different situations. Effectively comic and exaggerated as the language may be the first time, potential for comedy is amplified by repetition (or echo) either in similar or in strikingly dissimilar circumstances. For example, the reader will recall, compare, and assess the narrator's use of Medea to characterize first the desperate but ample-hearted Mrs. Quiverful and later the enraged warrior Mrs. Proudie. The fact that the two women are leagued together makes the shared—but very different—use of Medea effective.

The narrator not only creates patterns and repeats them but also occasionally and deliberately blurs the lines between his fanciful creation of patterns and a character's own internal monologue. (I have referred to this blurring in the Introduction with the discussion of Lady Mason's thoughts about her confession.) We are not always sure whether we are reading a piece of the narrator's purely comic interpretation of the character's thought or whether the character does occasionally think the very thoughts transcribed or whether the quality of thought of the character has been represented by the allusions and clichés the narrator repeats. The blurring is intensified when certain clichés or allusions supposedly offered fancifully by the narrator are later actually spoken by the character. As Trollope's career developed there were fewer and fewer purely comic blurrings (though there are numerous somber and ironic ones), but in *Barchester Towers* they contribute substantially to the creation of an almost uniformly comic mode for the story. Many of the characters and the narrator seem to conspire to augment the boisterous comedy of thwarted power and frustrated intrigue.

So far I have argued that the whole structure of *Barchester Towers* is ironic, that Septimus Harding is a part of the ironies but is also apart from them, that the narrator directs and controls the comedy by creating and repeating certain comic patterns and formulas, and that the uniform tone of the novel is sustained by a blurring of the narrator's voice with internal monologue supposedly representative of the character's thoughts. In order to explore these aspects of the narrator's control and his treatment of Harding, we should consider the patterns created and repeated in the book by the narrator-character.

The narrator uses cliché and Latin and French tags and borrows extensively from literature—most often from drama and the Bible and the classics, but also from Scott, Fielding, Sterne, and Thackeray. The characters themselves (apart from Harding) also borrow from and use these same resources or are associated in the reader's mind with certain borrowings the narrator has used to describe them. (In Trollope's later novels it is the characters themselves who usually use the borrowings.) In *Barchester Towers* the playful narrator prepares the reader for the novel's allusive richness and for the similarities between narrator and characters.

Look at a tiny sample of the narrator's language and preoccupations. He summarizes ambition in the tag "'last infirmity of noble minds!'" (I); says of the daily press "'Cassandra was not believed'" (II); speaks of clergymen as "'the bore of the age, the old man whom we Sindbads cannot shake off'" (VI); warns Slope of his danger with the old lines[9] "It's gude to be off with the auld luve / Before ye be on wi' the new" (XXVII); or echoes Milton playfully when describing the Ullathorne difficulties of "pandemonium" and "false Cerberus" (XXXIX). Dozens of similarly playful remarks work in concert with large and small patterns to enrich the reader's appreciation of characters and their interactions.

Even the many French and Latin phrases, though they often seem more ornamental than functional, help to establish connections and patterns structurally and linguistically. In fact, within the context of the whole book, the French and Latin expressions make an ironic extension of the Ullathorne Sports satire; the French words recall the detested Normans; the Latin, the old church establishment. There are more French words in this novel than in any of Trollope's others—perhaps he was remembering his abortive *La Vendée*—and a fair sprinkling of Latin (though we find the Latin tags put to better use in *The Last Chronicle of Barset, The Prime Minister,* and *The Way We Live Now*).

There are some repetitions between narrator and character, but the narrator has the greater number of distinctive language features generally. Some of the French words and phrases, apart from such anglicized borrowings as *élite* or *protégé,* are *carte du pays* (VI), *ci-devant* (XI), *de trop* (XVI), *coup de main* (XXXIV), *dénouements* (XXXIV), *déjeuner* (XXXVI), *cortège* (XXXVI), *désoeuvré* (XLII), *chef d'oeuvre* (XLV), *décolleté* (XLV), *soupçon* (twice XXVII, XLV), *fait accompli* (XLVII), *congé* (L), *couleur de rose* (LI), *mêlée* (LII). Trollope could easily have used English words, but the French reminds us of Grantly's secret copy of Rabelais, extends the satire in the observation early in the book on how politicians really spend their time (rather than "preparing his thunder for successful rivals," the former minister ". . . was sitting easily in a lounging chair, conning over a Newmarket list, and by his elbow on the table was lying open an uncut French novel on which he was engaged" [I]), and suggests the playfulness and artificiality of the novel form. It is no accident that Miss Thorne's Sports are *fête champêtre*.

The narrator uses fewer Latin words than French, but they, too, find echoes with the characters: *rarae aves* (III), *Labor omnia vincit improbus* (XX), *particeps criminis* (XXVIII), *Deus ex machina* (XXXIV), *status quo* (XXXIV), *quid pro quo* (XXXVI), *detur digniori* (XLIII), *nil admirari* (L). The expression *nolo episcopari* (I do not wish to be made a bishop) is particularly interesting since it encapsulates much of the novel's good-humored satire of ecclesiastical struggles for power: "the *nolo episcopari*, though still in use, is so directly at variance with the tendency of all human wishes that it cannot be thought to express the true aspirations of rising priests in the Church of England" (1). In an aside, the narrator despairs of the bishop's thralldom: "Oh, my aspiring pastors, divines to whose ears *nolo episcopari* are the sweetest of words, which of you would be a bishop on such terms as these?" (XXVI).

We feel the control of the narrator-character whether he is alluding to Disraeli—"the family of Sidonia" (XIX)—or to Dickens—the bishop "read the last number of the 'Little Dorrit' of the day" (XLIII)—or to the "melodrame" within his own novel—the Stanhopes conclude "this little family comedy" (XLII). Besides the interweaving of small patterns—created from references to a variety of literary works—there are several larger repeated patterns that the narrator invites us to enjoy. The most encompassing of these comes from drama. *Barchester Towers* is full of references to drama, but also as a whole exploits techniques of stagecraft. Two large, complementary parts of the novel, the Proudie Reception and the chapters of Ullathorne Sports, are dependent on stagecraft for their full comic effect. And many of the novel's important interchanges also hinge on the narrator's creation of scenes.

In a novel about clergymen and especially about stern Evangelicals against High and High and Dry churchmen, it is ironic and therefore appropriate that Trollope should choose to use techniques of drama.[10] He had already tried his hand at writing a play and he had read some thirty-five Beaumont and Fletcher plays while he was writing *The Warden*.[11] Since Trollope's devotion to drama was lifelong, we would expect to find his most heavily allusive and fanciful novel[12] filled with stagecraft. And this is the case. The most memorable parts of the novel are scenes, and the narrator and other characters make frequent satiric references to the conventions of the theatre. Doctor Proudie is called a "play Bishop," and at the close of the novel when the cheerfully ironic narrator tells us (mischievously alluding to the conclusion of *Vanity Fair*) that the end of the story must be like a children's party, we are reminded of the quality of "play" with the various puppets of the performance. Doctor Gwynne is even referred to as the wished-for "*Deus ex machina* who was to come down upon the Barchester stage, and bring about deliverance from these terrible evils" (xxxiv).

One of the most celebrated scenes of the novel takes place at Mrs. Proudie's reception; Bertie's accidental rending of Mrs. Proudie's dress is a perfect example of Trollope's use of stagecraft. The scene is pure farce. We are attached intimately to none of the characters—neither Madeline, nor Bertie, nor Mrs. Proudie—and it is time Mrs. Proudie had a set-down before the Barchester community as a whole. Who better to administer the dose to Mrs. Proudie than the children of the Italianized Dr. Stanhope, whom Mr. Slope and Mrs. Proudie together have recalled to Barchester to assist in putting down the Grantly and High and Dry faction? Mrs. Proudie demands her lace train from the kneeling Bertie (the wheel of Madeline's sofa having caught in and ripped apart the train from Mrs. Proudie's dress). With as much dignity as the tragic Druid warrior queen Bonduca in one of Trollope's collections of Beaumont and Fletcher,[13] Mrs. Proudie booms, "'Unhand it, Sir!'" and Trollope slyly remarks, "From what scrap of dramatic poetry she had extracted the word cannot be said; . . ." (xi). The mishap has been set up as a scene in a play, and then Mrs. Proudie uses an archaic word that the narrator, as though giving stage directions, identifies as coming from old drama. Trollope's extensive reading of old drama probably encouraged the scene painting and the pointed joke. Mrs. Proudie would style herself a tragedy queen; the narrator exposes her as an angry clown.

The techniques of drama are again openly used in another major part of the novel—Ullathorne Sports. This section, like the Jael and Sisera story in *The Last Chronicle*, has been called extraneous to the rest of the work.[14] When we look at the Sports chapters as a microcosm of the novel, and as an end-of-novel (or third-volume) counterpart to the Proudie reception, they make perfectly good sense artistically and thematically. The division of the Sports into acts (just as the Proudie reception is divided into two parts) suggests that something of real significance is going to happen during them. Something does, but not what the reader expects from the beginning of the novel and from the emphasis on battle given in the chapters on Arabin. In the Sports we focus on Eleanor's love concerns, not the struggle for control of the bishop.

Each of the acts in the three-part melodrame apparently chronicles some misadventure in Eleanor's confused relations with Arabin. The Barchester ecclesiastical war is entirely ignored; it has disappeared and the romance is uppermost. The climax of the melodrame appears to be Eleanor's resounding slap of the tipsy Mr. Slope. But since the Sports themselves are an ironic miniature of the whole novel, we would expect, and indeed we find, that even this climax is false. The really significant event of the Sports is not Eleanor's dismissal of Slope but Harding's discovery that Eleanor despises Slope; after that discovery, the farce of Eleanor's slap and the narrator's elaborately disingenuous apology for her are but further parts of the novel's comic miscuing. And in keeping with this irony, we find that the most interesting characters are not Eleanor or Slope or Arabin or even Mr. Harding. The narrator lavishes his dramatic know-how between the actual acts of the melodrame, and on the scenes with Madeline and with the Lookalofts and the Greenacres. (Who can read the description of Madeline's triumph over Lady De Courcy and not applaud the comic staging of the piece? Madeline's remark to Mr. Slope could serve as the motto for the Sports and for the novel as a whole: "'Ha, ha, ha. Well, that's as good as a play.'" The narrator follows up Madeline's remarks immediately by saying, "It was good as a play to any there who had eyes to observe it, and wit to comment on what they observed" [XXXVII].)

Trollope makes the Ullathorne acts richly allusive and humorous, using comic exaggerations to emphasize the themes of the novel. The Sports themselves are reminders of the Eglinton Tournament and the British obsession with Sir Walter Scott, which I will discuss later. The melodrama of the Sports is also supported by the narrator's comic uses of Shakespeare. Three quotations from Shakespeare embellish the comedy of the Sports chapters. When the narrator is describing love at first sight for the older man (here Wilfred Thorne's sudden infatuation with Madeline Neroni), he uses lines from *Love's Labour's Lost* (IV.iii.334–36; 340–41). The narrator says, "But for real true love—love at first sight, love to devotion, love that robs a man of his sleep, love that 'will gaze an eagle blind,' love that 'will hear the lowest sound when the suspicious tread of theft is stopped,' love that is 'like a Hercules, still climbing trees in the Hesperides'—we believe the best age is from forty-five to seventy; up to that men are generally given to mere flirting" (XXXVII). Though the narrator is being playful here, he is not entirely fanciful. We are invited to smile at the Thornes, but it is with the seniors[15] in the Barchester society we find the true values that must endure. Even Arabin and Eleanor, by no means youthful, are young in Trollope's apparent scheme of things: they flounder and fumble; Arabin, because as a previously sheltered Oxford don he is experiencing what must be called emotional adolescence; Eleanor, because she is a vine fluttering in the breeze, waiting for the right wall or tree or column around which to cling and grow (the Thackerayan ivy image is used with Eleanor in both *The Warden* and *Barchester Towers*).[16]

The second quotation, or adaptation, is from *Henry IV, II* (V.iii.37). The clerical feasting in the tents at Ullathorne is described with "'Twas merry in the hall when the beards wagged all'" (XXXVIII).¹⁷ The foolery and light-heartedness of the play are perfectly reflected in the general atmosphere of the Sports. And a comparison of Slope and Falstaff could be instructive.

The third quotation comes, ironically, from *Macbeth*. As Slope, tipsy from champagne, pursues Eleanor across the lawn so that he can propose to her, he quotes to himself, "'That which has made them drunk has made me bold'" (XL). Slope's unconscious pun on Eleanor's last name is characteristically clumsy. And one wonders, is it Slope or Mrs. Proudie who acts as the novel's Lady Macbeth?

Shakespeare is used other times in the novel, and each light use acts as a repetition or echo of the novel's numerous comedies of error. A quotation at the end of the novel encourages us to look back at the mock melodrame as a kind of distorted *As You Like It*, with Eleanor as a rather harried Rosalind and Slope as a darkly repulsive Jaques. Ullathorne then becomes the forest of Arden, a gloriously isolated spot separate from yet deliberately exposing the foibles and concerns of the larger world outside.¹⁸ This play within the play technique, the melodrame within the Barchester comedy, borrowed from Elizabethan and Jacobean drama, allows the narrator to suggest, lightheartedly, parallels within the text. At the end of *Barchester Towers* the narrator quotes from *As You Like It* to finish his own tale: "The last scene of all, as all last scenes we fear must be,

Is second childishness, and mere oblivion,
Sans teeth, sans eyes, sans taste, sans everything (LI).

Trollope's references to Shakespeare are usually richly echoic.

In Mrs. Proudie's Reception and Ullathorne Sports the narrator alludes to events and ideas in current society as well as to literature, and he fully exploits the techniques of stagecraft. The techniques used in these two prominent (melo)dramatic pieces in the novel are reinforced by the novel's many other allusions to drama (and other literature) and especially by the creation of scenes. A perfect example of the quality and extent of the narrator's deliberate repetitions and parallel uses of staging is found in the description of the three "wraths"—Grantly's,

Mrs. Proudie's, and Slope's. In each of these three we experience the narrator's use of different devices (measured syntax, mock-heroic tone, literary allusion) and are at the same time reminded of the other comic characters' anger.

Since the narrator controls the major patterns of the novel—the scenes and acts, the mock-heroic flavor of battle, the comic and ironic use of literature of all varieties—we would naturally expect to find in the individual characters echoes and continuations of the narrator's preoccupations. And so it is with all except the centrally important Harding. Archdeacon Grantly's repeated tag "Good heavens!" marks him as a comically explosive character in the battles and intrigues. The French and Biblical expressions offered by him, or by the narrator interpreting him, are consistent with the individual character of the man and with the narrator's established voice. The passage declaring Grantly's "noble wrath" (echoed in Mrs. Proudie's "divine wrath" and Slope's "furious wrath") is an excellent example of Trollope's use of tag and sentence structure to create a miniature comic scene:

"Good heavens!" exclaimed the archdeacon, as he placed his foot on the gravel walk of the close, and raising his hat with one hand, passed the other somewhat violently over his now grizzled locks; smoke issued forth from the uplifted beaver as it were a cloud of wrath, and the safety-valve of his anger opened, and emitted a visible steam, preventing positive explosion and probable apoplexy. "Good heavens!"—and the archdeacon looked up to the gray pinnacles of the cathedral tower, making a mute appeal to that still living witness which had looked down on the doings of so many bishops of Barchester (VI).

The structure of the sentence between the two "good heavens" exemplifies Trollope's deliberate control. The first exclamation is followed by exactly sixty-four words with a semicolon making a short pause between the two thirty-two-word parts. Each of the two sections in the sentence is divided by three commas which mark and emphasize the accumulation of detail. The first "good heavens" is followed by the description of the archdeacon's actions: he "exclaimed"; he "placed his foot"; while "raising his hat" he "passed the other [hand] somewhat violently over his now grizzled locks." The word *somewhat* is the only distraction from the catalogue of actions. The second part of the sentence balances the first by supplying descriptions of the actions. We see "smoke," "cloud of wrath," "safety-valve of his anger," and "visible steam." Reading the sentence aloud, as it was probably frequently read by Trollope's public,[19] reveals a distinct pattern to the pace. The first section is read quickly and relates the actions; the second gives a vivid picture and is read slowly because it requires more effort from both the imagination and the voice. The last part of the second section, "preventing positive explosion and probable apoplexy," is neatly balanced by its deliberate parallel of "explosion" and "apoplexy" to slow down to the full stop. The next "good heavens" redirects the reader's attention from the description of the archdeacon to the archdeacon himself as he wistfully views the cathedral tower, which, in the past, has represented his stable and friendly world.

This "wrath" passage opens the chapter entitled "War," which immediately follows the sedately titled "A Morning Visit," during which Harding and Grantly are insulted deliberately by Mrs. Proudie and Mr. Slope. This courtesy visit to the new bishop is itself wonderful comedy, with Mrs. Proudie, Slope, and the bishop's creating a grating, out-of-tune calliope; as the wife and chaplain blare at their guests, the bishop squeaks, and the former harmony of Barchester is shattered in a few painful measures. Grantly suppresses his rage until he leaves the Palace, when the reader expects a full description of his explosion. The tightly controlled sentence and the significant tag "good heavens!" offer a full play in miniature.

The narrator presents Mrs. Proudie's corresponding "furious wrath" five chapters later in the dramatic piece already mentioned, "Mrs. Proudie's Reception—Concluded." A woman who quotes Scripture *at* clergymen and regains dignity with archaic expressions richly deserves the narrator's tribute of a mock-heroic departure. In the manner of Fielding, the narrator describes Mrs. Proudie's "furious wrath" as her dress is ripped apart by Bertie:

So, when a granite battery is raised, excellent to the eyes of warfaring men, is its strength and symmetry admired. It is the work of years. Its neat embrasures, its finished parapets, its casemated stories, show all the skill of modern science. But, anon, a small spark is applied to the treacherous fusee—a cloud of dust arises to the heavens—and then nothing is to be seen but dirt and dust and ugly fragments.

We know what was the wrath of Juno when her beauty was despised. We know to what storms of passion even celestial minds can yield. As Juno may have looked at Paris on Mount Ida, so did Mrs. Proudie look on Ethelbert Stanhope when he pushed the leg of the sofa into her lace train (XI).

Whenever Mrs. Proudie or the archdeacon is incensed, there is the flavor of mock-grand style. The narrator is careful to make us feel that his "noble wrath" and her "furious wrath" have much in common. Mrs. Proudie's anachronistic "Unhand it, Sir!", shouted at Bertie, is as characteristic and compelling as Grantly's "good heavens!"—and both people are called "Juno" in their ire. The parts of warrior and outraged deity suit equally the archdeacon and Mrs. Proudie, and the narrator's careful directing makes us appreciate the comic bond between the two.

Slope's "divine wrath" exposes his sanctimoniousness as clearly as Grantly's wrath shows his offended self-importance and Mrs. Proudie's suggests her only lightly restrained bellicosity. This third "wrath" occurs, as with Mrs. Proudie's, as a scene within a scene, this time in the third act of Ullathorne Sports when Eleanor slaps Slope. The narrator invokes the muse and dramatic precedents from Greek theatre and finally resorts to Slope's ancestor, Dr. Slop, from Sterne's *Tristram Shandy*. As with Grantly and Mrs. Proudie, the choice of mock-grand language is characteristic of the narrator but also of the comic character himself: "But how shall I sing the divine wrath of Mr. Slope, or how invoke the tragic muse to describe the rage which swelled the celestial bosom of the bishop's chaplain? Such an undertaking by no means befits the low-heeled buskin of modern fiction. The painter put a veil over Agamemnon's face when called on to depict the father's grief at the early doom of his devoted daughter" (XL). This mock-heroic aside gives way to allusions to Sterne: "He stood motionless, undecided, glaring with his eyes, thinking of the pains and penalties of Hades, and meditating how he might best devote his enemy to the infernal gods with all the passion of his accustomed eloquence. He longed in his heart to be preaching at her. 'Twas thus he was ordinarily avenged of sinning mortal men and women. Could he at once have ascended his Sunday rostrum and fulminated at her such denunciations as his spirit delighted in, his bosom would have been greatly eased" (XL). This scene with Eleanor marks the mock climax of the Ullathorne melodrama, and we know that this part of the melodrama itself was constructed to gratify the reader with a full view of Slope's failure. With him the concept of battle is carried to ridiculous extremes. Through the description of this third "wrath" we appreciate how neatly the narrator has combined, confused, blended, and repeated the novel's wars, melodramas, and romances in the different yet similar scenes.

The reader is prepared to enjoy the scenes and to relish the novel's repetitions because of the way allusions, tags, and clichés are used and repeated—with different characters throughout the novel. If we turn now from the larger patterns of *Barchester Towers* to the individual characters, we will see how thoroughly the boisterous comedy of the narrator is echoed by each of the major characters—except, of course, the purposely separate Mr. Harding.

Building on *The Warden*, the narrator in *Barchester Towers* makes Grantly's "good heavens!" his emotional index, as we have just seen with his "noble wrath." Each time Grantly uses the expression, as with Dickens's Barkis or Sarah Gamp, we feel how "dramatically" alive is the archdeacon. Grantly greets Mr. Harding's news about the deanship with "'Good heavens!' said the archdeacon, and sank back exhausted in an easychair" (XLVII). Later, when Harding announces Eleanor's engagement to Arabin, the archdeacon exclaims "good heavens!" five times, ending, "'Well, well,' said he. 'Good heavens! good heavens!' and the tone of the fifth exclamation made Mr. Harding fully aware that content was reigning in the archdeacon's bosom" (L).

Mrs. Grantly reflects the archdeacon's energy and responds to Eleanor's engagement to Arabin by echoing her husband: "'Good heavens!' she exclaimed—it was the general exclamation of the rectory" (XLVIII).

Like the narrator, the archdeacon is fond of French. He says of Slope and Eleanor: "'I see it all. . . . The sly *tartuffe*! He thinks to buy the daughter by providing for the father. He means to show how powerful he is, how good he is, and how much he is willing to do for her *beaux yeux* . . .'" (XVIII). The narrator reinforces the archdeacon's words: "The archdeacon . . . at last remained firm in his own conviction that he was destined, *malgré lui*, to be the brother-in-law of Mr. Slope" (XXXIV). Grantly contemplates Mr. Harding's proposed deanship and the narrator reflects his thoughts: "And then the great discomfiture of that arch-enemy of all that was respectable in Barchester, of that new Low Church clerical parvenu that had fallen amongst them, that alone would be worth more, almost, than the situation itself " (XLVII). And we see, with the help of *parvenu*, that the archdeacon's traditionalism extends from his religion to the very furniture of his home. The narrator says: "In his eyes there was something democratic and *parvenu* in a round table. He imagined that dissenters and calico-printers chiefly used them, and perhaps a few literary lions more conspicuous for their wit than their gentility" (XXI).

Grantly is a convincing archdeacon, and the reader never doubts his faith, thoroughly mixed though it is with materialism. Naturally, his sermon reinforces what we know of him from his own words and from the narrator's. When Grantly introduces Arabin to his new congregation in St. Ewold's, he uses verse 10 of Philemon: "I beseech thee for my son Onesimus, whom I have begotten in my bonds" (XXIII). The narrator paraphrases Grantly's message, assuring us that though "he deprecated any comparison between himself and St. Paul," he also "took a little merit to himself for having studiously provided the best man he could without reference to patronage or favour; but he did not say that the best man according to his views was he who was best able to subdue Mr. Slope and make that gentleman's situation in Barchester too hot to be comfortable" (XXIII). Even in his choice of text Grantly exposes his militancy and pride. Though he demurs about St. Paul, he asserts his power in the diocese since the message to Philemon rests on Paul's claim for respect and obedience: "If thou count me therefore a partner, receive him as myself."[20]

The language used to develop Mrs. Proudie is an effective combination and blurring of the narrator's fancifulness and Mrs. Proudie's own indomitable spirit. The archdeacon's archrival has the "eyes of Argus" (III) for those who offend against Sabbath observances, and she is an "episcopal Argus" (XVII) when she confronts Slope with his unclerical attentions to Madeline Neroni. We find this expression later used by some political underlings to describe the duchess of Omnium in *The Prime Minister* and understand then, as here, the implied insult to the prying female.

Mrs. Proudie is primarily a warrior, and the narrator reflects her thoughts in terms of the glories of battle. When Slope and the bishop rebel together against her, she withdraws to her own room, and there: "The air of that sacred enclosure somewhat restored her courage, and gave her more heart. As Achilles warmed at the sight of his armour, as Don Quixote's heart grew strong when he grasped his lance, so did Mrs. Proudie look forward to fresh laurels, as her eye fell on her husband's pillow" (XXVI). When the vanquished bishop stammers that he thought to mollify his wife by proposing Slope for dean, the narrator likens Mrs. Proudie to a hyena and then a cannibal as he tries to suggest the fury in her response to the bishop:

Pleased at having her enemy converted into a dean with twelve hundred a year! Medea, when she describes the customs of her native country (I am quoting from Robson's edition), assures her astonished auditor that in her land captives, when taken, are eaten.
"You pardon them?" says Medea.
"We do indeed," says the mild Grecian.
"We eat them!" says she of Colchis, with terrific energy.
Mrs. Proudie was the Medea of Barchester; she had no idea of not eating Mr. Slope. Pardon him! Merely get rid of him! Make a dean of him! It was not so they did with their captives in her country, among

people of her sort! Mr. Slope had no such mercy to expect; she would pick him to the very last bone (XXXIII).

Only a few chapters before (XXV) the narrator used Medea to embellish the internal monologue of the distressed but kindly Mrs. Quiverful. The contrast between the anxious mother there and the bloodthirsty woman here is the more striking since Mrs. Proudie champions Mrs. Quiverful's cause. The narrator suggests that Mrs. Proudie's crusade for the "fourteen living children" is certainly more Medean than quixotic. The bishop wisely concludes that there is no hope in tilting "against a warrior so fully armed at all points as was Mrs. Proudie" (XXXIII).

In the final pages of the book the narrator describes Mrs. Proudie's battle tactics with a different analogy. Of her struggles with Slope he says: "They had gone through a competitive examination of considerable severity, and she had come forth the winner, *facile princeps*" (LI) (an easy first). Everything is a contest to Mrs. Proudie; she is always campaigning to prove or gain power. She uses her religion as a kind of weapon to subdue less aggressive competitors. (Mrs. Proudie uses her knowledge of the Scriptures the same way that Ferdinand Lopez in *The Prime Minister* uses his of literature: his quotations are insidious; hers are bellicose; but both realize the power of association.) When she first meets Mr. Harding she corners him and preaches: "'Neither thou, nor thy son, nor thy daughter, nor thy manservant, nor thy maidservant,' said she impressively, and more than once, as though Mr. Harding had forgotten the words. She shook her finger at him as she quoted the favourite law, as though menacing him with punishment..." (V). With Dr. Gwynne she frowns and gestures while she quotes: "'"Suffer little children, and forbid them not,"' said she. 'Are we not to remember that, Dr. Gwynne? "Take heed that ye despise not one of these little ones." Are we not to remember that, Dr. Gwynne?' And at each of these questions she raised at him her menacing forefinger" (XLIII). It is fitting that Mr. Crawley later should finally conquer Mrs. Proudie with Scripture in *The Last Chronicle of Barset*.

With Mrs. Proudie the narrator uses Scripture, myths, and

mock-heroic language (itself a kind of allusion) and drama, mixing together her own angry or ill-considered words with suitably exaggerated allusion. Two allusions to Shakespeare illustrate the effective combination of the incongruous and the appropriate. The narrator quotes from *Othello* (v.ii.347) to suggest, perhaps, her warrior cunning in cajoling her repentant husband on his return to the Palace: "Nothing, however, could be more affectionately cordial than the greeting he received; the girls came out and kissed him in a manner that was quite soothing to his spirit; and Mrs. Proudie, 'albeit, unused to the melting mood,' squeezed him in her arms, and almost in words called him her dear, darling, good, pet, little bishop" (XXXIII). The outlandish contrast between the grandeur of Othello's final speech and Mrs. Proudie's domestic flummery (spoken, too, at a time when she is again triumphant) is appropriate to the high jinks of the novel. She is best characterized, however, by an allusion to *The Taming of the Shrew*: "In truth, Mrs. Proudie was all but invincible; had she married Petruchio, it may be doubted whether that arch wife-tamer would have been able to keep her legs out of those garments which are presumed by men to be peculiarly unfitted for feminine use" (XXXIII). Mrs. Proudie is both victrix and vixen.

With Obadiah Slope the narrator and Slope together use a variety of allusions and echoes from Sterne, Dickens, Shakespeare, Bunyan, Milton, and the Bible that expose Slope's comic villainy. As mentioned earlier, Slope is introduced by the narrator as a direct descendant of Dr. Slop from Sterne's *Tristam Shandy*:[21] "I have heard it asserted that he is lineally descended from that eminent physician who assisted at the birth of Mr. T. Shandy, and that in early years he added an 'e' to his name, for the sake of euphony. . ." (IV). The now Protestant Slope (Sterne's Dr. Slop was Catholic) "has recourse, like his great ancestor, to the fulminations of an Ernulfus: 'Thou shalt be damned in thy going in and in thy coming out—in thy eating and thy drinking.' . . ." (IV). Trollope's readers no doubt appreciated this insult to Slope, remembering Dr. Slop's embarrassment at the virulence of Ernulphus's formula for excommunication.

The description of the red-haired Slope and his clammy handshake is unmistakably reminiscent of Uriah Heep. This comic combination of Slop and Heep quotes from *Macbeth*, as we have mentioned earlier, to give him the courage to propose to Eleanor, and it is words from *Hamlet* that transfix him when Madeline later taunts him with his failure with Eleanor: " 'Tis conscience that makes cowards of us all.' He felt on his cheek the sharp points of Eleanor's fingers, and did not know who might have seen the blow . . ." (XLVI). It is not clear whether Slope thinks of these words himself or whether the narrator supplies them, but it matters little—they are too appropriate a condemnation of his arrogance and guilt. He recognizes, perhaps, his own position in "vanity fair" (XL) and knows that "idolaters round the altars of Baal" (XL) deserve no better. The narrator dismisses him at the end of the book with a fanciful twist of the last lines of "Lycidas": "At last he rose, and twitched his mantle blue (black), / To-morrow to fresh woods and pastures new" (LI).

Slope fights battles in Barsetshire on two different levels, and his part in the novel provides links between the mock-heroic battles of ecclesiastical power and the melodramatic struggles of false romance. Allusions to Sterne, the Bible, and the classics connect the two different spheres of conflict. His first assault is from the pulpit. He chooses II Timothy 2:15 for his text: "Study to show thyself approved unto God, a workman that needeth not to be ashamed, rightly dividing the word of truth" (VI). He perverts the interpretation of the Scripture so that he can "ridicule, abuse and anathematize" the practises of his High and Dry congregation. Trollope's readers will probably recall the appropriateness to Slope and his audience[22] of the companion chapter, I Timothy 2, which gives advice to archdeacons and bishops and in advising the treatment of women foreshadows Slope's own doom: "Let the woman learn in silence with all subjection. But I suffer not a woman to teach, nor to usurp authority over the man, but to be in silence" (I Timothy 2:11–12). At any rate, Slope's attack is successful because he does, by innuendo and statement, set "all Barchester . . . by the ears" (VII).

The narrator tells us that Slope is an "abhorrent Gamaliel" (VII)[23] who knows "the wiles of the serpent" (VIII) and has "pharisaical arrogance" (XIII). "A rich wife was a great desideratum to him" (XV); he regards Eleanor as his "embryo spouse" (XIX), tries to dupe her about the hospital with an explanation of "wheels within wheels" (XVI), and brushes aside her hesitations with "Rome was not built in a day" (XVI). He tries to make his usurpation of Mrs. Proudie a *fait accompli* (XXVI). He tries to charm Madeline by telling her that if he destroys her letters "'they perish worthily, and are burnt on a pyre, as Dido was of old'" (XXVII). Mr. Slope's language, and that associated with him by the narrator, assures us that he is a clever, resourceful man. He is an unsuccessful soldier, and an unfortunate lover, and so is the perfect comic "male devil" for the Barchester battles and melodrama.

False romance, which is the key ingredient of the novel's melodrama, is personified in Madeline Neroni. Madeline is artificial; everything about her suggests contrivance.[24] She herself reminds us of the novel as a novel because she thinks of herself as part of a colorful and continuing fiction. She arranges intrigues, creates scenes, dazzles her followers with wit, allusion, and repartee. Her chief object in life is to fascinate, to make scores of men fall in love with her. She personally is what Ullathorne Sports is structurally: a self-parody. She thrives on fantasy and suggests her own superficiality in the cynical extremes of her charades. She is too realistic to have genuine pride in her conquests, and too desperate not to indulge herself constantly with them. In keeping with the novel's lightness, Madeline's desperation is almost entirely effaced. Instead, the narrator and Madeline herself encourage laughter over her numerous exploits.

The narrator repeats the word *basilisk* to summarize Madeline's deadly charms: "She was a basilisk from whom an ardent lover of beauty could make no escape" (IX), a "voluptuous Rubens . . . with the power of a basilisk" (XVI); ". . . Mr. Thorne . . . yielded himself up to the basilisk . . ." (XXXVIII). She is a "painted Jezebel" (XI), as Mrs. Proudie tells us, who has eyes "bright as Lucifer's" (IX). She, like Becky Sharp, is a "noxious siren" (XXVII) who in revenge can be "as active as Grimaldi" (XI). Madeline is most fittingly characterized as a huntress in various forms: she regards Mr. Thorne as a "pheasant" "worth bagging for family uses" (XXXVIII); she fishes for Thorne first, and "The fish took the bait, was hooked, and caught, and landed" (XXXVII). At Ullathorne, too, she decides "to entrap Mr. Arabin into her net" (XXXVIII); with Slope she is merciless, because ". . . the signora was a powerful spider that made wondrous webs, and could in no way live without catching flies" (XXVII); and of Slope she "spitted him, as a boy does a cockchafer on a cork, that she might enjoy the energetic agony of his gyrations" (XXVII). The signora's charms are addictive and men are driven to her repeatedly, the narrator says, "As the Eastern idler swallows his dose of opium, as the London reprobate swallows his dose of gin . . ." (XXXVIII). Madeline's "lustrous glances" (XLI)—the pun must be intentional—captivate Slope and Arabin, the bishop and Mr. Thorne.

Signor Neroni's eyes attack and attract. She duels through eye contact with Lady De Courcy, as we have mentioned earlier, and sends her "shambling" out onto the Ullathorne lawn. Her dramatic beauty and bold techniques change most of her conversations into superb scenes. Ullathorne, itself the excuse for an elaborate "melodrame," is the perfect background for Madeline's antics.

Madeline sharpens her wit and perhaps feeds her imagination with a variety of literary pursuits. She makes more allusions in her speech than any other character in *Barchester Towers* and has a greater density of patterns associated with her than any of Trollope's characters except Josiah Crawley. Unlike Crawley, who nurtures his imagination with the classics, Madeline is an inveterate letter writer who ". . . wrote also a kind of poetry, generally in Italian, and short romances, generally in French. She read much of a desultory sort of literature, and as a modern linguist had really made great proficiency" (IX). She studies the catechism so she can remark to Slope about a proposed Sunday School, "'I will teach them, at any rate, to submit themselves to their spiritual pastors and masters'" (XXVII). She can taunt Slope with his duplicity because she has read of St. Paul (XXVII). Her nature is most pointedly exposed in her allusions to the heroines of Shakespeare, Byron, and the classics. She mocks Dido because she fell between two stools; she mocks love in general because:

"Who was ever successful in true love? Success in love argues that the love is false. True love is always despondent or tragical. Juliet loved, Haidee loved, Dido loved, and what came of it? Troilus loved and ceased to be a man."

"Troilus loved and was fooled," said the more manly chaplain. "A man may love and yet not be a Troilus. All women are not Cressids."

"No, all women are not Cressids. The falsehood is not always on the woman's side. Imogen was true, but how was she rewarded? Her lord believed her to be the paramour of the first he who came near her in his absence. Desdemona was true and was smothered. Ophelia was true and went mad. There is no happiness in love, except at the end of an English novel" (XXVII).

Madeline's cynicism adds some strength to the novel's playful criticism of sanctimony. With another allusion to Shakespeare she openly attacks Slope: "'Why—what gulls do you men make of us,' she replied. 'How you fool us to the top of our bent; and of all men you clergymen are the most fluent of your honeyed, caressing words'" (XXVII).

Perhaps it could be noted here that Madeline's freedom with Shakespeare and her general vitality suggest similarities between her and Glencora of *The Prime Minister*. It seems no accident that these attractive and vocal women, along with Lady Carbury in *The Way We Live Now* (XVI), use Trollope's word *boody* (*Barchester Towers*, XXVII; The Prime Minister, LXXVI).[25] The differences between Madeline and Glencora, neither in her *première jeunesse* (XXVII), reveal some changes in Trollope's writing in the 1850s and the 1870s. Both "ladies" support and amplify the narrator's tone, but the repetitions and allusions with Madeline are consistent with the narrator's ebullience; Glencora's irreverent references and expressions implement the narrator's later use of deflation and irony.

Though the Thornes are not major characters in the novel, they are important because of the structural and emblematic significance of the Ullathorne Sports. The *fête champêtre* is given in honor of Arabin, the new vicar of St. Ewold's, and it sets the tone for his change to Barsetshire ways. The Sports, like the battles Arabin was called on to join in Barchester, are not what they seem. The Sports occasion Eleanor's melodrama; Arabin's crusade in Barchester results in his adoption of Harding's spirit of tolerance.

In keeping with the narrator's spirit of celebration of literature, Ullathorne Sports is not only a melodrama, but also a satire on Scott and the kind of medieval mania that produced the Eglinton Tournament.[26] Miss Thorne herself alludes to Eglinton when she despairs of creating her own tournament: "She would no doubt have been anxious for something small in the way of a tournament; but, as she said to her brother, that had been tried, and the age had proved itself too decidedly inferior to its forerunners to admit of such a pastime" (XXXIII). She decides to have amusements from the time of Queen Elizabeth; nevertheless, it is the spirit of *Ivanhoe* that enlivens the Sports. As she stands at the quintain, Miss Thorne becomes the Lady Rowena: "'Shall I begin, ma'am' said Harry, fingering his long staff in a rather awkward way, while his horse moved uneasily beneath him, not accustomed to a rider armed with such a weapon. 'Yes, yes,' said Miss Thorne, standing triumphant as the queen of beauty, on an inverted tub which some chance had brought thither from the farmyard" (XXXVI). The narrator likens her to another character in *Ivanhoe* when he first introduces her: "In some respects she was not unlike Scott's Ulrica, and had she been given to cursing, she would certainly have done so in the names of Mista, Skogula, and Zernebock. Not having submitted to the embraces of any polluting Norman, as poor Ulrica had done, and having assisted no parricide, the milk of human kindness was not curdled in her bosom" (XXII). Wilfred Thorne is also introduced with allusion to *Ivan-*

hoe: "He counted back his own ancestors to some period long antecedent to the Conquest; and could tell you, if you would listen to him, how it had come to pass that they, like Cedric the Saxon, had been permitted to hold their own among the Norman barons" (XXII).

The narrator uses other literary works to satirize the Thorne's antiquated tastes (XXII). Mr. Thorne is compared to Fielding's Squire Western. He reads Montaigne and Burton, "and he knew more perhaps than any other man in his own county, and the next to it, of the English essayists of the two last centuries." He has sets of the *Idler, Spectator, Tatler, Guardian,* and *Rambler.* In politics he is (as Grantly is in religion) a pure Conservative, nearly collapsing after "Sir Robert Peel's apostasy" but recovering when he began to regard himself and other Tory protectionists as "true depositaries left of certain Eleusinian mysteries." He looks upon others as a Greek scholar is likely to look upon those who do not know Greek, or thinks of himself as a Cato "who gloried that he could kill himself because Romans were no longer worthy of their name." (It is interesting to compare Mr. Thorne and Felix Carbury, with whom this reference to Cato is also used in *The Way We Live Now.*) When Mr. Thorne becomes the object of Madeline's wiles, he falls back on his eighteenth-century reading: "Mr. Thorne went on thus awhile with antediluvian grimaces and compliments which he had picked up from Sir Charles Grandison. . ." (XLVI). In Ullathorne Sports the narrator recalls Madeline's use of Shakespeare and Thorne's literary interests by describing Thorne's captivation with the lines from *Love's Labour's Lost* quoted earlier. The exaggerated lengths of Thorne's reaction are perfectly in keeping with the characterization of Madeline, the atmosphere of false romance, and the "labour lost" on the antiquated sports.

Miss Monica Thorne is a "living caricature of all his [Wilfred's] foibles" (XXII). She dotes on Addison, Swift, and Steele; praises Defoe and Fielding. The narrator says facetiously: "In poetry, she was familiar with names as late as Dryden, and had once been seduced into reading 'The Rape of the Lock;' but she regarded Spenser as the purest type of her country's literature in this line." Miss Thorne is a Druidess, who has adopted Christianity as a "milder form of the worship of her ancestors." At the Sports her guests discuss her eccentricities and identify her incongruence with her surroundings by this rather surprising but understandable comparison: "'She always makes me think of the Esquimaux and the Indians'" (xxxvii). Such a winsome combination of Elizabethan and Augustan preferences is the spirit behind the Ullathorne melodrama. Even her wardrobe is described by an analogy to Scott's lady of Branksome—"Nine-and-twenty knights of fame / Hung their shields in Branksome Hall" (xxii). Miss Thorne, who does not know the meaning of a *déshabilles* (xxxv), has "nine-and-twenty silken skirts" as her protection. Miss Thorne is an oddity even in a country proud of its past. She and her brother and the Sports themselves are reminders that times must change.

Arabin was initially introduced as one of the combatants of the Barchester War. Grantly invited him from Oxford because Arabin had already engaged in a battle with Slope through the press. Arabin seems happy at first with his part in the controversy, remarking on his new house: "'I shall have a beautifully complete view of my adversaries. I shall sit down before the hostile town, and fire away at them at a very pleasant distance. I shall just be able to lodge a shot in the hospital, should the enemy ever get possession of it, and as for the palace, I have it within full range'" (xxi). He describes to Eleanor the joys of war in terms that foreshadow Trollope's later themes in *Phineas Redux* and the *Prime Minister*: "'Wars about trifles,' said he, 'are always bitter, especially among neighbours. When the differences are great, and the parties comparative strangers, men quarrel with courtesy'" (xxi). He paraphrases Pope and again anticipates the serious criticism of Trollope's later political novels: "'I know no life that must be so delicious as that of a writer for newspapers, or a leading member of the opposition—to thunder forth accusations against men in power; to show up the worst side of everything . . . to damn with faint praise, or crush with open calumny!'" (xxi).

Barchester Towers 39

After Arabin is read in at St. Ewold's and delivers his sermon (the narrator naturally helps us to notice the contrast with Grantly's and Slope's) he begins to suffer from his love for Eleanor and his thoughts shift from ecclesiastical struggles to love. In his new preoccupation with his feelings the narrator shows us a revival of Arabin's youthful interests: "All that he had obtained, over and above the advantage of his character, was a gold medal for English verse, and hence was derived a strong presumption on the part of his friends that he was destined to add another name to the imperishable list of English poets" (xx). He is fascinated by the signora's beauty and the narrator uses a favorite cliché to suggest Arabin's reawakening to feelings; he "mothlike, burnt his wings in the flames of the signora's candle" (xxiv). In his unhappiness over Eleanor he recalls Henry Taylor's *Phillip Van Artevelde*: "How little flattering is woman's love." When he is galled by thoughts of Mr. Slope, he mutters to himself ten lines of the play (xxx). He castigates himself for neglecting his duties, by recalling Goethe's *Sorrows of Young Werther* (it matters little to the reader whether it is Arabin himself who thinks of Goethe's hopeless, romantic tale, or whether it is the narrator; in either case Arabin's exaggerated woe is comic): "He should have spent this afternoon among the poor at St. Ewold's, instead of wandering about at Plumstead, an ancient, love-lorn swain, dejected and sighing, full of imaginary sorrows and Wertherian grief " (xxxiv). Eleanor understands the hesitancies and broodings, and she likes him better because he is not, the narrator says, a "practised Lothario" (xxx).

Mr. Arabin is not only romantic but also old-fashioned. He shares something of the spirit of the Thornes, and he believes also in the beauties of Ullathorne: "'There is something about old-fashioned mansions, built as this is, and old-fashioned gardens, that to me is especially delightful'" (xlviii). When Eleanor questions him about his feelings for change he shows a cautious tolerance: "'If we believe in Scripture, we can hardly think that mankind in general will now be allowed to retrograde'" (xlviii). At the end of the novel Arabin accepts not only Eleanor and the deanship from Harding, but something, too, of the old man's gentleness. The onetime poet and warrior becomes, the narrator avers with mock solemnity, the unobtrusive scholar: "Dr. Arabin . . . is more moderate and less outspoken on doctrinal points than his wife, as indeed in his station it behoves him to be. He is a studious, thoughtful, hardworking man. He lives constantly at the deanery, and preaches nearly every Sunday. His time is spent in sifting and editing old ecclesiastical literature, and in producing the same articles new" (LIII). (This scholarly man is the best friend of that quintessential scholar, the Reverend Josiah Crawley.)

The narrator reintroduces Eleanor from *The Warden*, with a proverbial expression Sterne was also fond of: "But God tempers the wind to the shorn lamb" (II). She is gentle but headstrong and she causes pain to Arabin and confusion to herself because she wilfully misunderstands the Stanhopes and Slope. The narrator suggests her wrongheadedness in her allegiance to the Stanhopes. She thinks it a "thousand pities" that the archdeacon does not have more of the *savoir vivre* of the Stanhopes (XXI). She visits the Stanhopes often and joins in their trifling: "She played chess with them, walked with them . . . assisted them in writing stories in rhyme, in turning prose tragedy into comic verse, or comic stories into would-be tragic poetry" (XXXIII). When she realizes their design for her, she rejects them angrily, but with a little inspiration from Goldsmith, she braves Madeline's advice: "She despised the signora; but might she not stoop to conquer? It should be but the smallest fraction of a stoop" (XLV). She is the center of the melodrama, where, because she refused to accept Mary Bold as her Mentor (XLIV), she must endure Slope's and Bertie's attentions. The narrator describes her position in a jocund allusion to Homer that we see again later in *He Knew He Was Right* and in *The Way We Live Now*: "In striving to avoid that terrible Charybdis of a Slope she was in great danger of falling into an unseen Scylla on the other hand, that Scylla being Bertie Stanhope" (XXXVII). Her part at Ullathorne occasions the reappraisal of the novel's direction.

Eleanor's and Arabin's is the true romance of the novel, the one that counterbalances Madeline's heartless intrigues. It is typical of *Barchester Towers*, however, that their story is dashed with irony. Madeline is a Becky Sharp, and Eleanor is characterized by the ivy image associated with Amelia Sedley. At the beginning of the novel the narrator comments on her love for Bold: "Hers was one of those feminine hearts which cling to a husband, not with idolatry, for worship can admit of no defect in its idol, but with the perfect tenacity of ivy. As the parasite plant will follow even the defects of the trunk which it embraces, so did Eleanor cling to and love the very faults of her husband" (II). Near the end when she gives herself to Arabin the narrator again remarks, "When the ivy has found its tower, when the delicate creeper has found its strong wall, we know how the parasite plants grow and prosper" (XLIX). The end of Thackeray's novel is too similar to be ignored: "Good-by, Colonel—God bless you, honest William!—Farewell, dear Amelia—Grow green again, tender little parasite, round the rugged old oak to which you cling!"[27] We recall that Slope thought of Ullathorne as a "vanity fair" and realize that it could be as easily Thackeray's as Bunyan's that he remembered. James Kincaid outlines the similarities between stories of Becky and Amelia, and Madeline and Eleanor.[28] The comparison is a good one, but the analogy does not extend to Arabin. Nevertheless, Eleanor's and Madeline's similarities to the Thackeray women suggest parallels in the tone of the two novels. Their conclusions are much alike, as mentioned earlier: "Which of us is happy in this world? Which of us has his desire? or, having it, is satisfied?—Come children, let us shut up the box and the puppets, for our play is played out."[29] Trollope's closing chapter begins: "The end of a novel, like the end of a children's dinner party, must be made up of sweetmeats and sugar-plums" (LIII). The enduring tone of *Vanity Fair*, however, is cynical; there is always a barb in the humor. In *Barchester Towers* parallels to Thackeray are but a part of a genial narrator's allusive play.

Despite the good humor, Trollope conscientiously exposes the weaknesses of all his characters with the incisiviness Thackeray shows in *Vanity Fair*. No one escapes the humor of the narrator whether described as part of the war or the melodrama or the romance. Septimus Harding belongs to none of the exuberant levels of the novel, but even he, as moral core, is not entirely exempt from the narrator's raillery. He still plays an invisible violoncello whenever he is deeply troubled, as he did in *The Warden*; he has a "want of self-confidence" (XVIII) that makes him seem a "puppet" (XXXIV) to men of Grantly's verve. The narrator laughs at some of his instances of strength—when he refuses to give up his "*pied à terre*" (XLIV) in High Street, or when he refuses to question what he thinks is Eleanor's love for Slope: "There was but little of the Roman about Mr. Harding. He could not sacrifice his Lucretia even though she should be polluted by the accepted addresses of the clerical Tarquin at the palace" (XXVIII).[30] Ironically, it is in Harding's self-doubtings, in his persistent questions, that we see the firm faith of Barchester. To men such as Grantly and Proudie and even Slope little self-examination is ever required: "The school of men to whom he [Harding] professes to belong, the Grantlys, the Gwynnes, and the old high set of Oxford divines, are afflicted with no such self-accusations as these which troubled Mr. Harding. They, as a rule, are as satisfied with the wisdom and propriety of their own conduct as can be any Mr. Slope, or any Dr. Proudie, with his own. But unfortunately for himself Mr. Harding had little of this self-reliance" (XIII). Instead, when he sees what he may have to undergo with the new appointment to the wardenship, he questions his ability to become a martyr for his beliefs. He likens his own subjection to the Proudies and Slopes to the sacrifice of St. Bartholomew, St. Sebastian, and St. Lorenzo, but without a pride in the comparison that we find in Grantly's sermon on St. Paul and Onesimus.

Harding is a completely humble man, possessed of a firmness as unobtrusive as his "velvet step" (I). He acts as a structural and moral core for the novel in characteristically quiet ways. Though it is not immediately apparent, he poses the key questions of the novel and, by example, supplies their answers. He is a catalyst for the major campaign of the clerical war—the wardenship becomes a point of contention among Grantly,

Slope, and Mrs. Proudie. It is he, and not Mr. Arabin, who encounters and struggles with Slope face-to-face. It is from him that Arabin accepts the position of dean of Barchester. He opposes his powerful son-in-law, the archdeacon, concerning both the wardenship and the deanship. Structurally, he thus provides direction for the novel. Morally, he also directs the true spirit of Barchester. He rightly discerns Slope's philosophy of the times, and he shudders at the artificiality Slope advocates:

> We must talk, think, and live up to the spirit of the times, and write up to it too, if that cacoethes be upon us, or else we are nought. New men and new measures, long credit and few scruples, great success or wonderful ruin, such are now the tastes of Englishmen who know how to live. Alas, alas! Under such circumstances Mr. Harding could not but feel that he was an Englishman who did not know how to live. This new doctrine of Mr. Slope and the rubbish cart, new at least at Barchester, sadly disturbed his equanimity (XIII).

In later novels, *Phineas Redux, The Prime Minister,* and particularly *The Way We Live Now,* Trollope works out the serious implications of the frenzied "men, not measures" politics; here he uses Harding's insight into the shallowness of unthinking change as a counterpoise for the Thornes' unpractical, reactionary ways.

At the center of the mock battles and the fanciful melodramas and the boisterous allusions and patternings is Harding's faith in amelioration. Harding himself gets singular treatment from the narrator—though we smile at the mild old precentor and his violoncello, we see him as separate from the humor and the texture of the rest of the novel. It is as though the multiple linguistic devices in the whole work rest upon the simplicity of style used with Harding.[31] In characterizing him, Trollope's narrator never uses flights of mock-heroic style or dense patterns of associative phrases or allusions. And Harding's concept of change, his antidote to the poison of men like Slope, is devoid of fanfare:

> A tear came into each eye as he reflected that all this [familiar intercourse with the old bishop] was gone. What use would the hospital be to him now? He was alone in the world, and getting old; he would

44 Patterns of Repetition in Trollope

soon, very soon have to go, and leave it all, as his dear old friend had gone; go, and leave the hospital, and his accustomed place in the cathedral, and his haunts and pleasures, to younger and perhaps wiser men. That chanting of his!—perhaps, in truth, the time for it had gone by. He felt as though the world were sinking from his feet; as though this, this was the time for him to turn with confidence to those hopes which he had preached with confidence to others. "What," said he to himself, "can a man's religion be worth, if it does not support him against the natural melancholy of declining years?" And, as he looked out through his dimmed eyes into the bright parterres of the bishop's garden, he felt that he had the support which he wanted (XII).

In the sad musings of an old man we find the essence of Barchester. Harding is the emblem of humane tolerance, of gentleness and kindness which transcend the petty squabbles of passing controversies. He is not a philosopher but his beliefs, like his nostalgia, are instinctive, spontaneous—fundamental to the enduring strength of Barchester. Harding's elemental goodness is like Mr. Tryan's in George Eliot's *Scenes of Clerical Life*:

> Ideas are often poor ghosts; our sun-filled eyes cannot discern them; they pass athwart us in thin vapour, and cannot make themselves felt. But sometimes they are made flesh; they breathe upon us with warm breath, they touch us with soft responsive hands, they look at us with sad sincere eyes, and speak to us in appealing tones; they are clothed in a living human soul, with all its conflicts, its faith, and its love. Then their presence is a power, then they shake us like a passion, and we are drawn after them with gentle compulsion, as flame is drawn to flame.[32]

Barchester Towers is instinct with Septimus Harding's unassuming power. Because of him we see that change, tempered by honesty and humility, is not only good, but necessary. It is right that a worthy clergyman with fourteen children should be given a reasonable living; it is fitting that an energetic scholar and his youngish wife should come to the deanery. Unlike his belligerent son-in-law, Harding can accept parvenu clergymen and parvenu round tables, if the changes bring improvements.

Barchester Towers is a bustling novel, unique in all Trollope's writing for the density of repeated allusions, echoes, and patterns of language generally. He creates battles and melodramas and romances in an exuberant, narrator-dominated chorus of allusion, stock phrase, and proverb. The real triumph, however, is in the way we experience Harding's quiet charm through the boisterous good humor. Never again did Trollope write a novel so openly whimsical (and yet true)[33] as *Barchester Towers*. Yet even in this height of his exuberance we feel, through Harding's ascendancy, the subtle control that characterizes all of Trollope's good novels.

2
The Last Chronicle of Barset

Ten years and twelve novels after *Barchester Towers*, Trollope published *The Last Chronicle of Barset*. It was not, in fact, the last of Trollope's works set in Barsetshire,[1] but it was the last to include all of the familiar favorites. *The Last Chronicle* is one of Trollope's greatest novels—Trollope himself called it his best[2]— and it has enduring popularity because it provides more than a tidy farewell to the people and places of the series. It completes the stories of the major characters from the other five novels but also makes a memorable (if perplexing) psychological study of a former minor character. New characters from London and old characters from Barsetshire act as foils for Josiah Crawley's emotional drama. The novel's multiple focus explores self-reflection and the obstacles to honest self-reflection,[3] simultaneously concentrating attention on the Reverend Josiah Crawley's brooding intellect. Crawley is central to the structure and theme, and the numerous characters and subplots, intrinsically interesting in themselves, provide parallels for his struggles.

The novel is constructed around Crawley's alleged theft of £20. All of Barsetshire reverberates with the news, and the reader is allowed to examine how Harding, the Grantlys, the Thornes, the Luftons, the Greshams, the Dales, the Arabins, and the Proudies—the characters from the thousands of pages of the Barset novels—react to Crawley's trial of honesty. Each of the major characters undergoes some trial of his own, and each case is compared with Crawley's. Though Crawley by no means features in every chapter of the novel, he determines the reader's response to old and new characters.

The method of characterization of Crawley, the means of keeping him central to the farewell and to the study of honest self-reflection, shows how Trollope's technique has developed since *Barchester Towers*. The Barchester comedy operated on a number of levels, through a combination of playful strains—war, melodrama, romance. At the center of the novel, in a singularly unornamented position, is Septimus Harding. The very liveliness of the highly allusive style surrounding him makes his quiet presence powerful. The liveliest and most conspicuous character in the novel, a perfect foil for Harding, is the narrator. In *The Last Chronicle of Barset* the narrator's self-declaring presence is diminished, and a new voice supplements that of the jovial commentator. We frequently step into what C. P. Snow calls the "psychological stream" of the characters' own thoughts.[4] The narrator's and the characters' voices are so effectively blended that it is virtually impossible at times to separate them. As a result, we respond to a species of internal monologue, thinking of what may be summaries of events as transcriptions of the characters' patterns of thought. The knowledge of the characters is more intimate and the identification with them more complete than when the good-humored narrator-guide leads us to an appreciation of the story as a whole. This is not to say that the separation of the characters' thoughts and the narrative third person does not exist in *Barchester Towers*—but it does mean that the voice of the narrator-character does not dominate *The Last Chronicle of Barset*. The friendly asides and apostrophes are replaced by a uniformity and subtlety of tone that William West calls the "subliminal aura of warmth and light."[5]

In *Barchester Towers* the fabric of the novel is composed of numerous repetitions, literary allusions, clichés, and individual tags, and Harding's position is reinforced by the fact that few allusions and repetitions are used with him; in *The Last Chronicle of Barset* works of literature—quoted or alluded to by Crawley himself—are used by the reader to explore Josiah Crawley's mind as well as to assess other characters' relationships to him and to each other. The narrator revives the war imagery from *Barchester Towers* to characterize Grantly and the Proudies, but Trollope uses literary allusions and repetitions with a new subtlety. We find that the most serious and the most frivolous parts of the novel depend on a network of references and allusions. A variety of other linguistic devices revive the many characters from Barsetshire, all of whom undergo trials in their attempts at honest self-reflection.

The Last Chronicle has a complex structure. There are three centers of action—Hogglestock, the bishop's palace, and London; and five stories: Mr. Crawley's supposed theft of the check for £20, Mrs. Proudie's attempt to maintain supremacy in the diocese, Lily Dale's repeated refusal of Johnny Eames and his entanglement with Madalina Demolines, Major Grantly's love for Grace Crawley, and Mrs. Dobbs Broughton's aid in the painting of Jael and Sisera. In the interweaving of these places and plot lines Trollope's control is remarkable. Crawley's story is never obscured by the others; his imposing figure provides a powerful focus for a potentially sprawling narrative.

Crawley judges himself and others through literature; his own language reflects his love for classical writings and Scripture. The narrator and Crawley himself make us appreciate how important certain volumes and expressions are in analyzing the workings of his mind. In the introduction to Archdeacon Grantly in *The Warden*, we find a catalogue of his library that alerts us to his High and Dry prejudices as surely as his secret copy of Rabelais tells us of his more earthly side. The narrator shows us busts of Grantly's heroes: "Chrysostom, St. Augustine, Thomas à Becket, Cardinal Wolsey, Archbishop Laud, and Dr. Philpotts" (xii). Josiah Crawley's preferences tell even more about his preoccupations:

... the small space at which he wrote, was covered with dog's-eared books, from nearly all of which the covers had disappeared. There were there two odd volumes of Euripides, a Greek Testament, an Odyssey, a duodecimo Pindar, and a miniature Anacreon. There was half a Horace,—the two first books of the Odes at the beginning, and the De Arte Poetica at the end having disappeared. There was a little bit of a volume of Cicero, and there were Caesar's Commentaries, in two volumes, so stoutly bound that they had defied the combined ill-usage of time and the Crawley family. All these were piled upon the secretary, with many others,—odd volumes of sermons and the like; but the Greek and Latin lay at the top, and showed signs of most frequent use (IV).[6]

Crawley is a tireless scholar, exercising his playful and serious moments with literature. He reads books in Latin and French; recites "English poetry, lines after lines, stanzas upon stanzas, in a sweet low melancholy voice"; and even "translated into Greek irregular verse the very noble ballad of Lord Bateman,[7] maintaining the rhythm and the rhyme, and had repeated it with uncouth glee till his daughter knew it all by heart" (IV). After he is accused of stealing the check, he finds solace and inspiration in reading various works: when he hears that he must go before the magistrates, he reads Greek with Jane (VIII); after he expels Thumble they read *Seven Against Thebes* (XIII); to prepare himself for his meeting with the Proudies they read Oedipus (XVII); Grace reads Greek with him when she comes home and thus discovers that he is recovering from his illness (XLI); he recommends that Jane and Grace pass their idle hours with memorizing Antigone (XLI); he identifies himself with Polyphemus, Belisarius, and Samson (LXII); after a long and touching interview with Robarts he reads Pindar (LXVIII); he advises Jane to criticize Euripides rather than Thumble (LXIX); he accepts Grantly's friendship when the archdeacon presents him with a volume of the old bishop Grantly's sermons (LXXXIII).

His use of literature, in his troubled times, is occasionally playful, but is more often solemn. We achieve insight into his nature through his range of associations and reactions. His treatment of Thumble typifies the playful and serious sides of his nature. He calls Thumble an "angel," knowing that the little man will not understand the origin and use of the word. When he drives the bungling chaplain from his door he delights in Aeschylus's *Seven Against Thebes,* likening his own actions to the glories of Greek wars. From their knowledge of the play, Trollope's audience would have appreciated the full irony of Crawley's association. Eteocles' command to the female chorus in the play is Crawley's imagined rebuke to Mrs. Proudie, Thumble's chief:

War is no female province, but the scene
For men: hence, home; nor spread your mischiefs here.[8]

Another level to the reference is sadly ironic: at the seventh gate of Thebes, Eteocles and Polynices, by killing each other, fulfill the curse laid on Laius and Jocasta. Later in *The Last Chronicle of Barset* Crawley, too, laments the fact that his sins will be visited on his children. Perhaps the Greek drama inspires what his Old Testament (Exodus 20:5) reading substantiates: "'My child!' he said. 'My poor child! my darling! She has found grace in this man's sight; but even of that has her father robbed her! The Lord has visited upon the children the sins of the father, and will do so to the third and fourth generation'" (LXIII). Crawley mixes his classical and Scriptural knowledge to make more misery for himself.

In Crawley's great battle with the Proudies, we see a different combination of classical and Scriptural force: he himself is serious, and the result is a dignified comedy. On his way to the palace, he is:

... snorting like a racehorse at the expected triumph of the coming struggle. And he read much Greek with Jane on that afternoon, pouring into her young ears, almost with joyous rapture, his appreciation of the glory and the pathos and the humanity, as also of the awful tragedy, of the story of Oedipus. His very soul was on fire at the idea of clutching the weak bishop in his hand, and crushing him with his strong grasp (XVII).

During the interview Crawley ignores Mrs. Proudie with a determination that is nothing short of heroic. Mrs. Proudie will not withdraw and tries to scold the curate as she had once scolded Mr. Harding and Dr. Gwynne in *Barchester Towers*. Crawley's rebuke betokens the quality of his mind while the staging itself is reminiscent of the comic scenes of *Barchester Towers*:

"Peace, woman," Mr. Crawley said, addressing her at last. The bishop jumped out of his chair at hearing the wife of his bosom called a woman. But he jumped rather in admiration than in anger. He had already begun to perceive that Mr. Crawley was a man who had better be left to take care of the souls at Hogglestock, at any rate till the trial should come on.

"Woman!" said Mrs. Proudie, rising to her feet as though she really intended some personal encounter.

"Madam," said Mr. Crawley, "you should not interfere in these matters. You simply debase your husband's high office. The distaff were more fitting for you" (XVIII).

Mr. Crawley's dignity is inspired by the reading of *Oedipus,* but "distaff " comes from those familiar words in Proverbs describing the "virtuous woman." They end, we remember, with "She layeth her hands to the distaff, and her hands hold the spindle."[9] Mrs. Proudie is conquered by a sermon compressed into the one word *distaff.*

The most powerful passages in the entire novel show how Crawley identifies with the tragic figures of the classics and Scripture. We step directly into his thoughts and see how he responds to Polyphemus, Belisarius, and Samson:

"The same story is always coming up," he said, stopping the girl in her reading. "We have it in various versions, because it is so true to life.

> Ask for this great deliverer now, and find him
> Eyeless in Gaza, at the mill with slaves.

It is the same story. Great power reduced to impotence, great glory to misery, by the hand of Fate,—Necessity, as the Greeks called her; the goddess that will not be shunned! At the mill with slaves! People, when they read it, do not appreciate the horror of the picture. Go on, my dear. It may be a question whether Polyphemus had mind enough to suffer; but, from the description of his power, I should think that he had. 'At the mill with slaves!' Can any picture be more dreadful than that? Go on, my dear. Of course you remember Milton's Samson Agonistes. Agonistes indeed!" His wife was sitting stitching at the other side of the room; but she heard his words,—heard and understood them; and before Jane could again get herself into the swing of the Greek verse, she was over at her husband's side, with her arms round his neck. "My love!" she said. "My love!"

He turned to her, and smiled as he spoke to her. "These are old thoughts with me. Polyphemus and Belisarius, and Samson and Milton, have always been pets of mine. The mind of the strong blind creature must be sensible of the injury that has been done to him! The impotency, combined with his strength, or rather the impotency with the memory of former strength and former aspirations, is so essentially tragic!" (LXII).

This identification provides the key to Crawley's morbid musings. He prides himself on his similarity to the blind giants, and he prides himself on the fact that he can draw together and understand so many different stories from poetry. He sees himself as martyr and scholar, abused by those around him and manifestly grander. So much the reader can appreciate without knowing anything of Samson's further thoughts. But to the reader familiar with Milton's lines, there is the suggestion of another dimension of Crawley's suffering. The poem reads:

> Promise was that I
> Should Israel from Philistian yoke deliver;
> Ask for this great deliverer now, and find him
> Eyeless in Gaza at the mill with slaves,
> Himself in bonds under Philistian yoke:
> Yet stay, let me not rashly call in doubt
> Divine prediction; what if all foretold
> Had been fulfilled but through mine own default,
> Whom have I to complain of but myself?[10]

Samson has had to learn humility, and as Frank O'Connor says, "Crawley's sanctity has had to take a terrible beating from his vanity."[11] He prides himself on his similarities to the blind giants and on his ability to read them, and he is always struggling to understand the "default" of his position—that is, to remember where he got the check he is accused of having stolen. He believes that he got it from Arabin, but when Arabin denies it, Crawley attempts to achieve the humility of Samson by submitting himself to the dean. Accomplishing this perfect humility would leave Crawley with a desperate choice of the way to view his possession of the check: Did he steal it? Has he lost control of his memory and reason? Crawley's readings and his quotation from "Samson Agonistes" show his desire to do two opposing things: to revel in his strength and scholarship, which is to assert his sanity; to humble himself to the dean's word, which is to argue that he himself is mad. Even without knowing the words of Samson, we see that Crawley's is a losing battle against pride.

Crawley's test of honesty is really a battle against his pride. He judges himself by his intellectual merits, by the difficulty of his studies and the thoroughness of his identification with Scriptural solemnity and tragic grandeur. He cannot analyze his honesty without being driven to considerations of his sanity, and pride in intellectual pursuits is his reassurance that his mind is strong. In other words, Crawley judges himself by the literature he also uses for catharsis and inspiration. And this pride in scholarship makes him use literature as a gauge to assess the worth of those he feels the world considers superior to him. Scholarship is his touchstone.

Toogood is initially distasteful to Crawley, not only because he is jovial and eager, but also because Toogood prides himself on the education he has given his children. Crawley's intellectual snobbery bristles when Toogood proudly quotes from Dryden's "Alexander's Feast" to describe his wife obviously ignorant of the fact that Thais is a courtesan: "'"The lovely Thais sits beside you. Take the goods the gods provide you." I often say that to my wife, till the children have got to calling her Thais'" (xxxii). Toogood tells him that "'Educate, educate, educate; that's my word'" (xxxii) and then boasts of his children's erudition: "'And Lucy has read Lord Byron and Tom Moore all through, every word of 'em. By Jove, I believe she knows most of Tom Moore by heart. And the young uns are coming on just as well'" (xxxii). There could be no greater contrast between ideologies than between this industrious lawyer's and the ascetic clergyman's. We understand how far Crawley has conquered his pride when he can overlook Toogood's vulgarity—in his happiness at the end of the story, he puts aside his protective snobbery.[12]

By far a worse offender than Toogood is Arabin. At one time Arabin had had help from Crawley (we are told of this in chapter xx of *Barchester Towers*), and for a time Crawley looked upon him as a friend. In *Framley Parsonage*, where we see longer glimpses of Crawley, it is evident that the two are still close. But Crawley has become so poor in *The Last Chronicle of Barset* that he resents Arabin's success, reminding himself again and again that he is really the better scholar of the two. It is Arabin's access to scholarship that he resents more than anything else. He describes his feeling to Toogood: "'There were lying on the floor hundreds of volumes, all glittering with gold, and reeking with new leather from the binders. He asked me to look at his toys. Why should I look at them? There was a time, but the other day it seemed, when he had been glad to borrow from me such treasures as I had. And it seemed to me that he was heartless in showing me these things'" (XXXII). The contrast between Arabin's glittering volumes and Crawley's dog-eared ones is important. When Crawley is ill and delirious, he accuses Arabin of shallowness: "'He should have had my heart's blood if he wanted it. But now—look at his books, Grace. It's the outside of them he cares about. They are all gilt, but I doubt if he ever reads'" (XLI). It is not just that Crawley prides himself on what he knows and understands, but that he looks down on others for their lack of knowledge: "It was the fault of the man that he was imbued too strongly with self-consciousness. . . . It was not sufficient for him to remember that he knew Hebrew, but he must remember also that the dean did not" (LXI). And yet the dean, as we are told at the end of *Barchester Towers*, is considered, because of his scholarship, to be "the most promising clerical ornament of the age" (LIII). In Crawley's eyes, Arabin's offence is thus greater than Toogood's since Arabin has won recognition for work in which Crawley knows himself to be superior.

It is hard to begrudge Crawley his intellectual vanity when it is the only weapon he has against the pressures of the diocese. As long as he can pride himself on his scholastic powers, he can hold up his head among his more fortunate fellow clergymen: "Was there ever a man whose existence was so purposeless, so useless, so deleterious, as his own? And yet he knew Hebrew well, whereas the dean knew but very little Hebrew. He could make Greek iambics, and doubted whether the bishop knew the difference between an iambus and a trochee. He could disport himself with trigonometry, feeling confident that Dr. Tempest had forgotten his way over the asses' bridge. He knew 'Lycidas' by heart; and as for Thumble, he felt quite sure that Thumble was incompetent of understanding a single allusion in that divine poem" (LXII). Archdeacon Grantly discerns Crawley's pride and his love of scholarship when he calls him a gentleman and presents him with a volume of his father's sermons (LXXXIV). Crawley's most vulnerable point is, naturally, that which he has nurtured so carefully.

We recognize in his reliance on literature, and scholarship generally, a singular and remarkable mind. It is Crawley's constant, honest self-evaluation and his painful struggle with pride that establish the tone of the novel as a whole. His dependence on literature and his consequent bookish language inform all parts of *The Last Chronicle of Barset*. We feel we are listening to him rather than (as in *Barchester Towers*) to the narrator's interpretation of him. His preoccupations and his ideolect provide a standard against which to judge the other characters and their various trials of self-analysis.

The words of his familiar intercourse are as imposing as his knowledge. His speech is full of *seemeths* and *haths*; he uses the archaic *behoof* (LXI) and *nathless* (LXXIV) and calls himself *shandypated* (XXXII) (the *OED* cites Trollope here and in the earlier *Rachel Ray*). When we remember Mrs. Proudie's archaic "Unhand it, sir" we feel that they are suitable opponents. When he describes his feelings to his wife, assuring her that he will not commit suicide, he echoes *Hamlet* (III.i.76) and *Macbeth* (IV.i.25): "'. . . I will endure, though a bare bodkin or a leaf of hemlock would put an end to it" (XII). He thanks Robarts for his offers of friendship with forbidding formality: "'For yourself, as I was saying, pray believe me that though from the roughness of my manner, being now unused to social intercourse, I seem to be ungracious and forbidding, I am grateful and mindful, and that in the tablets of my heart I have written you down as one in whom I could trust—were it given to me to trust in men and women'" (XXI). There is something grand about Crawley that prevents his formality from sounding ridiculous. Of his thanks to Toogood after their first meeting the narrator says he ". . . reiterated thanks to his new friend in words which were touching in spite of their old-fashioned gravity. . ." (XXXII).

It is, in fact, this old-fashioned air that endears him to us and makes his preoccupations with literature and antiquity believable parts of his daily life. He has developed a singular manner of speech as a consequence of his scholarliness and as a preservative of it. He uses his formality as a weapon against adversity and as a support for pride as carefully but also as spontaneously as he refers to the classics for reassurance and inspiration. As Walter Allen says, he makes a carapace of his language to protect him from the ordinary world.[13]

When he first visits Toogood he says that he comes "*In forma pauperis*" (XXXII); when he imagines what people will say of him he puts his own archaic phraseology into their mouths: "'Lo! he confesses himself incapable!'" (XXXII). With "Roman fortitude" he writes to Arabin, "Nil conscire sibi, nulla pallescere culpa" (LXII) (to be conscious of no wrong, to turn pale at no accusation). In an elaborate sentence he rebukes Mr. Robarts for suggesting that we often feel more sympathy for those we know than for those we do not: "'No doubt the finite and meagre nature of our feelings does prevent us from extending our sympathies to those whom we have not seen in the flesh'" (LXVIII). And he discourages the use of familiar proverbs to comment on Mrs. Proudie's tyranny: "'When I hear jocose proverbs spoken as to men, such as that in this house the grey mare is the better horse, or that in that house the wife wears that garment which is supposed to denote virile command, knowing that the joke is easy, and that meekness in a man is more truly noble than a habit of stern authority, I do not allow them to go far with me in influencing my judgment'" (LXVIII). This is ironic, considering that Crawley resents Arabin's interference in his own marriage: "'A man's wife is his very own, the breath of his nostril, the blood of his heart, the rib from his body. It is for me to rule my wife. . .'" (LXXVIII). Occasionally Crawley is carried away by his own eloquence, just as he is often overproud of his scholarship. He declines Arabin's invitation to the deanery with "'It may not be that I and mine should transfer ourselves to your roof and sojourn there'" (LXXIX). But Crawley can also play with language, just as he could triumph over Thumble with Aeschylus, to show his good humor. He tells Arabin that he has escaped from his troubles with a "narrow squeak" and "The dean felt at the moment that not for many years had he heard the incumbent of Hogglestock speak either of himself or of anything else with so manifest an attempt at jocularity" (LXXIX).

The "attempt at jocularity," like the "uncouth glee" with which he created the Greek version of the ballad of Lord Bateman, prepares us for Crawley's regeneration. But for most of his story we identify him with tragedy and sad Scripture. Early in the book when he is trying to read Greek with his daughter, he exclaims in a reversal of Psalms 16:6: "'My God, what have I done against thee, that my lines should be cast in such terrible places?'" (VIII). The narrator tells us, in a tone altogether different from that used to make a similar statement in *Barchester Towers,* that Crawley was one "whose loaves and fishes are scanty" (X). He quotes Romans 12:19 and paraphrases Luke 6:29 when he boasts of his conquest of Mrs. Proudie: "'"Vengeance is mine. I will repay," saith the Lord,' answered Mr. Crawley. . . . 'To turn the other cheek instantly to the smiter can hardly be suitable in these days, when the hands of so many are raised to strike'" (XIX). We already know that he quashed Mrs. Proudie herself with the allusion to Proverbs. We have seen that Crawley believes, in his worst moments, the verse in Exodus, "'The Lord has visited upon the children the sins of the father, and will do so to the third and fourth generation'" (LXIII). It is fitting that when Toogood brings him news of his release, Crawley should break into Scripture, this time with the jubilance of Isaiah 52:7: "'. . . you are a messenger of glad tidings, whose feet are beautiful upon the mountains'" (LXXIV). The happiness is attuned to his "jocularity" with Arabin and his glee with his children, suggesting a subtle strain of potential joy running concurrent with his bitterest despair. This joy is part of Crawley's sense of humor, but for most of the book, we are made to concentrate, as he is, on the misery of his hopeless honesty and his thwarted pride.

In support of the sad Scripture and the tragedy we find another expression of Crawley's pride. He thinks of himself as greater than St. Paul. When his wife pleads with him to go to the magistrates instead of waiting for them to come for him he exclaims: "'Was St. Paul not bound in prison? Did he think of what the people might see?'" (VIII). He broods over the injustice of his degradation and thinks:

St. Paul could go forth without money in his purse or shoes to his feet or two suits to his back, and his poverty never stood in the way of his preaching, or hindered the veneration of the faithful. St. Paul, indeed, was called upon to bear stripes, was flung into prison, encountered terrible dangers. But Mr. Crawley—so he told himself—could have encountered all that without flinching. The stripes and scorn of the unfaithful would have been nothing to him, if only the faithful would have believed in him, poor as he was, as they would have believed in him had he been rich! (XII).

He visits the poor brickmakers because he "... felt himself to be more a St. Paul with them than with any other of his neighbours around him" (XII). The identification with St. Paul is harmful if, as with the blind giants, it prevents honest self-perception or humility. Yet, again, without this feeling of martyrdom, Crawley would have little support. His pride reaches its height when he identifies his sufferings with Christ's. He talks to Arabin about the Holy Land: "'... Rome makes my mouth water but little, nor even Athens much. I can realise without seeing all that Athens could show me, and can fancy that the existing truth would destroy more than it would build up. But to have stood on Calvary!' 'We don't know where Calvary was,' said the dean. 'I fancy that I should know—should know enough,' said the illogical and unreasonable Mr. Crawley" (LXXIX). Perhaps this is merely enthusiasm, but knowing Mr. Crawley as the careful allusions, echoes, and patterns lead us to know him, we feel that he, for a moment, and unconsciously, glorifies his own pains to the point of blasphemy.

For most of the book we examine Crawley's morbid introspections, but we are reminded at the beginning that he has had happier times. The jubilance of Isaiah suggests that those days may now return. He drops some of his intellectual snobbery and when Jane declares that Toogood is vulgar, he replies with this mild image: "'... when the jewel itself is good, any fault in the casket may be forgiven'" (LXXIV). Even more interesting is the recurrence of a homely expression to characterize his position. At the beginning he describes Proudie's advantage over him thus: "And the bishop would be in his own armchair—the cock in his own farmyard, while he, Mr. Crawley, would be seated afar off, in the cold extremity of the room..." (XVII). At the end of the book, dressed in his new frock coat, he complains to his wife: "'... you shall take a cock which is lord of the farmyard—the cock of all that walk—and when you have daubed his feathers with mud, he shall be thrashed by every dunghill coward. I say not that I was ever the cock of the walk, but I know that they have daubed my feathers'" (LXXXIII). It is typical of Crawley that he sees himself defeated by his new success. Perhaps the use of the homely expression itself indicates how far he feels himself to have fallen from the struggles of Greece or Calvary.

There is another level of irony involved in Crawley's use of the "bedaubed cock" analogy. The quality of the expression seems out of keeping with his archaic words and formal sentences until we realize a central irony of the novel: Crawley finds more strength in the brickmaker's words to him than he does in all the classical and Scriptural works he reads. Through them, in fact, he manages a semblance of humility that the great works denied him. Old Giles Hoggett advises: "'... there ain't nowt a man can't bear if he'll only be dogged. You go whome, Master Crawley, and think o' that, and maybe it'll do ye a good yet. It's dogged as does it. It ain't thinking about it'" (LXI).[14] Crawley repeats the words over and over to himself, and they eventually give him the strength to resign his living. He ennobles them somewhat in his own mind by associating them with a Latin tag, but it is still their essential homeliness that endears them to him. He thinks: "Let justice be done, though the heaven may fall" (LXII)—a translation of that favorite Latin tag Trollope uses in *He Knew He Was Right, Phineas Redux,* and *The Prime Minister,* "ruat caelum, fiat justitia"—but he is really only trying to reinforce "... that virtue which Hoggett had taught him" (LXII). Crawley achieves some humility through his acceptance of the expression, but even this humility is tinged with pride. When he condescends to be instructed by the brickmakers, it is as though, perhaps, he has been thrust into "the mill with slaves." It is no accident that after reflecting at length on Hoggett's maxim he recites to Jane from "Samson Agonistes." Nevertheless, we do feel that Crawley's sincere attempt to master Hoggett's advice suggests that he will eventually be able to shed the elaborate carapace his pride has constructed. The passage from Isaiah and the analogy of the bedaubed cock encourage faith in Crawley's happy recovery from his trial of honest self-reflection.

Mrs. Crawley understands better than anyone the struggle her husband has against his pride. She knows too well the false humility that makes him declare he will grovel before Mr. Toogood: "An unpleasant taste came across the palate of her mind, as such a savour will sometimes, from some unexpected source, come across the palate of the mouth" (XXXII). She knows the workings of his mind perfectly and reads him as easily as he reads Greek: "What she most dreaded was that he should sit idle over the fire and do nothing. When he was so seated she could read his mind, as though it was open to her as a book" (XII). But even though she fears his broodings, fears the "bare bodkin" he may use, she has a touching faith in him and their fate. She quotes to Lady Lufton the old proverb, "'We are told that He tempers the wind to the shorn lamb'" (L). Later when Crawley uses these same words to Dr. Tempest, we feel sure that Mrs. Crawley has been as much of an inspiration to him as Giles Hoggett: "'I can only trust that the wind may be tempered to them,' he said. 'They will, indeed, be shorn lambs'" (LXI). Mrs. Crawley's persistent humility and love reinforce our faith in Crawley's recovery.

The other major characters in the novel, like Crawley, have been introduced in other Barsetshire books. In *The Last Chronicle of Barset* Trollope revives the allusions and patterns of language associated with them in their earlier appearances. Crawley is central in their reintroductions, because his case provides an opportunity to draw in the diocese, and also because his own self-analysis seems to initiate theirs. A novel confined to Barsetshire alone would find a ready focus in Crawley, but *The Last Chronicle of Barset* is not confined to Barsetshire, and Trollope introduces some characters in London who have no place in Barsetshire at all. Even with them we feel Crawley's presence. Toogood is related to Crawley, and a comparison of the lawyer and clergyman is, as we have suggested, an important part of the characterization of Crawley. Other London characters, introduced through John Eames, become involved in a story that some critics have characterized as having no relationship to Crawley and his development. An examination of the patterns of language shows, however, that all of the London characters contribute to our assessment of the Hogglestock curate. The quality of allusions and clichés and repetitions used with Toogood and the numerous characters of the Jael and Sisera story provides a provocative contrast for those used with the scholarly Mr. Crawley.

Toogood's language is the opposite of Crawley's. Crawley's formal "in forma pauperis" is met by the unlucky reference to Thais, and the easy familiarity of "'Blood is thicker than water . . .'" (XXXII). He is proud of his large family, confiding to Crawley, "'I comfort myself with the text about the quiver . . .'" (XXXII). His words, though few, are full of a slangy verve that endears him to the reader and eventually to Crawley himself. When he gives Crawley the momentous news about his release, he uses a common expression: "'It's all right, old fellow,' he said, clapping his hand on Mr. Crawley's shoulder. 'We've got the right sow by the ear at last. We know all about it'" (LXXIV). He is equally jocose in talking of the dean of Barchester. He tells Johnny that he will probably find Arabin out of his "'armour . . . as the knights of old used to do'" (XLVIII).

There is no mock humility about Toogood, and he puts himself at his ease in talking about everything. He believes he and Mr. Crawley are of one mind about education, innocent of the differences between devotion to the classics and infatuation with Byron and Tom Moore. Lucy Toogood's words to Johnny Eames tell us what her education has provided: "'. . . I'd like to have a Corsair—or else a Giaour—I think a Giaour would be nicest. Only a Giaour wouldn't be a Giaour here, you know. Fancy a lover "Who thundering comes on blackest steed, with slackened bit and hoof of speed"'" and "'I know I'd go back and be Medora, if I could. Mamma is always telling Polly that she must be careful about William's dinner. But Conrad didn't care for his dinner. "Light toil! to cull and dress thy frugal fare! See, I have plucked the fruit that promised best"'" (XL). Trollope uses Byron frequently in his writing, and almost always to criticize shallow sentiment and affectation. Lucy's infatuation is innocent, and probably harmless, as was Ayala's (ultimately) in *Ayala's Angel,* but Mrs. Dobbs Broughton's, Lizzy Eustace's, and Lady Carbury's are not. There is the suggestion, as there always is in Trollope's use of Byron, that Lucy's time could have been more wisely spent. The contrast between the two conscientious parents is amusing and enlightening. Toogood is a good foil for Crawley, and Trollope brings this to our attention in a little joke on his own novel. Toogood comments on Crawley's struggle: "'Though he knew where he got the cheque as well as I know it now, he wouldn't say so, because the dean had said it wasn't so. Somebody ought to write a book about it—indeed they ought'" (LXXVII).

The characters of Jael and Sisera provide a different contrast to Crawley from that provided by Toogood, for they never encounter him directly. Instead, the reader is called on by the allusive technique used with them and by the general analytic tone of the novel to compare the central psychological character and the members of an apparently frivolous subplot. With Crawley the patterns of speech and the allusions betoken depth. The allusions in the story of Jael and Sisera suggest uniform superficiality. In fact the technique used in Jael and Sisera seems a parody of that used in the serious parts of the novel. Here Trollope plays on the differences between the classics and Byron.

Conway Dalrymple, Mrs. Dobbs Broughton, and Clara Van Siever, the chief figures of Jael and Sisera, are purposely slight creations. They are physical extensions of the sham wealth produced by speculation and are thus forerunners of the societies of the later Ferdinand Lopez and Augustus Melmotte. The very silver on the Broughtons' dinner table is plate; Conway works as an artist only that he might be "pelted with gilt sugar-plums." The entire story is composed of the exaggerated, artificial, and eventually perfunctory dialogues of Mrs. Broughton's and Conway's make-believe intrigue. Mrs. Broughton, though "not given to much reading" (XXXVIII), is infatuated with Byron. She plans to sacrifice her love of Conway, but:

> If, after that, some poet did not immortalise her friendship in Byronic verse, she certainly would not get her due. Perhaps Conway Dalrymple would himself become a poet in order that this might be done properly. For it must be understood that, though she expected Conway Dalrymple to marry, she expected also that he should be Byronically wretched after his marriage on account of his love for herself (LI).

She pictures herself as "romantic and poetic" (LI), and often her "mind was filled with a poetic frenzy" (LI). She quotes Byron's "Prisoner of Chillon" when complaining of their sorrows: "'Age does not go by years, ... We all know that. "His hair was grey, but not with years." Look here, Conway,' and she moved back her tresses from off her temples to show him that there were grey hairs behind. He did not see them; and had they been very visible she might not perhaps have been so ready to exhibit them" (LI). We feel that it is Mrs. Broughton more than the narrator who tells us about Conway's Turkish cap: "There was something picturesque about the cap, which might not have been incongruous with love-making. It is easy to suppose that Juan wore a Turkish cap when he sat with Haidee in Lambro's island" (LX). To protect herself from what people may say of her intrigue, she adopts the motto "Honi soit qui mal y pense" (XXXVIII), not understanding, perhaps, its meaning. She quotes *Lear* (III.iv.21): "'That way madness lies'" (XXXVIII) and offers so complete a contrast to her quotation that the narrator uses another Shakespearean allusion to reinforce the joke against her. Of the prospects of her running away with Conway the narrator says: "As to leaving Mr. Dobbs Broughton's house, and putting herself into the hands of another man—no Imogen of a wife was ever less likely to take a step so wicked, so dangerous, and so generally disagreeable to all the parties concerned" (XXXVIII). In their early meetings Conway alludes to the lines in *Love's Labour's Lost* (IV.iii.335–36) that the narrator used in *Barchester Towers* to characterize Madeline Neroni's conquest of Mr. Thorne. Here Conway is merely obliging Mrs. Broughton's need for romance. For Clara Van Siever, she tells him: "'You must climb the tree.' 'Still climbing trees in the Hesperides,' said Conway. 'Love does that, you know; but it is hard to climb the trees without the love.... the boughs are breaking with me, and ... I am likely to get a fall'" (XXVI). He tires of her posturing: "In his present mood he was not anxious for one of those tilts with blunted swords and half-severed lances in the lists of Cupid..." (LI).

The misguided, bothersome woman, who belongs to the class of "many Potiphar's wives who never dream of any mischief " (LI), is at her most ridiculous in her identifications with the story of Abraham and Isaac. As she prepares Clara for the picture of Jael and Sisera (the subject of the painting itself a mockery of the Bible): "She used to tell herself as she did so, that she was like Isaac, piling the fagots for her own sacrifice. Only Isaac had piled them in ignorance, and she piled them conscious of the sacrificial flames. And Isaac had been saved; whereas it was impossible that the catching of any ram in any thicket could save her. But, nevertheless, she arranged the drapery with all her skill, piling the fagots ever so high for her own pyre" (LI). Near the end of their story Conway offers money to her, apologizing for "however prosaic it may seem" (LX), aware that Mrs. Dobbs Broughton needs to keep up the false poetic frenzy in order to give her life interest. We see how necessary fiction is to her when she (in an action that suggests Trollope may have been influenced by Dickens's chilling analysis of the condemned Fagin) reacts to her husband's suicide by closing her mind: "Then she dropped his hands and walked away from him to the window—and stood there looking out upon the stuccoed turret of a huge house that stood opposite.... Her mind was paralyzed by the blow, and ... in the midst of it all she counted the windows of the house opposite" (LXIV). Mrs. Dobbs Broughton has, in fact, built a protective shell of her own from her narrow reading. The contrast of her dependence on Byron and convenient stories of Scripture to Crawley's reliance on epics, tragedies, and Commandments is instructive. Trollope has created the false world of the stockbroker's London to act as a foil for Crawley's solid virtues and palpable poverty. And Mrs. Broughton herself is a travesty of Crawley's preoccupations.

There is an ironic connection between the most serious and the most frivolous parts of this novel that makes them fully complementary: Mr. Crawley often resembles the Byronic hero Mrs. Broughton glorifies. At the beginning, when Crawley broods by his fireside, we feel that we are witnessing the decay of a once noble mind. He imprisons himself in morbid fancies and resembles Bonnivard in Byron's "Prisoner of Chillon," which Mrs. Broughton quotes. Crawley does recover some of his equanimity after Toogood brings him the news of his release, but it is typical of him that he does, as we have noted, feel defeated by his new successes with the archdeacon and St. Ewold's. In other words, he shares Bonnivard's reaction to his release from prison:

> And half I felt as they were come
> To tear me from a second home:
> . . . .
> My very chains and I grew friends,
> So much a long communion tends
> To make us what we are:—even I
> Regain'd my freedom with a sigh.[15]

Critics have claimed that Jael and Sisera, like Ullathorne in *Barchester Towers*, is an 'incongruous patch' on the narrative.[16] Instead, it seems that, like Ullathorne, Jael and Sisera contributes, by its very lightness, to the more serious purpose of the novel. We can more thoroughly appreciate the sterling qualities of Crawley and Barsetshire when we see the "Brummagem"[17] of London.

Johnny Eames, a main character of *The Small House at Allington*, calls the Broughtons "'Brummagem'" (XXIV) and is the means of introducing them and Madalina Demolines into *The Last Chronicle of Barset*. Madalina, bosom friend of Maria Broughton, is as fond of tragedies and epics as Mrs. Broughton is of Byron. Madalina's part in the novel is small, but she acts as a lively contrast to Lily Dale, whom Johnny really loves. Madalina is, in fact, part of Johnny's trial of honesty—he must free himself from her to be worthy of Lily. Madalina uses all of her histrionic energies to capture him. She calls him a "preux chevalier" (XLVI) and appeals to his sense of the dramatic when she relates Broughton's suicide: "'Man,' said Madalina, jumping from her chair, standing at her full height, and stretching out both her arms, 'he has destroyed himself!' The revelation was at last made with so much tragic propriety, in so excellent a tone, and with such an absence of all the customary redundancies of commonplace relation, that I think that she must have rehearsed the scene—either with her mother or with the page" (LXXV). She gives him all the details, and the narrator remarks: "She told her tale somewhat after the manner of Æneas, not forgetting the 'quorum pars magna fui'" (LXXV). With her the narrator revives the image that dominated *The Small House at Allington*: "The moth who flutters round the light knows that he is being burned, and yet he cannot fly away from it" (LXXX).[18] He also, with her, revives the images of beasts of prey and warriors from *Barchester Towers* to describe the campaign to conquer Johnny: ". . . he swore to himself that no union of dragon and tigress should extract from him a word that could be taken as a promise of marriage" (LXXX). Lady Demolines becomes a dishonest Mrs. Proudie: ". . . Lady Demolines, drawing herself back, and looking, in her short open cloak, like a knight who has donned his cuirass, but has forgotten to put on his leg-gear. And she shook the bright ribbons of her cap, as a knight in his wrath shakes the crest of his helmet" (LXXX). The antics of Madalina and her mother emphasize the comic elements in Johnny's own self-analysis.

    Johnny Eames is no longer the hobbledehoy of *The Small House*, but he is still a little too proud of his own romantic behavior to make the reader, or perhaps Lily either, take him seriously. Crawley's pride may lead him to compare himself to St. Paul, but Johnny takes comfort in identifying himself with the heroes in a hodgepodge of Biblical, Shakespearean, and romantic stories. He feels that if Lily now married Crosbie, ". . . anything so perversely cruel as the fate of John Eames would never yet have been told in romance" (xv). When he is again refused by Lily, Lady Julia reminds him of Jacob and Rachel (xxxv), but her reminder is unnecessary for he has already felt that he has "out-Jacobed Jacob" (xv). Later, on his travels to Europe in search of Mrs. Arabin, he prepares himself for another proposal with "His constancy had been as the constancy of a Jacob!" (xv). Later still, when he has proposed for what was supposed to be the last time, he thinks he might wait a few more years and try again, so that "In such a way would he not make himself immortal as a lover beyond any Jacob or any Leander?" (LXXX). Johnny occasionally laughs at his own determination and thinks any lover ridiculous who would go about like Malvolio: "'. . . I don't go about with my stockings crossgartered, and do that kind of business. . .'" (xxv).[19] He can tell Madalina honestly that he is as "jolly as a sandboy" (LXXX) and make playful allusions to Sir Charles Grandison (xxxix), but he is, too, always thinking of his "Excelsior" (LXX), as do all the characters in *The Three Clerks*.

Johnny's own use of literature, and the narrator's reinforcements, make him appealing but uninspiring. Twice he tries to sing lines from Wither's poem "The Lovers' Resolution" to dispel thoughts of Lily: "'If she be not fair to me, what care I how fair she be?'" (XLVI), and later: "'Shall I, sighing in despair, die because a woman's fair? If she be not fair to me, what care I how fair she be?'" (LXXVII). His quotations of Shakespeare seem either out of place or too lighthearted. He compares Madalina and Lily with thoughts of *Hamlet* (III.iv) and couples that reflection with Wither's poem: "Why had he left Lily to go to Madalina? As he thought of this he quoted to himself against himself Hamlet's often-quoted appeal to the two portraits. How could he not despise himself in that he could find any pleasure with Madalina, having a Lily Dale to fill his thoughts? 'But she is not fair to me,' he said to himself. . ." (XLVIII). It is difficult to despair with him when his thoughts are such a hodgepodge of glorification and abasement. *As You Like It* (III.ii.282–88) is more appropriate for him since he lacks Hamlet's powers of introspection: "He thought of Rosalind, and her counsels to lovers as to the keeping of time, and reflected that in such an emergency as his, he might really have ruined himself by that unfortunate slumber" (LXXVII).

The literary allusions used with Johnny suggest that he is an intelligent man but show that he overestimates his abilities. His resilience is charming, but it also makes him an object of the narrator's mild raillery. Mrs. Broughton's love of Byron characterizes her; Johnny's failure with Greek best reveals him. He resolves to abandon his job and take up the life of a private scholar, but when he discovers that he will have to learn the Greek alphabet all over again, he concludes, "Greek was not the thing for him. . ." (LXXX). The only thing to which he does stick with much energy is his scheme to marry Lily, and even it seems to become simply a habit too difficult to break. He paraphrases the words of *Henry IV, I* in complaining of Lily's unfair expectations: "The days for plucking glory from the nettle danger were clean gone by" (LXX),[20] and yet he realizes that there is something of vigorous gallantry lacking in him. The ease with which he laughs at Malvolio, quotes Wither, and abandons Greek suggests a complacency that can never win the lively intelligence of Lily Dale.

Johnny's honest self-evaluation makes him prefer to think of himself as a Jacob—he rids himself of Madalina and hopes to have no other waverings away from Lily Dale. Lily's trial of honesty is quite different. With so many people pushing her toward Johnny,[21] Lily is forced to analyze her own scruples. The reader discovers that what clouds her judgment is not sexual frigidity, as Laurence Lerner suggests,[22] but a tendency either to sentimentalize or to deride her own emotions. Lily's language shows that she never learns to reconcile her own energy and conservatism.

Lily's language, like Glencora Palliser's, is full of energetic and colorful slang. The whole of chapter XVI shows her command of vigorous expressions. Elsewhere she spices her speech as liberally: she wishes Lady Julia wouldn't use devious tactics "'... for then I could get up on my legs and answer her off the reel'" (XVI); she says of her uncle: "'He wears well, and he washes well...'" (XVI); when her mother reads the letter from Crosbie she declares, "'... out with it at once. What is the use of shivering on the brink?'" (XXIII); she calls her mother's a "pelican's love" (XXIII); she says easily: "'Out of the full heart the mouth speaketh—that is, the mouth does so when the full heart is allowed to have its own way comfortably'" (XXIII); she says playfully of Major Grantly: "'I have caught a major, mamma, and landed him'" (XXVIII); she teases Grace about him by saying, "'I am beginning to regard him as the one chevalier *sans peur et sans reproche*'" (XXIX); she shocks her mother with this bit of racy slang: "'Major Grantly has—skedaddled'" (XXXI);[23] she continues her military humor by telling Johnny that she and Grace will "convoy" (XXXV) him home; she summarizes her feelings for Grace and the major: "'I would take my best boots and eat them down to the heels, for Grace's sake, and for Major Grantly's'" (XXXI).

Throughout this novel, just as in *The Small House,* Lily is entertaining because she is often irreverent. She declares that she will put the letters *O.M.* after her name, "'O.M., for Old Maid. I don't see why it shouldn't be as good as B.A. for Bachelor of Arts. It would mean a great deal more'" (LXXVI).[24] But along with Lily's liveliness is a sentimentality that is often mawkish and maudlin. She uses the "won't wash" expression to sum up her feelings for her Apollo, Crosbie: "'The Apollos of the world—I don't mean in outward looks, mamma—but the Apollos in heart, the men—and the women too—who are so full of feeling, so soft-natured, so kind, who never say a cross word, who never get out of bed on the wrong side in the morning—it so often turns out that they won't wash'" (XVI). She speaks in vaguely ecstatic terms of forgiveness and what is her mother's duty in relation to Crosbie and heaven (XXIII), but when her mother paraphrases Scripture back to her, she refuses to listen and falls into the trite imagery of flowers and thorns: "'When a man has cheated you once, you think he will cheat you again, and you do not deal with him. You do not look to gather grapes from thistles,'[25] after you have found that they are thistles.' 'I still go for the roses though I have often torn my hand with thorns in looking for them.' 'But you do not pluck those that have become cankered in the blowing.' 'Because he was once at fault, will he be cankered always?'" (XXIII).

Lily knows her own weakness, but she cannot force herself beyond it. With her words to Mrs. Arabin she acknowledges to herself her own deficiency: "'I shall never become any man's wife. Mamma and I are all in all together, and we shall remain together.' As soon as these words were out of her mouth, she hated herself for having spoken them. There was a maudlin, missish, namby-pamby sentimentality about them which disgusted her" (LXXVI). When she gives her final refusal to Johnny, she struggles to be straightforward, but she ends by calling herself a "shattered tree" that is not fit for the center of any man's garden (LXXVII). Even when she wishes to be direct, she resorts to analogy. Like Josiah Crawley's, Lily's language is often used to defend, not reveal, her inmost thoughts. In her sentimentality and his formality we feel a similar perversity of spirit.

Lily's and Johnny's story is more interesting than the love story that is closest to Crawley—his daughter's and Major Grantly's. Henry Grantly and Grace Crawley belong to that list of Trollope heroes and heroines who have little life and few faults. Lily gives the major more attention than most readers will, for they see in him and in the images he uses to characterize himself, a stock formula. Henry "built various castles in the air" (VII), just as the three young girls do in *The Way We Live Now* (discussed in chapter VI) and felt that he must "... take upon himself the armour of a knight-errant for the redress of the wrong on the part of the young lady" (XIV). He justifies Lily's use of the military slang by his own image of his family: "It made him sad to think that he should cut the rope which fastened his own boat among the other boats in the home harbour at Plumstead, and that he should go out all alone into strange waters—turned adrift, as it were, from the Grantly fleet" (XXII). His consolation in his struggles is that after it all, Grace will be at the helm (XXII). Major Grantly's self-examination produces little that is interesting or moving, and Grace's blushing resolutions are as tame. Her father thinks her a great scholar, but we wonder at her brilliance when we see: "She had learned to read Greek and Italian because there had been nothing else for her to do in that sad house" (XXX). For a young scholar ripe with her father's love of quotation and allusion she is certainly dull. She makes a strange paraphrase of Exodus 20:17 in describing her relationship to Major Grantly. She is not his love: "'Nor his dog, nor his ox, nor his ass, nor anything that is his, except—except, Lily, the dearest friend that he has on the face of the earth'" (XXIX). Grace is supposed to be the picture of flurried prettiness, and this may be why she forgets her careful training and seems so vague in her references. She excuses herself with an allusion to Ecclesiastes 3:5 "'In the Bible it is said of some season that it is not a time for marrying, or for giving in marriage. And so it is with us.'" Since the actual verse says a "time to embrace, and a time to refrain from embracing" Trollope may be smiling at Grace's shyness. Major Grantly understands what season it is, and before he leaves he holds her in a passionate embrace (XXX).

However predictable their own story, Grace's and Henry's difficulties do provide the reader with an interesting view of Archdeacon Grantly. His struggle against pride and toward generosity is much more closely related to Crawley's own. Grantly is as proud of his material possessions as Crawley is of his scholarship. Each has to yield something in order to be generous to their children, Henry and Grace. Grantly's story has intrinsic interest in any case, for with him the spirit not only of *Barchester Towers* but of Barchester itself is present.

Grantly has aged since the days of *Barchester Towers,* but much in his spirit is the same. He now protects for others what he fought so strenuously to gain for himself in his younger days: "Now, in his green old age, he had ceased to covet, but had not ceased to repine. He had ceased to covet aught for himself, but still coveted much for his children. . ." (II). Trollope shows that his essential vigor is undiminished; the energetic "Good heavens!" is still there. When he hears of Henry's interest in Grace he cries, "'Good Heavens—!'" (II); when Henry tells him that the wealthy Griselda is not as clever as Grace: "'Griselda not clever! Good Heavens!'" (III). Mrs. Proudie is still to him a "she-Beelzebub" (X). Their encounters in the novel, like those in *Barchester Towers,* are full of hostility. At a dinner party Mrs. Proudie and the archdeacon discuss the American Civil War[26] and, naturally, take opposing sides. The entire evening is then filled with the "excitement of a half-suppressed battle" (XLVII). When Mrs. Crawley rebukes him for speaking ill of Mrs. Proudie after Mrs. Proudie's death, he says: "'The proverb of De mortuis is founded on humbug'" (LXVII). Their careers are commented on: "From the very first arrival of the Proudies at Barchester, Mrs. Proudie had thrown down her gauntlet to him, and he had not been slow in picking it up. The war had been internecine, and each had given the other terrible wounds" (LXVII).

There was no reflection required to wage war with Mrs. Proudie, but his difficulty with Henry requires him to examine his own priorities, to measure how much of his ambition he is willing to sacrifice. His first reaction, as the "Good Heavens!" indicates, is explosive. He then says, "'He has made his bed, and he must lie upon it'" (XXII), relying as unthinkingly on this expression as he does on his "Good Heavens!" But here the difference between *Barchester Towers* and *The Last Chronicle of Barset* is apparent. We respond warmly to the archdeacon because of the revival of the images and expressions we associate with him from other novels, but here we are also invited to step into his "psychological stream," to see how the father thinks of the son. In *Barchester Towers* we understood the quality of the archdeacon's anger against the Proudies when we analyzed the peculiar rhythm of the sentence opening the chapter "War" (discussed in chapter 1); its compression represents Grantly's swelling rage. In *The Last Chronicle* the interior view is more complete; the words approximate the process rather than the outcome of thought. As W. J. Overton says, with *The Last Chronicle of Barset* we see a ". . . Trollope, whose speciality is to recreate mental rhythms through repetition and rhetorical patterns of speech."[27] We understand Crawley's thoughts because we follow his repeated reactions to literature; we appreciate Grantly's "mental rhythm" by a different sort of repetition.

As Grantly goes to interview Grace, he repeats, with characteristic force, Lady Lufton's parting words to him, "Be gentle to her" (LVI). The first two long paragraphs of chapter LVII, "A Double Pledge," are masterly studies of Grantly's thinking; we see how he interprets this gentleness. We are immersed in his thoughts to see how he lets the word *gentle* trigger a series of expostulations, beginning: "Lady Lufton had beseeched him to be gentle with her. Was the mission one in which gentleness would be possible? . . . And how could this be properly explained to the young lady in gentle terms?" He imagines out the purport of his speech to Grace: "'Heaven and earth!' he must say, 'here are you, without a penny in your pocket, with hardly decent raiment on your back, with a thief for your father, and you think that you are to come and share all the wealth that the Grantlys have amassed, that you are to have a husband with broad acres, a big house, and game preserves, and become one of a family whose name has never been touched by a single accusation—no, not a suspicion?'" And when Grantly has finished this lecture, he returns to his friend's advice: "How was all that to be told effectively to a young woman in gentle words? And then how was a man in the archdeacon's position to be desirous of gentle words—gentle words which would not be efficient—when he knew well in his heart of hearts that he had nothing but his threats on which to depend." The word *gentle* almost overpowers him, knowing as he does his own love for his son, but then he sees a bill of sale for Henry's farm, and his better half is again repressed. Facing him is a list of Henry's possessions, and the worldly archdeacon despises Grace's poverty again when he sees item after item of the good things Henry must give up to woo her. Nettled by his son's disobedience and Grace's poverty he thinks: "Why had the foolish fellow been in such a hurry with his hideous ill-conditioned advertisements? Gentle! How was he in such circumstances to be gentle?" He slashes the sign with a final "Gentle, indeed!" All of the energy and emotion implied in the familiar "Good Heavens!" are revealed through the repetition of *gentle*. In these two paragraphs, however, we go beyond the mere external appreciation of the repetition to understand the process that produces them. We see that the archdeacon's repetitions are meant to convince him of what his own honest thoughts will not. If he disdains the word *gentle*, he may be able to avoid softheartedness with Grace; in the repetition he exposes his vigor and his vulnerability. In the interview with Grace that follows, he demonstrates his susceptibility when he poses on the hearth rug as a Mr. Brocklehurst whom Grace sees as the "impersonation of parsondom in its severest aspect" and then rushes across the room to her as a Parson Adams whose "tears formed themselves in his eyes, and gradually trickled down his old nose." The reader thus witnesses Grantly's trial of honesty and pride and sees him emerge somewhat abashed by his victory, just as Crawley is by his.

Grantly's newfound humility makes him share the spirit of tolerance and kindliness that Septimus Harding embodies throughout the Barsetshire series. At the end of *The Last Chronicle of Barset* Grantly recognizes his father-in-law's merits in a way he could not have in his younger, harsher *Barchester Towers* days. The expanded scope that the internal monologue offers suggests the way in which his thoughts have been transformed. At the end he says, "'He puts me so much in mind of my father'" (LXXXI). It is hoped that Grantly may eventually see that his own reaction to *gentle* betokens his kinship with Harding's spirit, and his claim, with Crawley, to heroism.

Not all of the characters from the former Barsetshire novels are rounded in the way Lily, Johnny, and Grantly are; some, like the Luftons and the Thornes, appear in the novel merely because it is a "farewell" and because their presence can reinforce the old diocesan divisions. They act as props for the

Barchester war and remind us of the far-reaching effects of Crawley's case. They also serve to bind together the numerous centers and plot lines into a consistent and believable whole. Lady Lufton represents opposition to the Palace and support for Grantly. Her son remarks to her that it is "'. . . rather hard that you should have to do all the work of opposition bishop in the diocese'" (x)—Mrs. Proudie is here regarded as the real bishop. Mrs. Thorne expresses diocesan feeling when she calls the magistrates "wiseacres" (x), and she directs our attention to Major Grantly's story by praising Grace's accomplishments: "'Everybody says that she talks Greek just as well as she does English, and that she understands philosophy from the top to the bottom'" (xiv). Mrs. Thorne becomes involved in Johnny's and Lily's romance as well as Henry's and Grace's, calling Johnny an "old Paladin" (lix) and warning Lily that she is letting a "horrid morbid sentiment" (lix) destroy her life. Mark Robarts, a chief member of the anti-Proudie party, lets us see that behind Crawley's humility is a "crushing pride," and he thinks that "There was something radically wrong within him, which had put him into antagonism with all the world, and which produced these never-dying grievances" (xxi). The lesser characters are thus bound to each other and are attached to the central story of Crawley's case. Despite their good intentions and their various reasons to champion him, they contribute to his anxiety because he knows that "The sympathy of the whole party had been with Mr. Crawley; but they had all agreed that he had stolen the money" (xiv). Crawley's innocence reproves both unthinking criticism and unthinking partisanship.

Mrs. Proudie's action on Crawley's case thoroughly revives the atmosphere of *Barchester Towers,* and yet she, like Grantly, is developed beyond the vigorous images associated with her. Her reintroduction assures us that she is, as Lady Lufton says, a "vulgar virago" (v), and a "vulgar, interfering, brazen-faced virago" (xi) as Grantly adds. She believes Lady Lufton is a "conceited old idiot" (v), regards Grantly as "an actual emanation from Satan" (xi), and thinks of Crawley as a "roaring lion" (xi). She welcomes fresh outbreak of war in Barchester, because "Mr.

Crawley belonged to the other party, and Mrs. Proudie was a thorough-going partisan" (xi). When the magistrates commit Crawley to the assizes, "Mrs. Proudie was ready for the battle, and was even now sniffing the blood afar off " (xi). The narrator's delight in mock-epic description (in the tradition of Fielding and Pope) makes the comic passages on Mrs. Proudie a joy to read. The catalogue of arms and the picture of "careless" power reintroduce the bellicose Juno from the earlier Barchester war. The voice of the narrator-character may be much diminished in the novel as a whole, but with Mrs. Proudie the exuberant chronicler laughs aloud. She appears before Thumble

... gorgeous in a dark brown silk dress of awful stiffness and terrible dimensions; ... And her bonnet was a monstrous helmet with the beaver up, displaying the awful face of the warrior, always ready for combat, and careless to guard itself from attack. The large contorted bows which she bore were as a grisly crest upon her casque, beautiful, doubtless, but majestic and fear-compelling. In her hand she carried her armour all complete, a prayer-book, a Bible, and a book of hymns (xvii).

The mock-heroic flavor of *Barchester Towers*' comic battle continues: "Then Mr. Thumble did retire, and Mrs. Proudie stood forth in her full panoply of armour, silent and awful, with her helmet erect, and vouchsafed no recognition whatever of the parting salutation with which Mr. Thumble greeted her" (xvii). The same strain continues to tell how she slammed the door behind her: "Then the conquered amazon collected together the weapons which she had laid upon the table, and took her departure with majestic step, and not without the clang of arms" (xvii). Since the narrator depicts Mrs. Proudie as a comic knight, it is appropriate that she should cross arms with the man who styles himself a crusher of kings.

In preparing herself for the encounter with Crawley, this mighty female warrior resorts to the common expression (or, rather, the narrator summarizes her thoughts as though she resorts to the expression) Crawley attributes to the bishop in summoning him to the Palace: "She understood how much louder a cock can crow in its own farmyard than elsewhere. . ." (XVII). The stock expression about the cock sounds as though it is her own because when she goads the bishop into forming a commission to investigate Crawley's case, she dismisses the need for delicacy or tact by saying peremptorily, "'It is all plain sailing'" (XXXIV). The narrator has earlier imitated what we find to be the character's own quality of speech. She declares that with the thought of Crawley her "'hair literally stands on end'" (XXXIV). She greets Dr. Tempest "in a full panoply of female armour" (XLVII). The dinner party given for Tempest goes off, as we have seen with Grantly, in the "excitement of a half-suppressed battle" (XLVII), and her struggle with Tempest himself is described in the familiar terms of battle. He thinks she has been "beaten out of the field" because he has silenced "his foe" and prepared himself for a "final retreat." But when he goes to the bishop to discuss Crawley, she is "on the field of battle as though she had never even been wounded" (XLVII). Dr. Tempest can only ignore her and "draw upon his courage and his strategy for the coming warfare" (XLVII). Mrs. Proudie loses the battle against Tempest, but the bishop's despair over her interference is what causes her ultimate defeat.

Up to this point in the novel Mrs. Proudie's part is really only a continuation of the comedy of *Barchester Towers,* but after this encounter with Tempest we are allowed a glimpse of her mind and are, as with Grantly, thus given an explanation for her behavior. Grantly's self-examination allies him to the spirit of Septimus Harding; Mrs. Proudie's self-analysis kills her. Whether we believe Trollope's own explanation in *An Autobiography* (XV) of his decision to kill Mrs. Proudie, we accept her death as believable for two reasons: in a complete reading of the book her death appears close to Dobbs Broughton's and is approaching Harding's and seems part of the tidying up of the novel's close; more importantly, we accept it because Mrs. Proudie's brief introspection is consistent with the pattern of self-examination Crawley's case establishes. We do not step into her thoughts in the way we do into Crawley's and Grantly's, but we are aware of their nature: ". . . she was a woman not without a conscience, and by no means indifferent to the real service which her husband, as bishop of the diocese, was bound to render to the affairs of the Church around her. Of her own struggles after personal dominion she was herself unconscious; and no doubt they gave her, when recognised and acknowledged by herself, many stabs to her inner self, of which no single being in the world knew anything" (LXVI). It is these "stabs" to her conscience that make Mrs. Proudie's story a foil for Crawley's.

The bishop's altered response to his wife is suggested through a number of repetitions. He tells her repeatedly that she "has broken his heart," and he becomes "so silent, so sullen, and so solitary" (LXVI) that she is afraid of him. The thoughts that fill his mind after his release from her are summarized in the repetition of *tyranny*: "Yes, he was a widower, and he might do as he pleased. The tyrant was gone, and he was free. The tyrant was gone, and the tyranny had doubtless been very oppressive. Who had suffered as he had done? But in thus being left without his tyrant he was wretchedly desolate. Might it not be that the tyranny had been good for him?" "There was no one else of whom he was afraid. She had at least kept him out of the hands of other tyrants" (LXVII). In his confusion the bishop mixes relief and sorrow, as his adaptation of Scripture indicates: "The Lord sent the thorn, and the Lord has taken it away. Blessed be the name of the Lord" and "'Blessed be the name of the Lord' . . . but he did not stop to analyse what he was saying" (LXVII). It is ironic that after all the trouble he has allowed his wife to cause Mr. Crawley, he should characterize the unhappy curate as "'Sitting among the potsherds, like Job, has he not, Mr. Dean?'" (LXXXII). Even though at the end of the book the bishop, without his wife, lacks the "beautiful head and richness of waving foliage" (LXXXII), he fits more comfortably into the spirit of Barchester. When he joins the procession at Septimus Harding's funeral, we feel that at last the true spirit of Barchester is fully triumphant.

As in all the other Barsetshire novels, in this one, too, Harding epitomizes tolerance and moral strength. It is fitting that a farewell to Barsetshire should end with Harding's death. Even though the High and Dry church party, to which he ostensibly belongs, is now gone,[28] and even though he himself dies, we see that the spirit he personifies will endure. As in *Barchester Towers,* so here he espouses amelioration and shows that some old truths abide. Harding himself is like Grantly's 1820 port— loved to the end for its mellowness; his philosophy, like his recollections, is mild but convincing. In *Barchester Towers* when Harding looked out over the bishop's gardens and remembered his former happiness in his old friend's company, he realized that he knew the meaning of faith. In this novel he again thinks of his old friend, suggesting that old Bishop Grantly, like him, would approve of many of the changes in the Palace: "'I think he would, upon the whole. I'm sure of this: he would not disapprove, because the new ways are changed from his ways. He never thought himself infallible. And do you know, my dear, I am not sure that it isn't all for the best. I sometimes think that some of us were very idle when we were young. I was, I know'" (XXII). Harding feels no bitterness in his approaching death, though he does sorrow over the loss of his violoncello and his cathedral visits: "Old as he was, and in some things almost childish, nevertheless, he thought of this keenly, and some half-realised remembrance of 'the lean and slippered pantaloon' flitted across his mind, causing him a pang" (XLIX).[29] He is able to say to Eleanor truthfully: "'Do not cry, Nelly—not till I am gone; and then not beyond measure. Why should anyone weep for those who go away full of years—and full of hope?'" (LXXVIII). Harding has good advice to give, too, in his characteristically mild way when he tells Henry to forgive his father, reminding him of the Fifth Commandment: "'Honour thy father—that thy days may be long in the land'" (LVIII). His is the proper reaction to Mr. Crawley's case. He tells Toogood: "'What does the Latin proverb say? "No one of a sudden becomes most base"'" (XLII). And he is responsible at the novel's end for restoring Crawley himself. He requests that Grantly give the living of St. Ewold's to Crawley, and the offer is made to Crawley in Harding's name.

Crawley is central to the novel even though many of the familiar characters claim more of our affectionate interest. There is a consistency in the treatment of all of the characters, whether they are fully developed or not, which makes analysis of Crawley and appreciation of the work as a whole effortless. The repetition of linguistic and structural patterns in the book encourages our reaction. And the narrator-character, though much less prominent in this book than in *Barchester Towers*, is here, too, important in our assessment of the fabric of the narrative. The tone, though supportive of the self-analysis pattern, is frequently playful: of Robarts and Crawley is said "'So, when two dogs have fought and one has conquered, the conquered dog will always show an unconscious submission to the conqueror'" (XXI); of Toogood, that he did not belong to the "Quirk, Gammon and Snaps of the profession, or the Dodson and Foggs, who are immortal" (XXXII);[30] of Mrs. Proudie, that she had never "taken a licking from anyone" (XXXIV); of Crosbie, that he was treated as the "needy knife-grinder" (XLIV);[31] of the archdeacon's concern for trapping a fox on his property: "I wonder whether he would have been so keen had a Romanish priest come into his parish, and turned one of his Protestants into a Papist?" (LVIII); of mankind in general: "How common with us it is to repine that the devil is not stronger over us than he is" (XXXIII); and of his central character and subject: "Had I written an epic about clergymen, I would have taken St. Paul for my model; but describing, as I have endeavoured to do, such clergymen as I see around me, I could not venture to be transcendental" (LXXXIV).

There are repetitions of some key expressions that tie the book together in an ironic manner. The image of the cock in its own farmyard is used with the Proudies, Crawley, and even the Misses Prettyman: "No one knew better than Miss Prettyman that a cock can crow most effectively in his own farmyard..." (VI). The contrasts among these different spheres of power is amusing. The Latin tag "Ruat caelum, fiat justitia," that Trollope uses in many of his novels, is here used by Crawley when he really means "it's dogged as does it," and by the narrator in commenting on Grantly's hypocrisy: "'Ruat caelum, fiat justitia' [let justice be done though the heavens fall] was said, no doubt, from an outside balcony to a crowd, and the speaker knew that he was talking buncombe. The 'Rem, si possis recte, si non, quocunque modo' [get money, honestly if you can, if not, by any means get money], was whispered into the ear in a club smoking-room, and the whisperer intended that his words should prevail" (LVI). The comparison of Crawley and Grantly is thus reinforced, and the justification of their self-righteousness is questioned. The Prettymans paraphrase the Latin tag with which Harding clears Crawley. The old ladies question, "'Whoever heard of anybody becoming so base as that all at once?'" (VII). These subtle, sometimes playful, repetitions support the larger thematic and allusive repetitions.

The Last Chronicle of Barset is a fine novel in itself, but it also gives the fitting conclusion to a whole series of novels. As an independent work and a farewell it has a thickly peopled, dense structure. Trollope maintains control by keeping Josiah Crawley and his self-reflection in plain view. Crawley's preoccupation with literature and his special archaic expressions pervade the entire novel. It is in Crawley's spirit of questioning that the other main characters of this novel and from the series end their careers. For this reason, Trollope could have given no better ending to this work, no more suitable conclusion to the series, than to have Crawley read in as the vicar of St. Ewold's. There the scholar and antiquarian will be closely allied to the Thornes of *Barchester Towers,* whose literary preoccupations and ancestor worship make them, like Crawley, anachronistic. There is a dash of unconscious humor in this last request of Harding's: the combination of Saxon and Greek is suitably eccentric. Crawley's case is thus relegated to its proper place and the harmony of Barchester is again restored. Harding's gentle spirit has its way over the mock battles of Barchester Close as well as over the imagined struggles of *Seven Against Thebes.*

3
He Knew He Was Right

Trollope's twenty-third published novel, *He Knew He Was Right* (1869), has been underrated by most scholars. Until recently critics usually included it in their overviews of Trollope's work, but failed to give it the thorough analysis its brilliance, albeit fragmented, deserves. With the Barsetshire chronicles completed and the Palliser series well under way (*Can You Forgive Her?* and *Phineas Finn* had been published), Trollope made a bold experiment[1] in *He Knew He Was Right*. He challenged conventional understanding of marriage and power with a sophisticated combination and reversal of genres and expectations. As he experimented with technique and focus he ran the risk throughout of losing the somber implications of Trevelyan's monomania in the effervescence of numerous romantic subplots. The novel was not popular, and Trollope himself lamented that he had not created sympathy for the main character Louis Trevelyan,[2] but many readers will find that the richly ironic parallels and echoes make *He Knew He Was Right* an uneven but compelling work.

What makes *He Knew He Was Right* uneven? The answer lies with the narrator and with the integration of tragedy and comedy. This is a difficult novel to analyze satisfactorily because its strengths also create its difficulties. The portrait of Trevelyan is a masterly study in obsession and self-destructive rigidity, and the novel has been rightly praised for Trollope's sensitive and shrewd depiction of him. But the narrator's treatment of Trevelyan is not always clear, and Trevelyan's relationship to the world around him is sometimes hard to understand. Two recent critics' responses to the novel suggest some of the reader's difficulties in interpretation. Christopher Herbert argues that Trevelyan is himself a victim of the hopeless schizophrenia of the Victorian patriarchal system, which makes him think it is his right and duty to annihilate his wife's will if it opposes his own but at the same time requires that he live the unacknowledged fiction of a companionate, moral equality in his marriage.[3] Jane Nardin, on the other hand, sees Trevelyan as destructive and culpable. She argues that *He Knew He Was Right* is a deliberate combination of tragedy, farce, and comedy meant to show us that inflexible and weak characters must fail (tragedy and farce) and characters who are willing to grow and learn from their mistakes will succeed (comedy).[4] The fact that both of these interpretations are plausible suggests, I believe, how difficult it is at times to determine one's own response to the narrator's voice and the combination or upheaval of genres. Perhaps Trollope intended for us to sympathize with Trevelyan's deficiencies (whether or not they are emblematic of society's destructive restrictions) while also seeing that flexibility and accommodation answer best in this world. However we interpret Trevelyan and however positively we respond to the novel as a whole, we are probably going to have trouble reconciling parts of the work. Maybe some of the confusion was a necessary part of the experiment.

As in *Barchester Towers* and in *The Last Chronicle of Barset,* and indeed in all of Trollope's good novels, in *He Knew He Was Right* the narrator is a skilled creator, director, or repeater of patterns of allusions and expressions. With the Heavitree intrigues of Mr. Gibson and Camilla and Arabella French, the narrator is as relentlessly boisterous as the *Barchester Towers* narrator. Using the techniques of the Ullathorne Sports or Jael and Sisera narrators, the narrator here makes Gibson's self-deluding, self-congratulatory allusions to tragedy (supplied by Gibson and by the narrator) act as grotesque echoes of Trevelyan's serious delusions. The love stories of Dorothy, Nora, and Caroline are treated with the pleasantry that characterizes the story of Grace Crawley (despite Grace's sad family life and despite these three young women's complicated family problems). The farcical and comical patterns and parallels of *He Knew He Was Right* resemble those in the Barsetshire novels. But when we look at Trevelyan and compare him with Josiah Crawley, those helpful allusions and repetitions of the narrator (and the narrator and character together) reveal a fundamental difference in the stories, the men, and the narrators presenting them.

In *The Last Chronicle of Barset* Josiah Crawley's preoccupation with the classics and with Scripture help him to define himself and the world around him. In *He Knew He Was Right*, Trevelyan studies echoes and perversely calls himself Othello (without acknowledging Othello's mistake). Crawley identifies with Greek and Biblical tragedy and sees himself as a martyr, who yet may be avenged; when Trevelyan identifies with Othello (and even with Lear) he sees himself as a maligned, pitiable victim. We admire—even if we do not like—Josiah Crawley's smoldering energy; we find Trevelyan willful, petulant, and finally pathetic. The larger and smaller patterns of allusions and expressions, in both novels, create and sustain these radically different reader responses: with Crawley there is detached, even ironic respect; with Trevelyan there is impatience and then a grudging perhaps irritated sympathy when he has driven himself, and been driven, mad.

Trevelyan is the most important character in the novel, and he is the most difficult to assess fairly. (This difficulty, interestingly enough, could have been the object of Trollope's experiment or it could have been the flaw in it.) From the first the narrator encourages our distaste for Trevelyan's egotism and stubbornness, and even as Trevelyan's obsession twists into painful madness, the narrator never lets the reader fully forget the man's vanity and rigidity. Whether in tantrum or in mad flight, Louis Trevelyan is treated with some degree of irony. The quality of allusions, repetitions, and expressions associated with Trevelyan helps to determine a mixed reaction to him.

By the world's standards Trevelyan is an unexceptionable young man. He is intelligent, sensitive (he has published a volume of poems), and financially independent. But the narrator warns us about his true nature with an ominous repetition of the expression "pearl among men." It is repeated so often in the first few paragraphs that the reader grows suspicious. By the third page of the introduction, the expression has been used three times, and then the warning is explained: "He could talk on all subjects, was very generous, a man sure to be honoured and respected; and then such a handsome, manly fellow, with short brown hair, a nose divinely chiselled, an Apollo's mouth, six feet high, with shoulders and legs and arms in proportion,—a pearl of pearls! Only, as Lady Rowley was the first to find out, he liked to have his own way" (I). We thus know from the first few paragraphs that Louis Trevelyan is imperious.

If Louis were merely imperious, perhaps the reader could like him, but he is also ridiculous; the narrator sometimes caricatures his gravity. By the end of the first chapter Louis and his bride have disagreed about Colonel Osborne, and Louis has decided to conquer his wife's opposition by making her feel the enormity of her disobedience. Emily is calm in opposition, and Louis tries to divert himself by working on a scientific article on, most appropriately, echoes: "He was intent on raising a dispute with some learned pundit about the waves of sound,— but he could think of no other sound than that of the light steps of Colonel Osborne as he had gone up-stairs" (II). Many of Louis's reflections are pompous, and the reader feels that he deserves some of his unhappiness. The narrator invites censure of him by reflecting his thoughts: the language is either too simple or too elevated to be innocent and suggests that Louis's self-importance is irrepressible. He wants to discuss his problems with Hugh Stanbury, but thinks sententiously: ". . . it is a great ease to tell one's trouble to a friend; but then one should always wash one's dirty linen at home" (IV). Shortly after this decision he thinks of himself and his situation. He cannot refrain from priding himself on how much he has given his wife, and how much she owes to him, and the narrator reminds us to compare Trevelyan's apparent generosity with King Cophetua's[5] (as Sir Marmaduke, ironically does later [LXXVIII]): "King Cophetua did nothing for his beggar maid, unless she were to him, after he married her, as royal a queen as though he had taken her from the oldest stock of reigning families then extant" (V). He does not heed the promptings of his own better nature, congratulating himself through the entire novel on what he believes is his unappreciated selflessness. His self-congratulation and self-excuse are evident in this bit of logic: "Even though a man be false, a woman is not shamed and brought unto the dust before all the world. But the slightest rumour on a woman's name is a load of infamy on her husband's shoulders. It was not enough for Caesar that his wife should be true; it was necessary to Caesar that she should not even be suspected" (v). With such a precedent, the scholarly Trevelyan (unlike the later Palliser) cannot doubt his reactions. A few pages later he again has recourse to the classics. This time he adapts the Latin tag we also find in *The Last Chronicle of Barset, The Prime Minister,* and *The Way We Live Now*—"Ruat caelum, fiat justitia"—to excuse himself from asking his wife's pardon: "He had pointed out to his wife her duty, and she had said she would do her duty as pointed out, on condition that he would beg her pardon for having pointed it out! This he could not and would not do. Let the heavens fall,—and the falling of the heavens in this case was a separation between him and his wife,—but he would not consent to such injustice as that!" (v). The reader is made to feel, before the monomania is apparent, that Louis Trevelyan's reasoning is unfair and distasteful.

Trevelyan insists that it is not really Osborne that he fears, but Emily's refusal to submit herself to his own authority. Nevertheless, Osborne is the catalyst for the difficulties, and eventually, when Trevelyan imagines himself Othello, Osborne's treachery has to be at the root of his identification. When Trevelyan is thoroughly mad, he loses sight of his wife's disobedience and returns to his initial jealousy. (The detective Bozzle's whole purpose is to find out whether Emily is an adulteress.) The reader's problem is relating to an arrogant hero and a lifeless villain. In the early parts of the novel the reader turns gratefully to Exeter for relief, but knows that the Stanbury story is only to occupy a small part of the real interest: ". . . the little tale shall be told before this larger tale is completed" (IV). When the Exeter stories, apart from Heavitree, have spun themselves thin, the Trevelyan story is only just beginning in earnest.

The condition of Trevelyan's mind is not seriously appreciated until he makes his first trip to Italy, approximately one-third of the way through the novel. The narrator has stated before this that Trevelyan is mad, but he has done so concerning episodes that seemed more ridiculous than insane. Trevelyan hires Mr. Bozzle to spy on Emily and Colonel Osborne, and the narrator says: "In these days of his madness, therefore, he took Mr. Bozzle into his pay. . ." (XIX). Bozzle himself is so pathetic and ludicrous a character that the reader feels more indignation over Trevelyan's hiring him than concern for Trevelyan's state of mind.[6] Up to this point, Trevelyan is the immature young man who refuses to countenance opposition; during his first trip to Italy, however, the pettiness disappears from his dejection. His melancholy is believable, often understandable, and he grows in dramatic stature.

The descriptions of Trevelyan's fully developed madness are masterly. One critic has called *He Knew He Was Right* "Trollope's *Timon of Athens*,"[7] and Trevelyan's mad eloquence is impressive. Louis's agony drives him to poetic intensity. We recognize Shakespeare in Trevelyan's illness just as we do Mrs. Browning in Phineas Finn's and the classics in Josiah Crawley's. The language, apart from the allusions themselves, supports Trevelyan's elevated self-analysis.

Trevelyan's illness forces him into a gloom that is comparable to Lear's. He cuts himself off from everyone except Bozzle, because "Trevelyan had now become so accustomed to being told by everybody that he was wrong, and was at the same time so convinced that he was right, that he regarded the perversity of his friends as a part of the persecution to which he was subjected" (XXXII). He prides himself on believing he is above the common experience, above relief, as this remark to Glascock indicates: " 'The truth is that when one is absolutely unhappy one cannot revel in the imagination. I don't believe in the miseries of poets' " (XXXVII). It is ironic that we associate his disorder with literature, and often with poetry. He writes to Mr. Outhouse, who is caring for his wife, and recalls Bunyan when he tells him that his situation is a "slough of despond" (XLV). He paraphrases *Hamlet* (v.i.299) (as Lady Laura will do in *Phineas Redux*) when he rebukes Sir Marmaduke: "'She is my wife, sir, and that is ten times more. Do you think that you would do more for her than I would do,—drink more of Esill? You had better go away, Sir Marmaduke'" (LXXVIII). Emily pleads with him to forget the past, to keep silent on the wrongs they have done to each other: "'Will it not be best that there should be no word spoken?' '"Forgiveness may be spoken with the tongue,"' he said, beginning to quote from a poem which had formerly been frequent in his hands" (LXXIX).

When he wants to be jocular with Mr. Glascock, and to prove his soundness of reasoning, he refers to *Richard III* (I.iv.277): "How grand a thing would wine really be, if it could make glad the heart of man. How truly would one worship Bacchus if he could make one's heart to rejoice. But if a man have a real sorrow, wine will not wash it away,—not though a man were drowned in it, as Clarence was'" (LXXXVI). He convinces Glascock, as he convinces the reader, only that a generous and perhaps even gifted mind has been wasted through obsession. Glascock has come to take Louey away, and the father turns from jocularity to Scriptural outburst: "What matters it whether the fiery furnace be heated seven times, or only six;—in either degree the flames are enough!" (LXXXVI).[8] As Glascock waits for Louey, the mad father wanders out among the olive trees in his austere Italian garden. What follows are probably the most powerful and insightful lines Trollope wrote: "Mr. Glascock followed him to the window and stood looking at him for a few moments. But Trevelyan did not turn or move. There he stood gazing at the pale, cloudless, heat-laden, motionless sky, thinking of his own sorrows, and remembering too, doubtless, with the vanity of a madman, that he was probably being watched in his reverie" (LXXXVI). Trevelyan's self-consciousness is now pitiable, showing the effects of stubborn pride and monomania. His condition worsens when Louey is away. When

Hugh Stanbury tries to persuade him to go back to England, Trevelyan's madness has reached an alarming pitch. He greets Hugh in a gaudy dressing gown and dirty nightshirt; his hair is long and a beard covers his face. Hugh knows that "There could be no mistake as to the restless gleam of that eye" and then Trevelyan rants in a pathetic jumble of politics, poetry, and pride:

"They have been telling us since the world began so many lies, that I for one have determined never to believe anything again. Labour leads to greed, and greed to selfishness, and selfishness to treachery, and treachery straight to the devil,—straight to the devil. Ha, my friend, all your leading articles won't lead you out of that. What's the news? Who's alive? Who dead? Who in? Who out? What think you of a man who has not seen a newspaper for two months; and who holds no conversation with the world further than is needed for the cooking of his polenta and the cooling of his modest wine-flask?" (XCII).

As Trevelyan echoes *Lear* (v.iii.8–19), we marvel at the extent of his own madness, and we admire Trollope's ability to make Trevelyan's insane flights a believable distortion of his earlier speech.

The force, even grandeur, of Lear (also partly responsible for his own madness) is unmistakable in the crazed Trevelyan, but there is also the identification with Othello, and that, because of Bozzle, lowers rather than elevates the tone of Trevelyan's distress. Our sympathy for Trevelyan is mixed with irritation at his refusal to analyze his own preoccupation with *Othello*. The narrator first makes the comparison for us when Bozzle has been working for Trevelyan for some time: "We remember Othello's demand of Iago. . . . But Trevelyan, though he had in truth given the order, was like Othello also in this,— that he would have preferred before all the prizes of the world to have had proof brought home to him exactly opposite to that which he demanded" (XLV). When Bozzle uncovers some information for him, we find Trevelyan's thoughts reflected in these words of the narrator: "He had sent his wife first into a remote village on Dartmoor, and there she had been visited by her— lover! How was he to use any other word? Iago;—oh, Iago! The pity of it, Iago! Then, when she had learned that this was discovered, she had left the retreat in which he had placed her, ... Oh, Iago; the pity of it, Iago!" (XLV). We are told that there was a "method in Trevelyan's madness" (XLV)[9] in finding out about his wife, but we find no further allusion to *Othello* until the end of the novel. Here Trevelyan himself quotes the lines of the play to Emily in a way that tells us he has never stopped making the analogy in his own mind: "He would speak of dear Emily, and poor Emily, and shake his head slowly, and talk of the pity of it. 'The pity of it, Iago; oh, the pity of it,' he said once. The allusion to her was so terrible that she almost burst out in anger, as she would have done formerly. She almost told him that he had been as wrong throughout as was the jealous husband in the play whose words he quoted, and that his jealousy, if continued, was likely to be as tragical" (XCV). The reader wonders why Trevelyan, as sensitive as he is to literature, did not see the irony of his insistent identification, especially since he was sure he was right, as Othello was sure.

Compare, for a moment, Trevelyan's use of Shakespeare and Crawley's use of the classics. Trevelyan seems to be controlled by what he has read—he identifies an idea or situation from his life with one in a work of literature and, after the idea is safely (and in a way that reflects well on Trevelyan) categorized, *then* is Trevelyan proud of his situation and the poetic intensity surrounding it. Literature has the models for behavior, and Trevelyan is merely (in his own mind) acting out the inevitable conclusion of his position. He does not have the independent stature of a Lear or an Othello; instead he identifies with the way they were betrayed and seems to rush toward tragedy himself. Crawley, on the other hand, identifies with the power and freedom of the classics as much as with the misery. Whether quoting Greek classics or the Bible, he is defying his enemies, positively asserting his own will. When he identifies with tragedy, it is as the indomitable soul who, in the face of doom, strikes out and demands that his dignity be acknowledged, even submitted to. Both men are proud, even vain, but Crawley's allusions show his wresting spiritual victory from defeat; Trevelyan identifies with the pitiable, betrayed spirit and then in mock humility bows his thwarted will to the dictates of tragedy. Crawley would be a blazing martyr (made even more glorious by his refusal to contradict the dean); Trevelyan would be a lamented victim.

The identification with *Othello* and *Lear* cannot be separated from other patterns in the narrative. Just as identification with *Othello* colors our response to Trevelyan's use of *Lear,* so the other patterns and repetitions in the narrative work to limit sympathy with Trevelyan. Some of the repetitions with Trevelyan are worthy of Ibsen, but these are read in a larger context that qualifies our compassion. In that splendid chapter "Trevelyan Discourses on Life," Louis lapses into unconscious repetition[10]: " 'My wife can remain at Siena if she pleases, or she can go to England if she pleases. She must give me the same liberty;—the same liberty,—the same liberty' " (XCII). (Some readers will be reminded of the powerful repetition at the end of Ibsen's *Ghosts.*) These repeated words should be especially moving because they follow Trevelyan's energetic paraphrase of *Lear* quoted previously. In fact the whole of this chapter is beautifully turned—the descriptions of the heat, the house, the conversation are some of the best Trollope ever wrote. But we do not forget that the Lear paraphrase and the echoes have been preceded by scenes that show Trevelyan's consciously melodramatic posing. In the earlier chapter "Sir Marmaduke at Willesden," Trevelyan and his father-in-law argue about possession of young Louey and the return of Emily: " 'She has but to say a word, and I will devote my life to her. But that word must be spoken.' As he said this, he dashed his hand upon the table, and looked up with an air that would have been comic with its assumed magnificence had it not been for the true tragedy of the occasion" (LXIX). Shortly after, he continues: " 'If I had put her from me, as you said just now, it might have been otherwise. But she shall be as welcome to me as flowers in May,—as flowers in May!' " (LXIX). This repetition, slightly different in quality from the later one in "Trevelyan Discourses on Life," yet possibly suggesting the deterioration that the later words illustrate, elicits little sympathy because of Louis's evident pride in his pain. Trevelyan's self-consciousness tinges with irony even his later genuinely tragic outbursts.

Louis's death scene, in the penultimate chapter of the novel, is touching despite (perhaps because of) Emily's apparently relentless single-mindedness. After Louis dies, she retires, in a "flood of tears" with Nora. Then the last chapter of the novel opens with these chilling yet consistently ambivalent words: "At last the maniac was dead..." (XCIX). The rest of the chapter, tying up all the loose ends as Trollope's last chapters always do, is peculiar. There is a subtle bitterness to it, a cynicism in the apparent jauntiness. In the same paragraph with the callous dismissal of Louis Trevelyan, the narrator remarks on the possibility of Emily's remarriage: "... and she felt that of such a career there could be no possibility. Anything but that! We all know that widows' practices in this matter do not always tally with wives' vows; but, as regards Mrs. Trevelyan, we are disposed to think that the promise will be kept" (XCIX). The forced lightness is jarring, even offensive, yet is consistent with the narrator's refusal to reconcile the conflicting elements of the narrative or to give a simple key to the reversals of tragedy and comedy.

Perhaps Louis's story, and the novel as a whole, is designed to make us question what is comic and what is tragic as we question the nature of marriage and the healthy relationship of man and wife. At any rate, throughout the book we constantly deal with reversals of genre and expectation and watch characters prove themselves to be other than what they thought themselves to be or other than what we thought they would be. The arrangement of the subplots, the repetition of expressions and allusions, encourages the ironic assessment of relationships and self-concepts.

In keeping with the ambivalence of the narrator's treatment of Louis Trevelyan, we find that Trevelyan's self-delusions and stubborn self-destruction are mirrored in the novel's most conspicuous and most heavily allusive comic subplot. The spineless Gibson is a grotesque complement for the too-rigid Trevelyan.

He Knew He Was Right 93

Both men muddle their lives; both misapply literature to their situations. The lengthy farce of Gibson's matrimonial difficulties parallels the disintegration of Trevelyan's mind and his marriage. With Gibson the narrator's position is unequivocal: Gibson is a dishonest fool and deserves some punishment for his vanity. Farce, Trollope suggests, is simple to judge. The ambivalent narrator of Trevelyan's story leaves the companion question—does Trevelyan deserve his punishment?—with the reader.

With Camilla and Gibson, Trollope creates a mock-heroic melodrama reminiscent of the tone of Ullathorne Sports in *Barchester Towers*. Camilla and her sister say little that is interesting, but the narrator's interpretations of their thoughts and actions make their story worth reading. The absurdity of Heavitree is established through this crude picture of the two scheming sisters: "As two pigs may be seen at the same trough, . . . so had these young ladies lived in sisterly friendship, while each was striving to take a husband from the other" (XLIV). Camilla dubs the captive Gibson a "naughty Lothario" (L) ("Lothario" is mentioned six times in the novel, three times with the aged dandy Osborne and three times with Gibson), and shortly afterward she is described as a harpy or as a predator as Gibson tries to escape: "Then he left the house, before Camilla could be down upon him from her perch on the landing-place" (LIV). Most of the allusions in the Heavitree chapters are concentrated in Gibson's speech, and it is the narrator who supplies Camilla's part in the mock battle. The narrator uses a favorite reference also found in *Barchester Towers, Phineas Redux,* and *The Way We Live Now* when he says, "Camilla French had never heard of Creusa and of Jason, but as she paced her mother's drawing-room that morning she was a Medea in spirit" (LXV). And with her family Camilla's position is equally exaggerated and ridiculous. Tongue-in-cheek the narrator says of her battle over an excessive trousseau: "Between Camilla and her mother, too, there had come to be an almost internecine quarrel on a collateral point" (LXXIV). To interpret the egocentric Camilla's fury over Gibson's defection, the narrator pretends that Camilla would invoke all of literature: "No history, no novel of most sensational interest, no wonderful villainy that had ever been wrought into prose or poetry, would have been equal to this" (LXXIV).

Gibson himself is delightfully stupid. His weak intellect and large ego are characterized by a hodgepodge of secular and sacred quotations and adaptations that act as uncomfortable reminders of Trevelyan's Shakespearean and Biblical allusions. With strong feelings of superiority, Gibson calls Brooke Burgess a "Merry Andrew" (XXXI). Shortly afterward, with galling condescension, he proposes to Dorothy and responds to her protestations with a favorite Trollope (Shakespearean) quotation: "The labour we delight in physics pain" (XLII). When he recoils from Arabella French's chignon, he reflects his classical studies in "Monstrum horrendum, informe, ingens!" (XLVII).[11] When Mr. Gibson wants to be truly impressive he paraphrases Scripture. The way he muddles II Kings, Job, and Matthew with Aphra Behn suggests the depth of his religion (and makes an engaging travesty of the Reverend Josiah Crawley's careful scholarship): "'I am afraid your aunt is very ill, Miss Dorothy.' 'She is ill, certainly, Mr. Gibson.' 'Dear, dear! We are all as the grass of the field, Miss Dorothy,—here to-day and gone tomorrow, as sparks fly upwards. Just fit to be cut down and cast into the oven'" (LIV).[12] He turns to Matthew again later when he reminds himself that he must 'turn the other cheek.' The irony is that he is as proud of the title "Lothario" as he is of the fact that he can find support in the Scriptures (LXXXIII). Perhaps we enjoy Gibson most when he is driven beyond the comfort of his pat Biblical references and turns to the classics. In the narrator's rendering of Gibson's mental rhythms we hear an echo of Trevelyan's energetic self-justification:

> He was prepared to throw up his living, to abandon the cathedral, to leave the diocese,—to make any sacrifice rather than take Camilla to his bosom. Within the last six weeks he had learned to regard her with almost a holy horror. He could not understand by what miracle of self-neglect he had fallen into so perilous an abyss. He had long known Camilla's temper. But in those days in which he had been

He Knew He Was Right 95

beaten like a shuttlecock between the Stanburys and the Frenches, he had lost his head and had done,—he knew not what. "Those whom the God chooses to destroy, he first maddens,"[13] said Mr. Gibson to himself of himself, throwing himself back upon early erudition and pagan philosophy. Then he looked across to the river Exe, and thought that there was hardly water enough there to cover the multiplicity of his sorrows (LXXIV).

Gibson absolves himself of all responsibility while magnifying his importance; he sees himself as threatened and toyed with and then chosen by the very gods for some especially cruel, undeserved punishment. His farcical self-delusions surely encourage an ambivalent response to Trevelyan's stubbornness.

Gibson is shallow and self-righteous; his comic part in the novel's investigation of marriage and male-female relationships is appropriately summarized in one of the narrator's favorite metaphors, that of the angling guardian and the hooked male: "Mr. Gibson, though he was not yet gasping in the basket, had some presentiment of this feeling, which made his present seat of honour unpleasant to him" (XXXI). The clumsy fish thinks of himself as a "Paladin" (XXXV), as an "Orlando" (XLII), and as a "clerical Don Juan" (L). When he has lied to Miss Stanbury and has proposed to both of the French sisters within a few days he dramatizes (or the narrator does for him) his dilemma so that he is a guiltless Greek adventurer: "Charybdis in the Close drove him helpless into the whirlpool of the Heavitree Scylla. He had no longer an escape from the perils of the latter shore. He had been so mauled by the opposite waves, that he had neither spirit nor skill left to him to keep in the middle track" (XLVII). Gibson's pride in his problems prepares us, perhaps unsympathetically, for Trevelyan's melodramatic posturing in the slightly later chapter "Sir Marmaduke at Willesden" (LXIX) cited earlier. Here Gibson fancies himself the innocent, will-less victim of a mystical predestination: "'And I have meant to be so true. I fancy sometimes that some mysterious agency interferes with the affairs of a man and drives him on,—and on,—and on,—almost,—till he doesn't know where it drives him.' As he said this in a voice that was quite sepulchral in its tone, he felt some consolation in the conviction that this mysterious agency could not affect a man without embuing him with a certain amount of grandeur,—very uncomfortable, indeed, in its nature, but still having considerable value as a counterpoise" (LXV). Ultimately Gibson thinks of himself as a "successful man of intrigue" (LXXXIII), but the narrator offers the final appropriate prototype for him: "Such men have their glory in their own estimation. We remember how Falstaff flouted the pride of his companion whose victory in the fields of love had been but little glorious. But there are victories going now-a-days so infinitely less glorious, that Falstaff's page was a Lothario, a very Don Juan, in comparison with the heroes whose praises are too often sung by their own lips" (LXXXIII).

Gibson is the unrivaled buffoon of the novel, but he, like Trevelyan, is embroiled in difficulties of honor and contract with women and he—unlike Trevelyan—survives because he can leave the larger issues of right and power undebated. Interestingly enough, the other romances and marriages of the novel also leave the major issues of right and power uncontested. Gibson is left with a loveless, even slightly ridiculous, marriage because he is dishonest in his dealings with the women around him; he deserves a set-down and belongs to the realm of farce. Trevelyan's imperiousness makes him brutally honest with Emily—he demands his rights as a Victorian male and husband and his marriage fails miserably. The clown fares better than the tyrant in this novel. The novel's other romances shun dishonesty but also have (what the novel suggests to be) a healthy ability to sidestep the confrontation of searching questions. In fact, in the light, comic romances of the novel, impediments to happiness can be dismissed as morbid or eccentric distortions of normal life. Certainly the narrator's ambivalence toward Trevelyan and dismissal of Gibson encourage the reader's identification with the sane, balanced, predictable love stories of Dorothy, Nora, and Caroline.

The successful, sane romances are found in Exeter and Florence. Two eccentrics, Jemima Stanbury and Wallachia Petrie—one in England and one in Italy—for a while pose obstacles to the marriages, but the narrator is quick to show us what their opposition is really worth. The Heavitree melodrama is an outgrowth of Exeter; Trevelyan's story is staged in both England and Italy. The comic, farcical, and tragic stories are thus constantly crossing and overlapping; instructive comparisons of the characters and their responses to courtship are inevitable. The narrator encourages these comparisons, too, with repetitions and echoes of the allusions and quality of expressions we have seen with Trevelyan and Gibson.

The heart of Exeter lives in Jemima Stanbury. Her letter inviting Dorothy to live with her has all the crustiness and promised generosity of a missive from Betsey Trotwood. She ends it characteristically: "'I shall expect her to be regular at meals, to be constant in going to Church, and not to read modern novels. . . . I hope the young lady does not have any false hair about her'" (VIII). She is strongly religious, opinionated, and humorous; the narrator uses melodrama and mock epic, as he does in *Barchester Towers*, to encourage laughter and sympathy, but here the vein of humor is not maintained; her invigorating crispness does not last the length of the Trevelyan story. Nevertheless, while she is still at her crotchety best, she sustains the comic narrative.

Miss Stanbury rules the Close in Exeter; she controls the spineless Rev. Thomas Gibson, and she dictates to him about doctrine as she does to Dorothy about sewing. Her power and her ignorance are supreme: "Since Judas, there had never been, to her thinking, a traitor so base, or an apostate so sinful, as Colenso; and yet, of the nature of Colenso's teaching she was as ignorant as the towers of the cathedral opposite her" (VII).[14] To summarize Aunt Stanbury's spirit of independence the narrator paraphrases the catechism in the Book of Common Prayer: "But for the ordinary authority of spiritual pastors and masters she shewed more of abstract reverence than of practical obedience" (XXII). Her religion, though undoubtedly sincere, is of a convenient kind. She may bless Dorothy for returning to her by calling her the "returned prodigal" (LXXIII), but she is also perfectly comfortable in condemning Dorothy's mother and sister for their contact with Colonel Osborne by reflecting smugly the words of Ecclesiastes 13:1: "'You can't touch pitch and not be defiled, my dear'" (XXII) (the very expression Wallachia Petrie uses about Caroline's defection and Roger Carbury uses with self-righteousness and then self-pity in *The Way We Live Now*). She dismisses Hugh by calling him a "Paladin" (XV) and derides Dorothy's dislike of Mr. Gibson by adapting Thomas Brown's quip (as Phineas does in *Phineas Finn* [VIII]): "'I do not like thee, Dr. Fell;—why I cannot tell'" (XXXVI).[15]

Miss Stanbury's sharp words, dramatic actions, and warmth make her charmingly comic. After their first quarrel, she makes up with Dorothy by pouring out a generous dose of port and striking the pose of a Mrs. Siddons: "'Come, drink it. Do as I bid you.' And she stood over her niece, as a tragedy queen in a play with a bowl of poison" (XII). Miss Stanbury, somewhat like her less attractive though not less admirable counterpart in *Barchester Towers*, is the most impressive when she is inspired with divine anger. We hear an effective echo of the mock-heroic language of Mrs. Proudie's "furious wrath" when Miss Stanbury finds that rumor is maligning Dorothy:

A base rumour was spread about the city that Dorothy Stanbury had been offered to Mr. Gibson, that Mr. Gibson had civilly declined the offer,—and that hence had arisen the wrath of the Juno of the Close. . . . The man had behaved like an idiot, Miss Stanbury said; but he had been brought into a little dilemma, and nothing should be said about it from the house in the Close. But when the other rumour reached Miss Stanbury's ears, when Mrs. Crumbie condoled with her on her niece's misfortune, when Mrs. MacHugh asked whether Mr. Gibson had not behaved rather badly to the young lady, then our Juno's celestial mind was filled with a divine anger (XLVII).

Miss Stanbury confronts Mrs. French and her daughter Camilla: "In this instance the Juno from the Close had come quite prepared to declare her casus belli as complete, and to fling down her gauntlet, unless the enemy should at once yield to her everything demanded with an abject submission" (XLVIII).

The fighting spirit deserts Miss Stanbury when she falls ill; her stubbornness and pride remain, but the narrator alerts us to her diminished role when he calls her "Poor old soul" (LXVI).

Miss Stanbury never recovers her former sharpness, and the allusions to Juno and the distortions of the Scriptures are finished. In her mellow state she is content to give Dorothy her blessing in a marriage she had before vigorously opposed. Miss Stanbury's change seems inevitable in the story, though regrettable, since she has presented an obstacle to both the marriage of Dorothy and the marriage of Hugh to Nora. In keeping with the genial spirit of successful romance, Miss Stanbury fades into benign eccentricity and her language and the narrator's are accordingly muted.

The most attractive aspect of Dorothy is Miss Stanbury's interest in her. She is one of Trollope's many sweet heroines, having the convincing purity and dullness of Grace Crawley before her, and Hetta Carbury after her. Her words—and thoughts—are largely from some stock formula, unclouded by interesting moral doubt. It is clear to her that Colonel Osborne is a "Lucifer" and a ". . . horrible roaring lion" (XXII). She shows more spirit, or the narrator does for her, in her rejection of Gibson: she will not marry ". . . a man who was like a donkey between two bundles of hay" (XXXI). Dorothy is so steady and unimaginative that when the narrator tells us she and Brooke discuss Tennyson's poetry (XXXV), the reader finds it hard to think what Dorothy would say. She is the most appealing when the narrator laughs at her. He makes a pun on Brooke's proposal: "To dive among the waters in warm weather is very pleasant; there is nothing pleasanter. But when the young swimmer first feels the thorough immersion of his plunge, there comes upon him a strong desire to be quickly out again" (LI). It is comically appropriate that quiet Dorothy should be the one to read from Jeremy Taylor's sermon on The Marriage Ring, thereby unwittingly uniting the many investigations of marriage in the novel.[16] Dorothy, like the three Woodward girls in *The Three Clerks*, is best characterized by stock imagery. At the end of the novel the narrator likens her to the flower that "should be warmed by the sun of life, and strengthened by the breezes of opposition, and filled by the showers of companionship. . ." (XCVII).

Dorothy's sister Priscilla is of stronger fiber. She has Hugh's intellect and determination and a large measure of her aunt's independence. We may doubt Dorothy's depth of analysis of Tennyson, but we would not doubt Priscilla's had she been given to reading poetry. We see little of her in the novel, hear few of her words, yet we are familiar enough with Trollope's technique to understand the importance of Priscilla's reaction to Nora Rowley and Emily Trevelyan: "Priscilla was a young woman who read a great deal, and even had some gifts of understanding what she read.[17] She borrowed books from the clergyman, and paid a penny a week to the landlady of the Stag and Antlers for the hire during half a day of the weekly newspaper. But now there came a box of books from Exeter, and a daily paper from London, and,—to improve all this,—both the new comers were able to talk with her about things she read" (xiv). Perhaps Priscilla, a kind of embryo eccentric, is in the novel to remind us about the (apparently) dull alternatives to marriage. She is a breed apart from the normal, healthy Dorothy, Nora, and Caroline. We could only wish that Trollope had included some of Priscilla's intelligent conversations with Emily so that we might appreciate something about Trevelyan's wife.

The narrator offers livelier language with the romance of Dorothy's brother Hugh and Emily's sister Nora. Miss Stanbury's disinheritance of Hugh makes his love for Nora seem hopeless and gallant. The narrator's genial humor with them is more entertaining than that used with the tame, sweet Dorothy, but it is obviously related to it.

The language associated with Nora—from Nora and from the narrator—is playful. Her disagreement with her mother is rendered thus: "Mr. Glascock was not an Apollo, not an admirable Crichton; but he was a man whom any girl might have learned to love" (xiii). She fills the role, so familiar in numerous Trollope novels, of the determined girl whose guardians object to her impractical engagement. Her resolve is perfectly captured in comforting cliché: she will "make her hay while the sun shines" (xiii). When she becomes good friends with Mr. Glascock's new infatuation, Caroline Spalding, in Florence, she cheers Caroline on to accepting his offer with a familiar allusion to Thais from "Alexander's Feast" (that Trollope also uses in *Barchester Towers* and *The Last Chronicle of Barset*): "'As for you changing now, that is quite impossible. If I were you, I would not say a word about it to any living being; but just go on,—straight forward,—in your own way, and take the good the gods provide you,—as the poet says to the king in the ode. And I think the gods have provided for you very well,—and for him'" (LXXX). Nora, like many of Trollope's trial-tested heroines, shows her worth through generosity, sense of humor, and comfortable self-knowledge. The narrator interprets Nora's temptation with Glascock with another familiar expression: "That had been her Rubicon. . . . there had been moments in which she had almost regretted her own courage and noble action, still, having passed the river, there was nothing for her but to go on to Rome" (LXXXVII). She goes, in fact, to Florence, and arrangements with Hugh eventually, inevitably, follow. Nora's words of teasing practicality assure us that she understands how to curb Hugh's impulsiveness: "'That idea of yours of walking out to the next church and getting ourselves married sounds very nice and independent, but you know that it is not practicable. . . . Of all things in the world I don't want to be a Lydia'" (XC). Nora responds in kind to Hugh, who has already referred to *The Rivals* in an earlier letter, "'For myself, I do not prefer clandestine arrangements and rope-ladders; and you, dear, have nothing of the Lydia about you'" (LXXI).

The narrator's treatment of Nora and Hugh is kindly; her liveliness and sense of proportion suit her to his rather comic gallantry. The narrator's introduction of Hugh brings to mind similar stock phrases used with the eager novice Phineas Finn: "'. . . he had won for himself reputation as a clever speaker, as a man who had learned much that college tutors do not profess to teach, as a hard-headed, ready-witted fellow, who, having the world as an oyster before him, which it was necessary that he should open, would certainly find either a knife or a sword with which to open it" (IV). Trollope's narrator frequently uses the expression "the world was his oyster" to characterize youthful zeal, and we are prepared to applaud Stanbury's energy. Almost the first words Hugh speaks suggest his colorful nature. The snobbish Trevelyan calls him a coward for having quit the bar to join the staff of a newspaper, but Hugh answers with spirit, "'Is a man faint-hearted when he finds it improbable that he shall be able to leap his horse over a house'" (IV). He is practical but can give way to the excesses of romance. One of Trollope's favorite ironic images for romance seems to come from lyrics in Tennyson's *The Princess*.[18] Trollope refers to the rocks and valleys of love and the excesses of sentiment often associated with the critical peaks and valleys of emotion (he uses the rocks and valleys extensively in two sections of *Can You Forgive Her?*). Here the narrator interprets Hugh's supposedly deep philosophizing with the obvious image:

> Was love to be ever a delight, vague as is that feeling of unattainable beauty which far-off mountains give, when you know that you can never place yourself amidst their unseen valleys? . . . Then, through the cloud of smoke, there came upon him some dim idea of self-abnegation,—that the mysterious valley among the mountains, the far-off prospect of which was so charming to him,—which made the poetry of his life, was, in fact, the capacity of caring more for other human beings than for himself. The beauty of it all was not so much in the thing loved, as in the loving. . . . Then he blew off a great cloud of smoke, and went into bed lost amidst poetry, philosophy, love, and tobacco (xxv).

Even though Hugh's gallantry is gently ridiculed, it is attractive, and though we may smile at his ennobled reflections, the shape and voice of the novel suggest that we should also admire his boldness and sincerity. (His willingness to bend, occasionally, makes him a moral complement for the inflexible Trevelyan.) The narrator's good-humored approval of Hugh is evident in the choice of quotation used to suggest the romantic vagueness of Hugh's financial account to Nora's parents. The narrator likens Hugh to Scott's charming Allen-a-Dale: "He had pleaded it [his case] well, and Lady Rowley's heart had been well disposed towards him; but when she asked of his house and his home, his answer had been hardly more satisfactory than that of Alan-a-Dale. There was little that he could call his own beyond 'The blue vault of heaven'" (LXX). Trollope's audience would have appreciated this allusion to Scott's well-known lyric (Trollope's misspelling of the name suggests that he was quoting from memory). The poem's central stanza runs:

> Allen-a-Dale to his wooing is come;
> The mother she asked of his household and home:
> "Though the castle of Richmond stand fair on the hill,
> My home," quoth bold Allen, "shows gallanter still;
> 'Tis the blue vault of heaven, with its crescent so pale
> And with all its bright spangles!" said Allen-a-Dale.[19]

Nora's parents display the same "prejudice" as this maid's, and Hugh, of course, shares Allen-a-Dale's eventual success. The narrator pokes tolerant fun at the kind of unthinking romance that probably instigates most marriages. Parental disapproval and the threats of poverty will not deter bold lovers.

The English romances are bound up with the Glascock-Spalding romance in Florence. In that story, again providing an ironic and comic contrast to Trevelyan's, the most interesting obstacle is Caroline Spalding's best friend, the feminist Wallachia Petrie. Though she may be a devastating commentary on Americans abroad and on American feminists, Wally Petrie has something in common with the very English, very conservative Jemima Stanbury.

Wally Petrie, the "Republican Browning," has the sharpness of Miss Stanbury, the social ineptness of Mr. Gibson, and a voluble but empty rhetoric that is all her own. With her, Trollope inverts the comic allusive technique he uses with Gibson. Gibson is a fool, and we expect to find the language surrounding him bland. Instead, Trollope inflates the language to expose Gibson's overblown ego. Expectations with Wally Petrie are the opposite. She is introduced as a talented, irascible poet, and we expect her language, and that concerning her, to be fresh and vigorous. Instead, we find an occasional bright statement overshadowed by numerous trite ones. The narrator prepares us for a stringent moral pronouncement but shows Miss Petrie's fiery indignation resolved comically in "you can lead a horse to water, but you can't make him drink." With Gibson we respond to overstatement; with Wally, understatement; with both the narrator uses comic expressions, repetitions, and allusions.

As with many of Trollope's satiric figures, Wally Petrie has some sense personally and some point to her criticisms. She attacks Mr. Glascock for England's underestimation of the Brownings. Perhaps Trollope's own friendly contact with the Brownings[20] accounts for this telling outburst by Miss Petrie (as it does for Phineas's use of Mrs. Browning in *Phineas Redux*):

"I am afraid," she said, looking up into his face with some severity, and rushing upon her subject with audacity, "that the works of your Browning have not been received in your country with that veneration to which they are entitled."

"Do you mean Mr. or Mrs. Browning?" asked Mr. Glascock,—perhaps with some mistaken idea that the lady was out of her depth, and did not know the difference.

"Either;—both; for they are one, the same, and indivisible. The spirit and germ of each is so reflected in the outcome of the other, that one sees only the result of so perfect a combination, and one is tempted to acknowledge that here and there a marriage may have been arranged in Heaven. I don't think that in your country you have perceived this, Mr. Glascock" (LV).

Wallachia Petrie's cynicism about marriage but idealization of the Brownings makes hers a curious presence in the continuing examination of courtship and relationship. The very fact that her friends call her the "Republican Browning" may be more of a just compliment to her than it is a rebuke to the United States (or to the Brownings).

Later, she again attacks Mr. Glascock (this time with an oblique reference to *Lear*) and her exuberance exposes his slowness: "'You English have no sympathy with a people who claim to be at least your equals. The clown has trod upon the courtier's heels till the clown is clown no longer, and the courtier has hardly a court in which he may dangle his sword-knot.' 'If so the clown might as well spare the courtier,' not meaning the rebuke which his words implied. 'Ah—h,—but the clown will not spare the courtier, Mr. Glascock. I understand the gibe, and I tell you that the courtier shall be spared no longer;—because he is useless'" (LVI). Wallachia's language is spirited

He Knew He Was Right 105

and the point indisputably hers, but she soon turns from the accomplished satirist into the self-righteous moralist. Immediately after she declares that the courtier will not be spared, she concludes lamely, "'He shall be cut down together with the withered grasses and thrown into the oven, and there shall be an end of him'" (LVI). This allusion to Matthew, that Gibson has muddled only twenty pages earlier, suggests Wallachia's sententiousness and aligns her with the antics of Heavitree. In fact the chapters are arranged so that the comparison is inevitable.

Chapter LIV is "Mr. Gibson's Threat"; in it Gibson gives Dorothy that medley of Scripture quoted earlier. The next chapter is "The Republican Browning," and Wallachia warns Caroline against marrying the titled Englishman by referring to the cymbals and brasses of Scripture[21]: "Miss Petrie had, with considerable eloquence, explained to her friend that that English title, which was but the clatter of a sounding brass, should be regarded as a drawback rather than as an advantage" (LV). Caroline hesitates: "She would put away from herself as far as she could any desire to become Lady Peterborough. There should be no bias in the man's favour on that score. The tinkling cymbal and the sounding brass should be nothing to her" (LV). It is ironic that Wallachia refers to the passages on charity when she is so critical of Mr. Glascock and the whole English nation.

Wallachia's words often prove to be as weak as Mr. Gibson's intrigues are foolish. When she learns that the engagement is settled, she resorts to stock (Biblical) phrase: "'Caroline,' said the stern monitress, 'you are already learning to laugh at principles which have been dear to you since you left your mother's breast. Alas, how true it is, "You cannot touch pitch and not be defiled"'" (LXXVII). It is amusing that Wally, who prides herself on originality and republican independence, should use the same expression as an old, conservative lady from England. In our last view of her the narrator again reveals a comic disjunction between the energy of Wallachia's thoughts and the simplicity of her language:

In the privacy of her little chamber Wallachia Petrie shed,—not absolute tears,—but many tearful thoughts over her friend. It was to her a thing very terrible that the chosen one of her heart should prefer the career of an English lord's wife to that of an American citizeness, with all manner of capability for female voting, female speechmaking, female poetising, and, perhaps, female political action before her. It was a thousand pities! "You may take a horse to water,"—said Wallachia to herself, thinking of the ever-freshly springing fountain of her own mind, at which Caroline Spalding would always have been made welcome freely to quench her thirst,—"but you cannot make him drink if he be not athirst." In the future she would have no friend (LXXXI).

Wallachia's comic blend of acumen and banality gives life to a part of the book which would otherwise serve merely as a light backdrop for the powerful scenes of Trevelyan's madness.

The other people of the Florentine group have some merit. Olivia Spalding advises her older sister Caroline from "Alexander's Feast" to "'take the goods the gods provide you'" (LV) just as Nora Rowley is to advise Caroline later (LXXX). Olivia is young and romantic, as two of her references (intentionally wry from the author's point of view) indicate. She exclaims to Mr. Glascock: "'Mr. Trevelyan! What a pretty name. It sounds like a novel'" (XXXVII), and later she calmly tells Carry that Carry cannot possibly know as much about English life as she can, because "'You haven't read so many of their novels as I have.'" To which Caroline replies, "'Who would ever think of learning to live out of an English novel?'" (LV). Caroline herself can be interesting, and at times she puts the modern reader in mind of Daisy Miller (just as Isabel Boncassen from *The Duke's Children* reminds us of Isabel Archer). It is especially pleasing to find a simple and fresh character in the midst of what is an amusing but sometimes wearing satire on Americans and Englishmen abroad. Wallachia's "crumbling marble" theory of Europe and Mr. Jonas Spalding's view on John S. Mill (LV) may be humorous, but they benefit from the "sane" romance of the Spalding girls. We are expected to find more sense, if less entertainment, in Livy's advice to Carry: ". . . I know a nice sort of man when I see him, and the ways of the world are not to be altered because Wally writes poetry'" (LV). Sanity and hopefulness are the predominant characteristics of the Florentine people—their main function in the novel is to provide a contrast and an alternative to Louis Trevelyan's philosophy and condition.

Caroline Spalding's marriage to Mr. Glascock is a kind of fairy tale: the American girl is transformed by love into English Lady Peterborough complete with attendant lord and lands. This story is a comic inversion of the sad Trevelyan tale. The novel, we remember, begins where the traditional fairy tale usually ends (the two references to the story of King Cophetua and the beggar maid [v, LXXVIII] are a reminder of the traditional pattern for Louis's gallantry). Beautiful but dowerless Emily Rowley has recently married the admirable, handsome, wealthy Trevelyan—but their happy wedlock quickly turns into bitter deadlock. The narrator's treatment of the various romances suggests that Dorothy and Nora and Caroline just may fare well in the marriage lottery; certainly their optimism is largely unreproved. The unfortunate Trevelyans are treated less kindly by the narrator, and we see clearly how much they are to blame for their own sorrows.

If Trevelyan himself is rigid and self-willed, his wife is correspondingly humorless and stubborn. Her own language and the narrator's suggest from the beginning that their story will be fraught with difficulty. Emily, about whose resistance the tragedy develops, can say nothing more dramatic than this about Louis's oppressive wrongheadedness: "'Louis intends to set the Thames on fire some day, and see what comes of it'" (v). Even in her moments of agonized pleading with her mad husband Emily is dull. It is not just that her speech is singularly devoid of allusions but that everything she says is predictable and uninspired. The narrator occasionally makes up for the deficiencies in Emily's speech by supplying vivid descriptions of Emily's reactions, reactions that Emily herself would be apparently unable to describe. For example, when Emily and Nora leave their uncle Outhouse's, they discuss their recent hosts. The reader knows that Emily and Nora have made the Outhouses miserable, but obtuse Emily merely reflects: "'I know that they have both been very good to us, . . . but I have never for a moment felt that they were glad to have us'" (LXI). Yet later in this same chapter, "Parker's Hotel, Mowbray Street," we sympathize with Emily's hysteria over her husband's kidnapping of their child because the narrator makes Emily's response credible and pitiable without letting Emily speak; instead, the narrator reports: "Mrs. Trevelyan had staggered against the railings, and was soon screaming in her wretchedness. . . . She in her frenzy declared that she would never see her little one again, . . . she again became hysterical in her agony, and could hardly be restrained from going forth herself to look for her lost treasure" (LXI). The narrator is frequently Emily's apologist.

We cannot blame Emily's dullness on a lack of literary allusions and references (either her own or the narrator's) to enrich her character, but certainly their absence is an indication of Trollope's assessment of and purpose for her. Her words after Louis's death are characteristically colorless, and then the narrator describes her physical reaction: "Some time after that she crept into Nora's room. 'Nora,' she said, waking the sleeping girl, 'it is all over.' 'Is he———dead?' 'It is all over. Mrs. Richards is there. It is better than an hour since now. Let me come in.' She got into her sister's bed, and there she told the tale of her tardy triumph. 'He declared to me at last that he trusted me,' she said,—almost believing that real words had come from his lips to that effect. Then she fell into a flood of tears, and after a while she also slept" (XCVIII). The phrase "tardy triumph" offers a shrewd but unkind comment on Emily's tenacity. It would have been difficult indeed to believe in Trevelyan's madness had Trollope not made it clear that Trevelyan's jealous obsession is not entirely with Emily herself but with his own right to power over her.

Power and privilege and the enduring contracts between men and women are the subjects of Trollope's impressive—if uneven—experimental novel. The narrator's attitude, revealed in the quality of asides, repetitions, and allusions, is ambivalent with Trevelyan and possibly with Emily; derisive with Gibson; and kindly ironic with the Exeter and Florence people. Trollope was evidently testing narrative control in a psychological novel

He Knew He Was Right 109

that itself reverberates with comic and ironic distortions of the unlikable main character's misguided introspection. Since the attractive comic characters operate comfortably within the moral and social codes that the unsympathetic main character's madness calls into question, the comedy of the novel inevitably undercuts the tragedy. Nevertheless, the very presence of Trevelyan's story poses questions about what might otherwise appear to be unthinking compliance with the accepted Victorian roles for men and women. Certainly the fates of the thwarted tyrant Trevelyan and the defeated feminist Wallachia Petrie together suggest that Trollope's novel advocates an accommodating middle course for relationships. The interweaving of the characters' language patterns suggests that the successful marriage could be modeled on the Brownings', may adjust to the occasional flights of an "Allen-a-Dale," may even endure the teachings of J. S. Mill, but will never survive morbid identification with *Othello* and *Lear.*

Poised between the Barsetshire series and the completion of the Palliser novels,[22] *He Knew He Was Right* shows Trollope experimenting with scope and tone and scene. Even in the test, he continues to use repetition as an organizing and unifying principle. Gibson repeats Trevelyan's mistakes; the successful romances repeat the familiar formula of attraction-problem-triumph that itself echoes Trevelyan's difficulties;[23] the narrator, throughout, repeatedly echoes the characters' quotations and allusions or offers the familiar expressions as ironic interpretations of the characters' thoughts and situations. The narrator's use of Sheridan, Thomas Brown, Scott, Tennyson, Thackeray,[24] the Bible, Bunyan, and Browning is consistent with the methods we have discussed with *Barchester Towers* and *The Last Chronicle of Barset.* The narrator's allusions to Shakespeare in *He Knew He Was Right,* as we have suggested, reveal the struggles of tragedy and comedy in the novel but also show the novel's kinship with later works. Trevelyan's confusion over *Othello* and *Lear* is like Phineas Finn's mistaken interpretation of Mrs. Browning's "A Musical Instrument" and Palliser's false identification with Caesar. In the later novels, however, the narrator's uniform irony shows the characters' making healthy reentries into the societies that have wronged them. Trevelyan's death is the inevitable result of his inability to accommodate, to grow, as Nardin says;[25] the narrator's ambivalence may thus reflect Trevelyan's own inadequacy. At any rate, Trevelyan's failure to bend focuses the novel's wonderfully complex comparisons of integration and disintegration.

4
Phineas Redux

The novel *Phineas Redux*[1] has received surprisingly little critical attention since it was first reviewed in 1874. Trollope's contemporaries, and many critics since his time, usually comment on the characters in it simply to remark on how well they have been continued from *Phineas Finn*. Trollope himself dismissed *Phineas Redux* in his autobiography as an extension of the earlier novel, mentioning it only as he praised a favorite character: "Lady Laura Standish is the best character in the two books,— of which I will speak here together" (xvii). But Lady Laura, as brilliant and attractive as she may be in *Phineas Finn*, is not the focus of the repetitions or the patterns of the second novel nor is she the best character in it; the narrator uses Phineas himself for an investigation of maturity, change, and balance. In the second novel Phineas's political and personal maturation is key to the numerous political and social ironies; through Phineas's trials we are repeatedly reminded that resilience and adaptability are essential for the public or private individual who refuses to be molded, deluded, or destroyed by dishonest rhetoric. Phineas's personal crisis forms the climax of the novel, and Lady Laura and many of the other favorites from *Phineas Finn* appear in parallel stories that comment, through contrast or similarity, on Phineas's position and choices. The equilibrium the mature Phineas achieves is a signal triumph over the rhetoric of numerous political and social imbalances.

The narrator's establishment and control of certain patterns of language are crucial to the shape and effectiveness of Phineas's story and the novel's multiple explorations. Phineas's own words and his transcribed or interpreted internal monologues reflect or are reflected in the three complementary levels of the novel. The language associated with Phineas is used to interweave politics, psychological tension, and conventional romance.

Phineas's professional awakening and political maturity involve the ironic use of slogans, maxims, and common expressions, themselves the language of dishonest politics. His personal development and the novel's psychological tension (echoed in several subplots) are explored through his identification with Elizabeth Barrett Browning's poem "A Musical Instrument." The conventional romance is expressed through the dissolution of poetic intensity with Phineas and his then ironic—even wise—use of cliché, as well as in the ascendancy of quiet harmony with Madame Max Goesler (whose best friend is herself master of a political patter and fund of ironic allusion that will be used later to point the lessons of *The Prime Minister*).

The first thirty-four chapters are deliberately, almost disarmingly, light; they reintroduce Madame Max and Lady Laura and begin the lengthy love stories of Lord Chiltern's guests, but they are also conspicuously filled with politics. The politics are presented by the narrator in what sounds like a whimsical blend of satire, sarcasm, and common sense. But the real degeneracy of government and its language is soon detected as they purposely reflect and attempt to mold Phineas's honest, naive admiration. Phineas's expressions are an innocent manifestation of what soon proves to be the highly contagious disease undermining English politics: empty rhetoric.

The first chapter of *Phineas Redux* alerts the reader to the importance (if not the purpose) of clichés, repetitions, and allusions in characterizing both Phineas and the political world he reenters. Daubeny and the Conservatives and Gresham and the Liberals are carefully reduced to a series of familiar, catchy expressions. First the Conservatives are called "birdlings with beaks wide open and craving maws," but this image is dropped in favor of a more playful one. The narrator recalls the rollicking freedom of Robin Hood's outlaws with "Mr. Daubeny and his merry men." Twice they are called "merry men" and then the narrator tells us that "fortune favoured them" and that it favored them when they "made their hay while the sun shone." Meanwhile the restless Liberals, made up of "good men—of men good and true" and "every good and true man," plan to wage war. The Liberals claim that the "cutting up of the Whitehall cake by the Conservatives was spoliation" because the Conservatives refused to get out of office when they had had their fair share of "the cake." It was even discovered that "the hay was still made even after the sun had gone down." The Liberals fear further deceit because it is believed "Mr. Daubeny had a scheme in his head—some sharp trick of political conjuring, some 'hocus-pocus presto' sleight of hand, by which he might be able to retain power...."

When the Liberals decide to wage war, they call back Phineas Finn (hence the *redux* of the title), who is reintroduced with the lightness used with the parliamentary "good men" and "merry men." The apparently lighthearted narrator interprets with clichés Phineas's dissatisfaction with tame Irish life: Phineas "had revelled in the gaslight, and could not lie quiet on a sunny bank. To the palate accustomed to high cookery, bread and milk is almost painfully insipid." The narrator then throws in a little Horace and shows Phineas transformed (as he is, no doubt, in his own imagination) ironically into a conqueror from antiquity: "Now Dublin was his Tibur, and the fickle one found that he could not be happy unless he were back again at Rome."[2] At the thought of London, Phineas is ready for war and feels the thrill of battle, and the narrator interprets his thoughts with a glib Biblical allusion: "Like the warhorse out at grass he remembered the sound of the battle and the noise of trumpets." With the letter from Barrington Erle, "he neighed like the old warhorse, and already found himself shouting 'Ha, ha,' among the trumpets."[3] Phineas believes he returns to England a mature man; his joy at the prospect of approaching political battle suggests his unthinking zeal. He is, in fact, immature and unwise and he has yet—in this novel—to pass through the suffering of Job before he attains balance. Within ten pages Trollope has established the tone of the novel and has shown Phineas's kinship with the political "characters." The surge of mixed metaphors and empty clichés complements the unreflecting Biblical allusion used to show Phineas's spirit. The rest of the first chapter reinforces the impression of windiness and also supplies most of the key expressions used in the novel to stigmatize emotional and political immaturity, irresponsibility, and general imbalance.

Phineas is obviously dazzled by "those wars of the gods at which he had been present" in London and never seriously considers rejecting Erle's offer. He says to himself, easily, "there is the bare bodkin," but the reader has only to recall Crawley's different use of this same expression (*Hamlet*, III.i.76) in *The Last Chronicle of Barset* to appreciate the superficiality of Phineas's trouble. Then the narrator shows that the whole of Phineas's debate can be reduced to clichés:

> We all know those arguments and quotations, antagonistic to prudence, with which a man fortifies himself in rashness. "None but the brave deserve the fair." "Where there's a will there's a way." "Nothing venture nothing have." "The sword is to him who can use it." "Fortune favours the bold." But on the other side there is just as much to be said. "A bird in the hand is worth two in the bush." "Look before you leap." "Thrust not your hand further than you can draw it back again." All which maxims of life Phineas Finn revolved within his own heart, if not carefully, at least frequently, as he walked up and down the long pier of Kingston Harbour (1).

Phineas's ingenuousness predetermines his reinvolvement as well as disillusionment with politics. His lightheartedness here is dangerously close to the irresponsibility of men noted for empty political rhetoric: "But what matter such revolvings? A man placed as was our Phineas always does that which most pleases him at the moment, being but poor at argument if he cannot carry the weight to that side which best satisfies his own feelings" (1). His new life and his ambitions are easily summed up with "the world as his oyster," the cliché Trollope uses throughout *Phineas Finn* as well:

> Then he would be penniless, with the world before him as a closed oyster to be again opened, and he knew,—no one better,—that this oyster becomes harder and harder in the opening as the man who has to open it becomes older. It is an oyster that will close to again with a snap, after you have got your knife well into it, if you withdraw your point but for a moment. He had had a rough tussle with the oyster already, and had reached the fish within the shell. Nevertheless, the

oyster which he had got was not the oyster which he wanted. So he told himself now, and here had come to him the chance of trying again (I).

Phineas contemplates the oyster again when he arrives in London and enters his old lodgings: "He had opened the oyster for himself once, though it had closed again with so sharp a snap when the point of his knife had been withdrawn" (VI). We find the spirit, if not the exact words of the other expressions from this first chapter informing the novel as a whole. As the novel develops, the clichés and expressions become signals of danger on a national scale.

Phineas also looks at the House as his "oyster" (I), and the other members of Parliament think of themselves and the House in terms as ready and meaningless as Phineas's own. Parliament promotes word games: Mr. Rattler, the Liberal whip, and his colleagues "bolt the bran" from their opponents' arguments (V); Rattler describes the movement of the party in Yankee slang—"'it's just as well to let things slide'" (V); when the Conservatives perceive that Daubeny is going to bring a bill to disestablish the Church, they, as a body, cry "Ichabod" in the House (VIII). The substance and purpose of party politics are neatly satirized in some widely accepted dictums: "A party can only live by having its share of Garters, lord-lieutenants, bishops, and attorney-generals. Though the country were ruined, the party should be supported" (VIII).

The general philosophy of politics is encapsulated in catchy, perverse maxims. The insidious undercurrents of the party system are disguised in abstraction or excused in motto: "'If we were all a little less in the abstract, and a little more in the concrete, it would be better for us.' . . . Laurence Fitzgibbon, when these words had been whispered to him by Mr. Bonteen, had hardly understood them; but it had been explained to him that his friend had meant 'men, not measures'" (VIII). Mr. Bonteen's words deliberately reverse the more honorable and less popular "measures, not men"[4] by declaring that party politics will be of more importance than the country's laws. Gresham and the Liberals vote against Disestablishment simply because

Daubeny and the Conservatives propose it. Gresham advises his party to reject the bill and: "It was a simple avowal that on this occasion men were to be regarded, and not measures. No doubt such is the case, and ever has been the case, with the majority of active politicians. The double pleasure of pulling down an opponent, and of raising oneself, is the charm of a politician's life" (xxxi). The narrator's tone of confidential candor enforces the severity of his criticism: he pretends to praise the Liberals for openly embracing a selfishness other politicians have long cherished but never dared admit. In truth, of course, the Liberals make no such declarations, but cover their greed for power with a thin veil of righteous indignation against the duplicity of the Conservatives. Both parties squabble over power, and the measures put before the country are merely incidental weapons in the constant battle for the Whitehall "cake."

The atmosphere of political corruption is sustained and exposed through the narrator's careful, often humorous, use of references and expressions. For example, in pretending to excuse Phineas's friends for never having bothered to write to him while he was back in Ireland, the narrator chooses the busy, canny Walpole for his analogy, an analogy that can only damn the friends: "A Horace Walpole may write to a Mr. Mann about all things under the sun, London gossip or transcendental philosophy, and if the Horace Walpole of the occasion can write well and will labour diligently at that vocation, his letters may be worth reading by his Mr. Mann, and by others. . ." (II). Out of sight, out of mind, is clearly implied. The Conservatives are condemned for their duplicity in supporting the Disestablishment of the Church, and the narrator imitates the Liberals' righteous contempt: "Doubtless they were all Esaus; but would they sell their great birthright for so very small a mess of pottage?" (IX). The clergymen's despair over the Conservative position is similarly and pointedly drawn: "Was it wonderful that parsons should be seen about Westminster in flocks with '*Et tu, Brute*' written on their faces as plainly as the law on the brows of a Pharisee?" (XXXIII). The old duke of St. Bungay, staunch

Whig politician, thinks of the sharing of power with Conservatives with a complacency that suggests how truly meaningless are the many changes of government. He quotes comfortably from the *Tempest* (II.ii.42): "They say that 'misfortune makes men acquainted with strange bedfellows'" (XL). The political mind delights in sensation and notoriety, as suggested through a comic distortion of Isaiah 52:7 that was so welcomely jubilant in *The Last Chronicle*. Phineas's agents are sorry he will not return with them to Tankerville after his much-publicized acquittal: "Messrs. Ruddles, Gadmire, and Troddles returned to Tankerville,—disappointed no doubt at not bringing with them him whose company would have made their feet glorious on the pavement of their native town. . ." (LXXI). An easiness of thought prompts the empty rhetoric of Parliament and its agents.

In Parliament, Daubeny and Gresham play with Biblical passages, Latin tags, and poetry. The great Disestablishment debate hinges on the interpretation of "Quod minime reris." Gresham introduces the Liberal position: ". . . pointing over the table to his opponents, he uttered that well-worn quotation, *Quod minime reris*,—then he paused, and began again; *Quod minime reris,—Graiâ pandetur ab urbe*. The power and inflexion of his voice at the word Graia were certainly very wonderful" (VIII).[5] But Daubeny is quick to twist the second part to his advantage: "He did not doubt that the Dissenting interests of the country would welcome relief from an anomaly, let it come whence it might, even *Graiâ ab urbe*, and he waved his hand back to the clustering Conservatives who sat behind him" (VIII). Later, in the real debate, Daubeny appropriates the quotation: "'See what we Conservatives can do. In fact we will conserve nothing when we find that you do not desire to have it conserved any longer. "*Quod minime reris Graiâ pandetur ab urbe*"'" (XXXIII). Gresham mixes the classics and Scripture when he tries to undermine the reference he has himself given the clever Daubeny: "The right honourable gentleman had prided himself on his generosity as a Greek. He would remind the right honourable gentleman that presents from Greeks had ever been considered dangerous. . . . The political gifts of the right honourable gentleman . . . had always been more bitter to the taste than Dead Sea apples" (XXXIII). The current issue is only an excuse for exhibiting pyrotechnics, and the Latin tags, like the ready clichés, suggest the extent of political falsity. The public applauds the trickery and showmanship and is even thrilled to believe that Daubeny may lead his own party to destruction: "There was a gratification in feeling that the country party was bound to follow, even should he take them into the very bowels of a mountain, as the pied piper did the children of Hamelin;—and this made listening pleasant" (XXXIII). Robert Browning's "Pied Piper of Hamelin" suggests the fate of those who are dishonest and who will not listen to warning; the presence of his disturbing piper makes an ironic complement to Mrs. Browning's "A Musical Instrument" and the restoration of harmony later in the novel.

Fairly early, the narrator sums up the difference between Gresham and Daubeny and suggests the extent of public corruption in the preference for Daubeny. He says that the man who loses his temper is probably telling the truth, but the "tranquil" man is preferred for public office even though he may be lying. With apparently unflappable heartiness, the narrator offers two cynical slogans to represent the thinking of those who support Daubeny's smooth lying: "We want practical results rather than truth. A clear head is worth more than an honest heart" (IX). These perverse mottoes can be added to the list of twisted clichés and stock expressions used to characterize the evils of unanalyzed rhetoric. Both leaders cultivate the wrongheadedness of a public easily swayed by histrionics. The real argument does not favor Gresham over Daubeny, but condemns the House and the public in general. The question of either leader's worthiness is subsumed in an attack on the public conscience. The Liberal party can promote "men, not measures," and the Conservatives can applaud Daubeny's tricks because the public, self-seeking and unprincipled, clamors for fireworks and jingles.

Both parties' principles, in keeping with the public they

serve, are distorted similarly by greed for power. In fact, the narrator shows us that the parties' views are actually identical. The colorful differences are created to distract a gullible public into feeling that whoever has power is important. The differences between the leaders are unimportant, and the differences in platform are determined by strategic opportunism. What is really important to politicians, the narrator shows, is who gets the most of what. Daubeny is a conjuror who leads his followers by the nose, altering the tenets of Conservatism to retain power; Gresham is greedy and hot-tempered, thoughtlessly offending his own party members and perverting the spirit of the Constitution. The narrator shrewdly questions, why should the public trouble itself with Daubeny's changes or with Gresham's tirades when both parties are the same? The narrator suggests that our godlike gladiators are really dogs fighting over a bone. The lengthy aside in Chapter XXXIII on similarities between the parties is a masterly bit of satire that echoes and focuses the many images and expressions used to make fun of politics.

The narrator pretends to explain away the dishonesty of partisan politics by likening the politicians to frustrated professional fighters, bored and restless and eager for an excuse to practice their apparently unnecessary skills. First the narrator says: "A man destined to sit conspicuously on our Treasury Bench, or on the seat opposite to it, should ask the gods for a thick skin as a first gift." The crucial lack of "thick skin" determines Palliser's downfall in *The Prime Minister*; here "The need of this in our national assembly is greater than elsewhere, because the differences between the men opposed to each other are smaller." Men with real differences "may cut each other's throats if they can find an opportunity; but they do not bite each other like dogs over a bone. But when opponents are almost in accord, as is always the case with our parliamentary gladiators, they are ever striving to give maddening little wounds through the joints of the harness." The narrator sharpens the gibe by pretending to excuse the boredom. What can be the issues, he says, when one of us wants to "put down the Queen, or to repudiate the National Debt, or to destroy religious worship, or even to disturb the ranks of society?" And finally this apparently tolerant, broad-minded advocate of parliamentary chicanery expands the satire to religious bigotry: "It is the same in religion. The apostle of Christianity and the infidel can meet without a chance of a quarrel; but it is never safe to bring together two men who differ about a saint or a surplice" (XXXIII). The narrator's own smooth irony is a powerful reflection of society's willingness to accept corruption and dishonesty if they are packaged acceptably. The twisted maxims are presented in a playful or an ominously calm tone; the most vital criticisms are delivered in eloquent, fanciful, and perverse repetitions and images, and the narrator maintains a delicate balance between imitation and satire.

Trollope's balance is not perfect; occasionally his own party bias threatens to outweigh the broader censure of general party politics. His distinct distrust of Disraeli makes the image of Daubeny the conjuror[6] so colorful that general criticism of the party system sometimes sounds tame by comparison. Trollope shares the misery over his own abortive attempt to get into Parliament in *Ralph the Heir* (1871), but he echoes his own speeches on the hustings in *Phineas Redux*. His election experience was bitter.[7] His speeches[8] in Beverley may explain the quality of attack he makes upon Disraeli (Daubeny) in this novel since he openly despised Disraeli's oratory and was suspicious of Conservatives who demanded it as their right to reform. Trollope attacked the Reform Bill of 1867, brought in by Disraeli's government, because he claimed Disraeli merely concealed Liberal measures in Conservative dogma. The shrewd words of Tadpole and Taper in Disraeli's *Coningsby* may have justified Trollope's accusation:

"The time has gone by for Tory government; what the country requires is a sound Conservative government."
"A sound Conservative government," said Taper, musingly, "I understand: Tory men and Whig measures."[9]

Disraeli's speeches alarmed the Liberals,[10] and at Beverley, infuriated by Disraeli's apparent duplicity, Trollope prepared the image of the magician that was to appear in *Phineas Redux*: "It will be hocus pocus, square round, fly away, come again, up and down, turn a somersault, come down on his feet, and present you with a most beautiful bill to disestablish and disendow the Irish Church, and very likely to abolish Protestantism generally."[11] If we substitute the Disestablishment of the Church of England for that of the Church of Ireland, we have the background for *Phineas Redux*.[12] In the novel, the narrator echoes Trollope's speech: "There would be a blaze and a confusion, in which timid men would doubt whether the constitution would be burned to tinder or only illuminated; but that blaze and that confusion would be dear to Mr. Daubeny if he could stand as the centre figure,—the great pyrotechnist who did it all, red from head to foot with the glare of the squibs with which his own hands were filling all the spaces" (XXXIV). Throughout the novel Daubeny is a conjuror and a charlatan who creates intrigue and manipulates language.

Daubeny, as one of Trollope's few pure caricatures, is persistently denounced for his trickery. Trollope calls him an "English political Von Moltke" (XIII)[13] and a Cagliostro (XIII, XXXIX) (the latter of which epithets, considering its frequent use in his novels to label deceit, is particularly damning). He gives summaries of Daubeny's speeches suggesting that he makes a show of his learning (and his religion), referring in one to Eli, the Levites, and the order of Melchisedek,[14] winding up with this deliberately confusing assertion: "By a clearly pronounced disunion of Church and State the theocracy of Thomas à Becket would be restored. . ." (XXXIII). As usual with Trollope's allusions, we are invited to analyze the references themselves along with the speaker and the occasion. Daubeny is clearly a master showman. Anyone who can make the unlikely combination of Jewish priests and Thomas à Becket a convincing commentary on the Anglican Church deserves the admiration if not the faith of his followers. The members of the House and the public, addicted as they are to maxim and rhetoric, are willing victims of Daubeny's "hocus pocus." The narrator's treatment of Daubeny may occasionally take the subtlety and the objectivity out of the satire, but it enlivens the novel.

Daubeny is derided—at length—as chief magician of a public manifestly corrupt, but this novel is not solely or primarily political. Under the splashy caricature and the deliberate understatement is a current of irresistible humor. The tone of the political sections prevents the reader from taking the Liberals, the Conservatives, or the narrator wholly seriously. Disraeli used stories as thin threads to bind together often cumbersome lectures on his own political theories. Trollope, though he may vent some of his political opinions, stresses the stories surrounding the political scenes and points them all with the same gentle irony. For example, the narrator relates a conversation about forming the new Liberal cabinet; the dialogue is serious and convincing. Suddenly the narrator destroys the illusion of authenticity with a burst into Horace reminiscent of the exuberant narrator of *Barchester Towers*:

> But whither would'st thou, Muse? Unmeet
>   For jocund lyre are themes like these.
> Shalt thou the talk of Gods repeat,
> Debasing by thy strains effete
>   Such lofty mysteries?[15]

The narrator demurs, "The absolute words of a conversation so lofty shall no longer be attempted . . ." (XL) and thus pokes fun at the reader for believing that a mere novelist can relate something so divine as a cabinet conference, at the reader for presumptuously feeling worthy of such eavesdropping even if it were possible, and, of course, at the politicians (and those who admire them) who evidently imagine their own backroom maneuvers to be lofty.[16]

The narrator's mocking use of Horace is a timely echo of the public's and the politicians' slogans, clichés, and ingeniously twisted Latin tags. The mottoes, maxims, and linguistic conjurings in *Phineas Redux* prove to be distant, kindly cousins of the sinister repetitions that would later shape *Brave New World* and *1984*. While the narrator creates and echoes the satiric and humorous patterns, he uses Phineas Finn as the focus for action and reaction. Thus the potential sweep of the satire is deliberately, ironically contained in the personal struggle between two rival Liberals, Phineas Finn and Mr. Bonteen.

Phineas's emotional maturation necessitates political disillusionment. The clichés and stock phrases of Phineas's untested enthusiasm act as extensions of as well as symptoms of parliamentary corruption. When Phineas outgrows the habits of thought that have made him idealize the system, his language, for a while, is charged with poetic intensity. His metamorphosis begins when he reacts to his demeaning squabbles with Bonteen and progresses rapidly while he is in prison, suspected of Bonteen's murder. The clichés of parliamentary life are thrust into the background of Phineas's psychological drama as he struggles to find genuine balance. In prison, Phineas's language, stripped of the comfortingly false phrases of his jaunty reentry into politics, is authentically, intensely emotional. Other characters associated with him, who undergo parallel forms of trial, also reveal themselves in impassioned speeches. The core of the novel, the moment when Phineas first reassesses himself in relationship to others, is marked by his identification with Elizabeth Barrett Browning's poem "A Musical Instrument." Phineas, as the narrator's repetitions reinforce, passes from hollow cliché to the fine, restorative harmony of lyric.

Phineas's imprisonment is the turning point in all three levels of the narrative. The politics (and the language associated with them) are pushed into the background, Phineas's anguish forces him into the tension of self-recognition, and Phineas's changes prepare him to accept the generous love of Madame Max Goesler. The quality of Phineas's suffering echoes in and is echoed by the other characters' private trials. In prison, Phineas's anger, then weary restraint, then bitterness permanently separate him from the naive, unthinking devotion to the system. The repetition of *who* imitates the repetition in Phineas's own head of his reasons for outrage:

Murder! They really believed that he had deliberately murdered the man;—he, Phineas Finn, *who* had served his country with repute, *who* had sat in Parliament, *who* had prided himself on living with the best of his fellow-creatures, *who* had been the friend of Mr. Monk and of Lord Cantrip, the trusted intimate of such women as Lady Laura and Lady Chiltern, *who* had never put his hand to a mean action, or allowed his tongue to speak a mean word! He laughed in his wrath, and then almost howled in his agony (LV). (italics mine)

Phineas's anguish is a reminder of the narrator's mocking words about energy and truth in politicians. Daubeny is preferred for public office because he is a "tranquil" (probably lying) man rather than an angry, honest one. Phineas's anger denotes that he is one of the men perhaps too honest for present politics.

Phineas's fury is expressed largely in internal monologue; with others his maddened "laugh" and "howl" are (after the first outbursts) painfully suppressed in flat, emotionless words. Others, then, must echo the language of his private thoughts. Both Lady Laura and the old cynical lawyer Chaffanbrass speak with energy akin to Phineas's own. Lady Laura (tormented by her own trial) visits Phineas and speaks with unrestrained passion:

> "I suppose, Phineas, it cannot be that you are really in danger?"
> "In the greatest danger, I fancy."
> "Do you mean they will say—you are guilty?"
> "The magistrates have said so already."
> "But surely that is nothing. If I thought so, I should die. If I believed it, they should never take me out of the prison while you are here. Barrington says that it cannot be. Oswald and Violet are sure that such a thing can never happen. It was that Jew who did it."
> "I cannot say who did it. I did not."
> "You! Oh, Phineas! The world must be mad when any can believe it!" (LV).

Her later internal monologues show this same abandon.

Phineas's mental rhythms are also echoed by the unlikely Chaffanbrass, the gruff, old lawyer Trollope readers would recognize from *The Three Clerks* and *Orley Farm*. Phineas's dignified control so impresses the lawyer that he confides to his colleague later "'I never did,—and I never will,—express an opinion of my own as to the guilt or innocence of a client till after the trial is over. But I have sometimes felt as though I would give the blood out of my veins to save a man. I never felt in that way more strongly than I do now'" (LX). (This is high praise indeed from the man who had been unmoved by Lady Mason's sad beauty in *Orley Farm*.) Even Chaffanbrass's performance in the courtroom seems to echo the novel's larger concerns with language, literature, and the expressing of honest, worthy emotion. Chaffanbrass invokes *Hamlet, Macbeth, Othello,* Scott's *Kenilworth,* and Bulwer's *Eugene Aram* to prove that murder is usually premeditated (LXI). Despite (perhaps because of) the histrionics, Chaffanbrass makes his point and we associate Phineas's sufferings with the poetic grandeur of Shakespearean tragedy as well as with the romance of popular fiction.

Ironically, after the magistrates commit Phineas to trial, Phineas fortifies himself with the Latin tag we recognize from Mr. Harding in defending Crawley in *The Last Chronicle of Barset*: ". . . he remembered an example in Latin from some rule of grammar, and repeated it to himself over and over again.—'No one at an instant,—of a sudden,—becomes most base'" (LV). The difference between Phineas's comfort in the old rule and his earlier ease with cliché is instructive. Phineas does not subvert the classics as do his parliamentary colleagues; instead, painful experience makes him turn to the classics and poetry for identification. Released from prison, he quotes Mrs. Browning. But just before he is released, the narrator shows us how depleted Phineas has been by weary vigil. The narrator's words here carefully prepare the reader for Phineas's interpretation of Mrs. Browning and then for his achievement of equilibrium.

The narrator suggests that Phineas is almost too exhausted to realize what has happened:

He had borne himself very gallantly during that week, having in all his intercourse with his attorney, spoken without a quaver in his voice, and without a flaw in the perspicuity of his intelligence. But now, when Mr. Low came to him, explaining to him that it was impossible that a verdict should be found against him, he was quite broken down. "There is nothing left of me," he said at the end of the interview. "I feel that I had better take to my bed and die. Even when I think of all that friends have done for me, it fails to cheer me. In this matter

I should not have had to depend on friends. Had not she gone for me to that place every one would have believed me to be a murderer."

And yet in his solitude he thought very much of the marvellous love shown to him by his friends (LXIV).

His cry that "'There is nothing left of me'" foreshadows his identification with "A Musical Instrument" already, perhaps unconsciously, shaping his own thoughts about himself. But the narrator, while preparing the way for identification with the poem, also suggests what will be the tenor of the restored Phineas's mind, when he has grown beyond his misreading of the poem. The fact that he "thought very much of the marvellous love shown to him by his friends" shows that Phineas has a saving resilience.

Before quoting Phineas's use of Mrs. Browning's poem, I would like to explain why the use of this poem was so important and why it may have been given such prominence in the psychological development of Phineas. Trollope mistook and objected to the logic of the poem initially, and his objection was conveyed to Mrs. Browning herself. She answered him and explained away the difficulty. The novel *Phineas Redux* seems to offer a delayed working out of the poem—in full agreement with Mrs. Browning's explanation. Perhaps Trollope is laughing at his former wrongheadedness when he makes Phineas misinterpret his own relationship to the poem, concentrating on the very aspect that has previously given Trollope difficulty. When Phineas has fully recovered, his own balance suggests that his initial identification with the poem was morbid and misguided. But it is only after his bit of melodramatic self-pitying that Phineas is able to shake free and to reemerge a new man in both politics and romance. Though Phineas himself does not again revert to the poem in his newly won equilibrium, the reader can clearly feel how the real meaning of the poem has at last asserted itself as Phineas becomes a useful, harmonious instrument.

"A Musical Instrument" was one of the last of Mrs. Browning's published lyrics and appeared in the 1860 issue of the *Cornhill* (which also contained chapters XIX to XXI of Trollope's first serial publication, *Framley Parsonage*). In the poem the "great god Pan" disturbs the quiet of the river bed when he splashes in to pull a reed. He strips the protective leaves from the reed and then hacks and hews it with his knife. The fourth stanza reads:

> IV
> He cut it short, did the great god Pan,
>   (How tall it stood in the river!)
> Then drew the pith, like the heart of a man,
> Steadily from the outside ring,
> Then notched the poor dry empty thing
>   In holes as he sate by the river.

He plays the pipe and the "lilies revived, and the dragon-fly / Came back to dream on the river." The poem concludes with the lines that bothered Trollope initially:

> VII
> Yet half a beast is the great god Pan
>   To laugh, as he sits by the river,
> Making a poet out of a man.
> The true gods sigh for the cost and pain,—
> For the reed that grows nevermore again
>   As a reed with the reeds in the river.[17]

Though the poem made a vivid impression on Trollope, he misunderstood what it implied about the poet's role in society, writing as follows to his brother:

> The lines are very beautiful, and the working out of the idea is delicious. But I am inclined to think that she is illustrating an allegory by a thought, rather than a thought by an allegory. The idea of the god destroying the reed in making the instrument has, I imagine, given her occasion to declare that in the sublimation of the poet the man is lost for the ordinary purposes of man's life. It has been thus instead of being the reverse; and I can hardly believe that she herself believes in the doctrine which her fancy has led her to illustrate. A man that can be a poet is so much the more a man in becoming such, and is the more fitted for a man's best work. Nothing is destroyed, and in preparing the instrument for the touch of the musician the gods do nothing for which they need weep. The idea, however, is beautiful, and it is beautifully worked.... In the third line of it [the seventh

stanza], she loses her antithesis. She must spoil her man, as well as make a poet out of him—spoil him as the reed is spoiled. Should we not read the lines thus:

> Yet one half beast is the great god Pan
> Or he would not have laughed by the river.
> Making a poet he mars a man;
> The true gods sigh, etc?[18]

Trollope thought Mrs. Browning was saying that a man would be lost to the "ordinary purposes of man's life" in becoming special. It is evident that Phineas makes this very mistake when he first believes he will never again be able to rejoin his fellow "reeds." He, like Palliser in the next political novel, mistakes the denuded reed for a permanently impaired man, forced from the comforting similarity and proximity of others. Through Thomas Adolphus Trollope and Isa Blagden, Mrs. Browning heard the criticism and answered Trollope thus:

> I meant to say that the poetic organisation implies certain disadvantages; for instance an exaggerated general susceptibility, . . . which may be shut up, kept out of the way in everyday life, and must be (or the man is *"marred"* indeed, made a Rousseau or a Byron of), but which is necessarily, for all that, cultivated in the very cultivation of art itself. There is an inward reflection and refraction of the heats of life . . . doubling pains and pleasures. . . .[19]

Whatever personal difficulties their disagreement may have caused were evidently repaired,[20] and Mrs. Browning's qualifications evidently satisfied Trollope. R. W. Chapman notes: ". . . Thomas Adolphus Trollope quotes a letter from Anthony who, while admiring this poem, was not convinced of its logic. That was in 1860; by 1874 the poem had its own way with him."[21] Phineas's sensitivity makes him lose political innocence and a sense of privacy (for a while), but it also allows him to become a clear-sighted, mature public servant. Phineas can find a new, sturdy balance, just as the atmosphere of the river-bed can be restored, because in unthwarted times his sensitivity tempers his good humor and his patriotic ardor. Phineas, like the reed, has gained, not lost, by his transformation.

Feeling hollow and abused, Phineas is released from prison

and reflects on "A Musical Instrument." This internal monologue reads as a direct transcription of Phineas's thoughts. The wording is inspired by the poem and suggests how deeply Phineas has been brooding over, perhaps relishing, the aptness of pictured violation and mutilation of the innocent reed:

> And now what should be his own future life? One thing seemed certain to him. He could never again go into the House of Commons, and sit there, an ordinary man of business, with other ordinary men. He had been so hacked and hewed about, so exposed to the gaze of the vulgar, so mauled by the public, that he could never more be anything but the wretched being who had been tried for the murder of his enemy. The pith had been taken out of him, and he was no longer a man fit for use. He could never more enjoy that freedom from self-consciousness, that inner tranquility of spirit, which are essential to public utility. Then he remembered certain lines which had long been familiar to him, and he repeated them aloud, with some conceit that they were apposite to him:—
> The true gods sigh for the cost and pain,—
> For the reed that grows never more again
> As a reed with the reeds in the river (LXVII).

Later that evening Phineas returns to the scene of the murder and walks back over the ground he imagines Emilius to have taken. He again recites the words of the poem:

> The reed that grows never more again
> As a reed with the reeds in the river (LXVII).

In the poem the god "hacked and hewed as a great god can" the reed he has taken from the river, and Phineas feels he has been "hacked and hewed about." The reed Pan fashions is almost beyond recognition: "There was not a sign of a leaf indeed / To prove it fresh from the river"; Phineas feels that he can "never more be anything but the wretched being who had been tried for the murder of his enemy." In the poem Pan destroys the essence of the reed: "drew the pith, like the heart of a man, / Steadily from the outside ring, / Then notched the poor dry empty thing / In holes as he sate by the river." Phineas feels: "The pith had been taken out of him, and he was no longer a man fit for use. He could never more enjoy that freedom from self-consciousness, that inner tranquility of spirit, which are essential to public utility." So far Phineas's identification with the poem is appropriate, and his conclusions, justified. However, the most important part of the passage comes not from Phineas, but from the narrator: "he repeated them aloud, with *some conceit* that they were apposite to him" (italics mine). These two words epitomize Trollope's technique throughout this novel and all of his good ones. He ballasts a character's morbid exaggerations with reason, distance, and judgment. Phineas is right to identify himself with the poem, but, as "some conceit" suggests, his analysis is incomplete. He dwells on the destruction of the reed and forgets the creation of music and the restoration of order. The narrator's irony is double-edged: he makes the reader smile at Phineas's boastful self-abasement; he lets the reader feel that a fully mature Phineas will qualify his own morbid exaggeration. As Juliet McMaster says of Phineas's response to the poem, "Phineas's sensibility has inevitably expanded, but for the moment he is crippled and incapacitated, and, like Hamlet, simply sickened by himself and the world."[22]

Phineas's initial withdrawal from society is a natural reaction to the painful publicity of his trial, but it is also the last stage in his painful metamorphosis. During his withdrawal the extent of Phineas's changed responses to the things which, prior to the trial, had been of utmost importance to him becomes apparent. His first act upon returning to society is to resign his seat in the House because he knows many of the constituents of his borough have thought him guilty. When he is reelected, he is reluctant to enter the House, and this hesitancy is caused by doubts about the value of the House itself and not just by morbid shyness.

In fact, the strain of the trial makes the clamor for office, before irritating, now abhorrent. Because Phineas completely loses his illusions about the House, he is no longer protected by his own enthusiasm among the other "reeds." He refuses office when Mrs. Gresham offers it, marries wealthy Madame Max, and afterward, in the stories of *The Prime Minister* and *The Duke's Children,* as a practical and experienced man, attains a number of influential posts, including secretary of the Admiralty and secretary for Ireland. His experience of the trial deepens him and makes him selfless and instrumental; he will never again endure the pettiness that he before mistook and accepted as part of the rough combat of the House.

In a long letter to Lady Laura he describes the nature of his altered feelings; his clear-eyed self-irony shows the maturity and balance of the new man:

"I used to have a faith that now seems to me to be marvellous. Even twelve months ago, when I was beginning to think of standing for Tankerville, I believed that on our side the men were patriotic angels, and that Daubeny and his friends were all fiends or idiots,—mostly idiots, but with a strong dash of fiendism to control them. It has all come now to one common level of poor human interests. I doubt whether patriotism can stand the wear and tear and temptation of the front benches in the House of Commons. Men are flying at each other's throats, thrusting and parrying, making false accusations and defences equally false, lying and slandering,—sometimes picking and stealing,—till they themselves become unaware of the magnificence of their own position, and forget that they are expected to be great. Little tricks of sword-play engage all their skill. . . . And I am aware that I have been soured by prison indignities. But still the conviction remains with me that parliamentary interests are not those battles of gods and giants which I used to regard them. Our Gyas with the hundred hands is but a Three-fingered Jack, and I sometimes think that we share our great Jove with the Strand Theatre. Nevertheless I shall go back,— and if they will make me a joint lord to-morrow I shall be in heaven!" (LXX).

Phineas's images here recall those the narrator used earlier to characterize the House: the "thrusting and parrying" and "little tricks of sword play" are usefully reminiscent of the narrator's impotent gladiators; "Gyas"[23] and "Three-fingered Jack" bring to mind the narrator's mock-apologetic flight into Horace, and the Strand Theatre is a reminder of Daubeny's and Gresham's theatrics. Phineas's resilience allows him to grow and change from his experience and to recognize the House as a potential circus. But Phineas is seriously committed to true government, and his all-important "Nevertheless" shows that he accepts the challenge of belonging to the House even though he sees its corruption. His laughter at his own willful ambition speaks eloquently of his stability.

The concept of "trial" is repeated with three other prominent characters; two are unsuccessful and one is a complement to Phineas's own. Kennedy's and Lady Laura's trials support the psychological tension of the novel and even extend the political satire. Madame Max's provides the triumph of Phineas's own romance. Each of the trials is closely related to Phineas's in the story line, and the repeated patterns of language and the allusions knit the parallels together.

Phineas is slandered during his trial by Mr. Quintus Slide, editor of a daily paper called *The People's Banner.* Slide champions Mr. Kennedy's pathetic case against Phineas because Slide himself hates Phineas. He drags Phineas's name into his paper by making innuendos about his relationship with Lady Laura Kennedy, accusing him of responsibility for Kennedy's madness, and then, later at the trial, insisting on Phineas's guilt. Even before the murder of Bonteen, Phineas's name is often in the public eye, and we recognize the word of the press as another manifestation of corrupt power. Mr. Kennedy's personal trial, his struggle against madness, provides the self-seeking editor with an excuse to vilify Phineas.

Slide's use of the press makes a sinister distortion of the "Musical Instrument" theme: "The People's Banner was the organ, and Mr. Quintus Slide was, of course, the organist. The following [an attack on Phineas] was one of the tunes he played, and was supposed by himself to be a second thunderbolt..." (XLIII). If a large part of the English public accepts the manufactured thunder of a charlatan such as Slide, "the Jove of The People's Banner" (XLIV), there is little wonder that a Daubeny is so successful. Slide understands the morality of his readers perfectly: "A highly-wrought moral strain would he knew well create either disgust or ridicule. 'If there is any beastliness I 'ate it is 'igh-faluting,'... The sentiment was the same as that conveyed in the '*Point de zèle*' of Talleyrand" (XXII). The press is as guilty of fraud as the government is of political high jinks.

Slide expands the political satire, but he also gives promi-

Phineas Redux 133

nence to Kennedy and Lady Laura. The conclusion of Kennedy's "trial" is inevitable because he relies on such men as Slide to help him. He succumbs to his obsession with religion and refuses to forgive his wife. He calls her Sunday afternoon gatherings "meetings of Belial" (x), and he accuses Phineas of being a "child of Apollyon" (x). The narrator makes fun of Kennedy's stinginess with the lighthearted language we associate with politics—"There are so many men by whom the *tenuis ratio saporum*[24] has not been achieved, that the Caleb Balderstones[25] of those houses in which plenty does not flow are almost justified in hoping that goblets of Gladstone may pass current" (x)—but the humor itself, ironically, makes us look sharply at Kennedy's obsession. On his deathbed he says this of Lady Laura's chances of salvation: "'Eh, mother;—nothing can soften the heart Satan has hardened, till it be hard as the nether millstone.'" The narrator adds: "And in that faith he died, believing, as he had ever believed, that the spirit of evil was stronger than the spirit of good" (LII). Kennedy had no will or spirit to grow or adapt; his inflexibility drives him mad as surely as Trevelyan's drove him.

The outcome of Lady Laura's trial is not so certain or so sensational as Kennedy's. Slide's slander is an annoyance, but Lady Laura's own thoughts torture her more than anyone else's words can. Compared with her situation, Kennedy's is melodramatic and unreal (and never so convincing as Louis Trevelyan's). Lady Laura is a notable creation, and this is why Trollope himself thought her to be the best character in the two Phineas novels. She is the best character in *Phineas Finn*, though Madame Max is a powerful rival by the end of that novel, but she loses ground entirely to Madame Max in *Phineas Redux*. (Robert Polhemus even says that she becomes a "self-lacerating neurotic bore" by the end of the novel.[26]) In the second novel Lady Laura's passion borders on hysteria, and at times, sadly, her eloquent love is tiresome (to Phineas and to the reader alike). Both the best and worst passages in the novel describe her and offer her words; occasionally her thoughts are intriguing, heartrending. But she abandons all the restraint that initially attracts Phineas (and possibly the reader) to her in *Phineas Finn*; the cool volcano (IV) we associate with her there, here bursts out uncontrollably.

Her love for Phineas is her "trial," and we are never quite certain what will become of her because of the violence of emotion she endures. Early in the novel Phineas goes to Dresden to visit her, and she tells him she will love him as a sister would. Soon, however, she blurts out the truth: "'I wonder why I should have brought you here to tell you my story. Oh, Phineas,' Then she threw herself into his arms, and he pressed her to his heart, and kissed first her forehead and then her lips. 'It shall never be so again,' she said. 'I will kill it out of my heart even though I should crucify my body'" (XII). When Phineas is committed to prison her vehemence startles Lady Chiltern and her husband. Lord Chiltern tells her that Phineas has been arrested for murder, and, "He had no time to go on, for his sister was crouching prostrate on the floor before him. She had not fainted. Women do not faint under such shocks. But in her agony she had crouched down rather than fallen, as though it were vain to attempt to stand upright with so crushing a weight of sorrow on her back. She uttered one loud shriek, and then covering her face with her hands burst out into a wail of sobs" (LI). This is the most unfortunate description in the novel, but it is curious that the passage's excesses make us criticize Lady Laura more harshly than the author. Perhaps the "crouch" is too readily linked by the reader with the earlier "crucify" to blame anyone but Lady Laura herself.

Readers familiar with *Phineas Finn* remember Lady Laura's coolness in characteristic remarks such as this one: "'. . . poetry is so usually false. I doubt whether Scotland would not have been as prosaic a country as any under the sun but for Walter Scott;—and I have no doubt that Henry V owes the romance of his character altogether to Shakespeare'" (XIV). At times in *Phineas Redux* she can be just as detached. When she writes to Phineas to welcome him back to London politics she speaks jocosely of her brother: "'But Oswald suddenly retricked his beams, and is flaming in the forehead of the morning sky'"

(VI). (Lady Laura's playful adaptation of "Lycidas" reminds us of the narrator's similar use of it in *Barchester Towers* and *The Way We Live Now*.) In the same letter she brings to mind the political jargon by her own ready use of it: "'For myself I hate to think of the coming severance; . . . But, as Barrington says, a horse won't get oats unless he works steady between the traces'" (VI). Her love for Phineas changes her nature, or, rather, releases its volcanic tendencies, as she demonstrates in the chapter "'I Hate Her'" discussed later. The once objective, restrained woman falls into the intensity she formerly mocked. The narrator comments on her fondness for Phineas with an adaptation of a familiar line from *Hamlet* (III.ii.408) that itself is ironic preparation for Lady Laura's later identification with Hamlet's desperation: "With Lady Laura Kennedy, Phineas did find some sympathy;—but then she would have sympathised with him on any subject under the sun. If he would only come to her and sit with her she would fool him to the top of his bent" (XLIV).

The masterly chapter "'I Hate Her'" traces Lady Laura's thoughts about Phineas. The narrator blends transcription and commentary to reveal how Lady Laura's intelligence and sensitivity lose the struggle to balance reason and passion; jealousy conquers her and she turns viciously on her rival, Madame Max. The concentration of paraphrase and allusion suggests the confused richness of her mind (while also making an odd echo of the Shakespearean tragedy associated with Phineas):

Would not she have drunk up Esil, or swallowed a crocodile against any she-Laertes that would have thought to rival and to parallel her great love? Would not she have piled up new Ossas, had the opportunity been given her? . . . This strange female, this Moabitish woman, had gone to Prague, and had found a key,—and everybody said that the thing was done! How she hated the strange woman, and remembered all the evil things that had been said of the intruder! She told herself over and over again that had it been any one else than this half-foreigner, this German Jewess, this intriguing un-feminine upstart, she could have borne it. . . . And then she was old enough to be his mother, though by some Medean tricks known to such women, she was able to postpone,—not the ravages of age,—but the manifestation of them to the eyes of the world. . . . Lady Laura hated her as a fair woman who has lost her beauty can hate the dark woman who keeps it (LXV).

This remarkably bitter passage comes from the woman who once awed Phineas with cool incisiveness. She now combines Shakespeare, the classics, the Bible, and common gossip to curse a rival. The narrator, in transcribing Lady Laura's thoughts, steps into her "psychological stream," actually blurring the distinctions between transcription and commentary, as he does with Grantly, Crawley, Trevelyan, Lady Mason, and Phineas Finn in their moments of intense pain. The identification with Shakespearean, classical, and Biblical figures reveals how Lady Laura thinks of herself and the cosmic injustice of her loss. Ironically, Phineas himself is lost in her fury and becomes a pitiable, will-less victim of her rival's schemes. Even the reference to Medea is not an attack on Jason (though a disturbed Lady Laura could argue that Madame Max is Creusa); Lady Laura sees Madame Max as a trickster, a Medean sorceress. But the narrator—as with the phrase "some conceit" used to qualify Phineas's identification—puts Lady Laura's accusations and self-justifications into perspective. All of the literary grandeur is reduced to the fact that the faded fair woman is jealous of the beauty of the well-preserved dark woman.

Lady Laura identifies most closely with Hamlet's anguish over Ophelia's death. In the play (v.i.297–306) Hamlet challenges Laertes with:

'Swounds, show me what thou'lt do:
Woo't weep? woo't fight? woo't fast? woo't tear thyself?
Woo't drink up eisel? eat a crocodile?
I'll do it. Dost thou come here to whine
To outface me with leaping in her grave?
Be buried quick with her, and so will I:
And, if thou prate of mountains, let them throw
Millions of acres on us, till our ground,
Singeing his pate against the burning zone,
Make Ossa like a wart!

Lady Laura's passion finds sympathetic vent in Hamlet's rage. She rightly chooses for herself the dominant, masculine role and for Phineas, that of the gentle maiden since throughout their mutual careers Phineas has been the less sophisticated and more vulnerable of the two. The identification of Madame Max with the Moabitish woman is less clear. Ruth is the best known Moabitish woman, but her self-sacrifice has nothing to do with the way Lady Laura uses the epithet. In the Bible the Moabites are frequently an accursed people. (In Zephaniah 2:9, for example, it is decreed, "Surely Mòab shall be as Sodom, and the children of Ammon as Gomorrah. . . .") Perhaps Lady Laura had in mind the words of Numbers 25:1: "And Israel abode in Shittim, and the people began to commit whoredom with the daughters of Moab." This accusation alludes to Lady Laura's belief that Madame Max had been the old duke's mistress.[27] In any case, the use of "Esil" [sic], "she-Laertes," "Ossas," "Moabitish woman," and "Medean tricks" together demonstrates Lady Laura's quality of introspection. She achieves tragic stature through *Hamlet*, just as Phineas does poetic intensity through "A Musical Instrument," and they are both reestablished as normally human and fallible by the narrator's comment within the internal monologue (to show Phineas's morbid self-absorption and Lady Laura's jealousy).

Lady Laura's intellect survives her "trial," but her spirit does not. She retreats to Saulsby, permanently broken and disillusioned. There is no regeneration for Lady Laura as there is for Phineas; her failure underscores the importance of his new perspective. It is a fitting tribute to the once proudly independent woman that in the final view of her, "The Last Visit to Saulsby," we find some of Trollope's best writing. The rhythm of this passage, for example, perfectly suggests Lady Laura's repeated struggles for control:

Then she suddenly turned upon him, throwing her arms round his neck, and burying her face upon his bosom. They were at the moment in the centre of the park, on the grass beneath the trees, and the moon was bright over their heads. He held her to his breast while she sobbed, and then relaxed his hold as she raised herself to look into his face. After a moment she took his hat from his head with one hand, and with the other swept the hair back from his brow. "Oh, Phineas," she said, "Oh, my darling! My idol that I have worshipped when I should have worshipped my God!" (LXXVIII).

The release and restraint in the passage reflect the power of her emotions and the self-destructive effort required for her to manage them. Phineas quietly supports her, and she turns from the savagery with which she attacked him earlier (in the chapter) to the despair that will characterize the rest of her life. The structure of the two first sentences contributes to an appreciation of her dilemma: each is divided into three balanced, deliberate parts, stressing the irrevocability of the parting they describe. The somberness of the words (and atmosphere) is enforced by the measured pace—the two commas with the significant "and."

Lady Laura's and Kennedy's trials are distorted echoes of Phineas's. He avoids their failure or madness because he has a saving resilience and develops a healthy self-irony. Madame Max's parallel trial of patience, as difficult and triumphant as Phineas's own, actually alters the focus of the novel. As Phineas matures we begin to feel that all of his difficulties merely prepare him to be worthy of Madame Max. Quietly, steadily, since the days of *Phineas Finn*, she has been perfecting her transformation from Circe to Calypso,[28] and now in *Phineas Redux*, it is he who must grow to catch up with her.

Madame Max's part in the novel, though prominent, is unobtrusive. She is the chief character of romance and is also the link between Phineas and dozens of minor characters. She revives the playful, allusive atmosphere of *Phineas Finn* but also unconsciously involves herself with Lady Laura's (later) powerful language when she borrows from *Hamlet* (III.iv.206) to comment to Phineas on Lady Glencora: "'... for a little job of clever mining, believe me, that there is not a better engineer going than Lady Glen;—not but what I've known her to be very nearly "hoist with her own petard,"'—added Madame Goesler, as she remembered a certain circumstance in their joint lives" (XXXVII). Madame Max's influence is subtly indispensable to the structure of the novel as well as to its tone. She is the old duke of Omnium's faithful friend, the tie between the Pallisers and the entire novel, the friend of the Chilterns, the benefactress of Adelaide Palliser and Gerard Maule, the thorn of Lady Laura, and the clever woman who virtually rescues Phineas. A tribute to her quiet command lies in this fact: at the end of the novel, when she is rewarded with Phineas, the reader wonders whether it has been Madame Max's interest in Phineas that has given Phineas importance throughout. Certainly Phineas's value is increased by the two women who vie, in two novels, for him.

Because Lady Glencora and Madame Max are best friends, we see something of the Pallisers in this novel. Palliser entertains himself with Adam Smith and Blue Books (LXXV), while Glencora schemes for social and political prominence, foreshadowing what is to come in *The Prime Minister.* Here, as in *The Prime Minister,* Lady Glencora says Palliser is an Othello because he has lost his occupation (XXVI), and she then gives her concept of philosophy and poetry that underlies the tone and theme of *The Prime Minister* as well as *Phineas Redux*: "'Romance and poetry are for the most part lies, Mr. Maule, and are very apt to bring people into difficulty. I have seen something of them in my time, and I much prefer downright honest figures. Two and two make four; idleness is the root of all evil; love your neighbour like yourself, and the rest of it'" (LXXVI). Lady Glen's sturdy, wholesome maxims offer a deliberate antidote to the catchy, perverse mottoes of politics. She adopts clichés, too, when she discusses with Barrington Erle strategy involving Phineas: "'... if you choose to put your shoulder to the wheel you can manage it; and I shall expect to have it managed'" (XXXVII). The narrator remarks on her efforts for Phineas: "A second Juno, she would allow the Romulus she hated to sit in the seats of the blessed, to be fed with nectar ... but ... Phineas Finn must be allowed a seat also, and a little nectar..." (XL) Her struggles for Phineas reinforce the political commentary, Phineas's difficulties, and Madame Max's prominence. Her language—and her rejection of "romance and poetry"—clearly reflect the tenor of the novel's resolution. Phineas himself learns to use the clichés and stock images of politics in an ironic, positive way and can abandon his morbid misreading of "A Musical Instrument." Lady Laura cannot forget her hatred for Madame Max or her own self-hatred in having married Kennedy, and she is forever trapped in tragedy. Madame Max's best friend thus epitomizes here, as in *The Prime Minister*, the durability of honest, straightforward (or even ironic) thoughts and the prose that conveys them.

The connection among Madame Max, the Chilterns, and the Spooner-Maule romance is not so close as that between the Pallisers and Madame Max. But the Spooner-Maule romances (like the Heavitree parts of *He Knew He Was Right*) offer light, almost frivolous parallel to the serious and moving studies of Lady Laura and Madame Max. Numerous little clichés, tags, and allusions echo back and forth between the Spooner-Maule romances and the larger patterns of romance, politics, and psychological tension. For example, Ned Spooner's pride in his knowledge of Latin reminds us of the narrator's mock humility and of the parliamentary debates. Ned analyzes Adelaide: "*'Ludit exultim metuitque tangi . . . nuptiarum expers'*" (XXIX).[29] The Spooners express their belief in Tom's success with cliché and tag: "'None but the brave deserve the fair'" and "'Labor omnia vincit'" (LIII). The superficiality of Adelaide Palliser's difficulties, and her ironic relationship to the stories of Lady Laura and Madame Max, is underscored by her self-pitying allusion to *Hamlet*: "She had thought of a nunnery, of Ophelia among the waterlilies, and of an early death-bed" (LXXVI). Mr. Maule, Senior, as a suitor for Madame Max, makes an interesting contrast to Phineas. The narrator tells us that the old dandy is not quite a Mr. Justice Shallow (XXI) and in his younger days ". . . he was considered to have got into a good set,—men of fashion who were also given to talking of books,—who spent money, read poetry, and had opinions of their own respecting the Tracts and Mr. Newman" (XXI). He reads French novels and tries to ingratiate himself with Madame Max by telling her an old story and then hunting up the reference for it (XXIV). Mr. Maule's interest, like Lady Glencora's, helps keep Madame Max prominent. His, and the other lesser characters' associations with literature, reinforce the patterns of language that are associated with the more interesting characters.

In many ways *Phineas Redux* is Madame Max's novel. In *Phineas Finn* she is introduced halfway through, and at the end of that novel Trollope himself has changed his mind about her. She is transformed, before the reader's eyes, from a siren into a generous, kind woman.[30] In the next novel of the series, *The Eustace Diamonds,* Madame Max is kept in the reader's view, but she plays the passive part of nursemaid to the querulous old duke. She endures three years of selfless servitude before Phineas reemerges into politics in *Phineas Redux.* The reader can enjoy *Phineas Redux,* ostensibly about Phineas and politics, as the climax to Madame Max's trial of patience. And Trollope has been careful in the language that he uses to cultivate this sympathy from the end of *Phineas Finn* to the end of *Phineas Redux.* We suspect that Madame Max is more intelligent and has been more ambitious than Phineas, and since her goal is love, Phineas's fate is determined. Sympathy with Madame Max sometimes makes Phineas's development and the political sections seem but interludes to the real story.

Perhaps this is the essential charm of *Phineas Redux*: each level of the narrative richly echoes the other parts of the entire work; each level contributes to the novel's persistent study (focused on Phineas) of the characters' successful or unsuccessful attempts to achieve equilibrium. The mutually illuminating interdependence of the novel's politics, psychology, and romance suggests Trollope's mastery of repetition and parallel. An interest in all of the major characters and a familiarity with their blended and contrasted patterns of language encourage us to imagine the far-reaching implications of Phineas's reinterpretation of "A Musical Instrument." With his own hard-won knowledge and with Marie's firm support, the balanced man can relieve the warhorse's trumpet of public skirmish with the inspiring harmony of Park Lane life. Thus the mature Phineas's irony even offers hope for the rhetoric of politics.

5

The Prime Minister

Phineas Redux was fairly popular with Trollope's readers, but the next novel in the Palliser series, *The Prime Minister*, was not.[1] This fifth of the six "political" novels brings to a climax the careers of Lady Glencora and Palliser and at the same time explores Trollope's own political and social theories. Trollope himself was fond of this new work and was surprised by the attacks from a vocal and hostile audience.[2] Faced with initial rejection of the book, Trollope inaccurately identified its failure in his creation of two separate novels in one novel: "The Lopez part of the book has only been to me a shoe-horn for the other."[3] The Lopez-Wharton story is lengthy and occasionally upstages the Palliser tale, but on the whole the two stories reinforce and comment on each other in a number of remarkable ways.

In both halves of the novel patterns of allusions, proverbs, and slang reveal the characters' natures while also binding together the threads of a full and complex narrative. Ironically, the essence of the political satire and the tone of characterization are found in Glencora's vigorous language. Lopez not only occasions some of her virulence, but also emphasizes the quality of her speech through contrast with his own. And when Lopez the interloper invades the solid social establishment, his resulting career exposes parallels between the Conservative Whartons and the Liberal Pallisers. The friendship between Lopez and Glencora involves multiple expositions in a densely populated tale.

Whatever the strengths or weaknesses of the Lopez story, the fact remains that the main part of the novel revolves around Glencora and Plantagenet Palliser, the new duchess and duke of Omnium. Trollope was confident of their importance and of the success of his portraiture:

The Prime Minister 143

I think that Plantagenet Palliser, Duke of Omnium, is a perfect gentleman. If he be not, then I am unable to describe a gentleman. She is by no means a perfect lady; but if she be not all over a woman, then am I not able to describe a woman. I do not think it probable that my name will remain among those who in the next century will be known as the writers of English prose fiction;—but if it does, that permanence of success will probably rest on the character of Plantagenet Palliser, Lady Glencora, and the Rev. Mr. Crawley (xx).

In the other novels of the series, Glencora and Plantagenet have been in the background, always developing, but also always consistent with our lengthy introduction to them in *Can You Forgive Her?* In this novel, they are in the foreground, and the narrator discloses the intimacies of their thoughts and the thoughts of those around them. Part of the charm of the exploration of Glencora and Plantagenet is that it involves principal favorites (and their familiar language patterns) from former novels, especially *Phineas Redux*. The Chilterns, the duke of St. Bungay, Phineas Finn, Madame Max (now Mrs. Finn) all contribute to this novel's investigations of communication, coalition, partnership, and politics. As usual, the narrator creates and repeats certain rhythms and patterns so that we appreciate the duke and duchess as prominent people in an enormously complex, interrelated society.

The Prime Minister, like *Phineas Redux*, has been accused of leaving out politics altogether,[4] but it really amplifies and completes what the earlier novel suggested. Like *Phineas Redux*, *The Prime Minister* uses irony extensively, but in *The Prime Minister* the ironies are darker, further-reaching than in the earlier novel. In the earlier novel, Phineas's immature enthusiasm was tested against the corruption of Parliament. Slogans, tags, and maxims encapsulate the self-seeking dishonesty of the system. Phineas, through his personal and legal trials, confronts his disillusionment and grows, and the novel ends cheerfully, with Phineas as a mature, balanced man. In *The Prime Minister* the ground shifts. The prime minister and his wife are the focus of attention and the corrupt political parties have now been forced into a coalition. This novel explores coalitions and partnerships of all kinds and the outcome is not so apparently cheerful. The duchess fails to hold the coalition together; the duke fails to control the wayward parties and his own ambition; the marriage between the duke and duchess itself survives but is irreparably fractured; Lopez kills himself. But since none of the characters here—not even the stiff duke—is as hopelessly rigid as Louis Trevelyan, there is also another way to interpret the ending: the duchess is willing to look to the future for new schemes and strategies; the duke is relieved of the burden of office; the duke and duchess declare a truce with each other; rid of Lopez, the Whartons and Fletchers reassert the solidity of the Conservative party and society. In both deeper and broader ways, *The Prime Minister* ultimately reinforces the perceptions of *Phineas Redux*: politics is corrupt and will corrupt; words must be sincere and considered if they are to earn trust and promote honesty.

The Prime Minister's narrator, as usual, has a key part to play in the pointing of parallels and the exploration of ironies. Here, as in Trollope's other good novels, the narrator creates and repeats revealing patterns of language. Appropriately, in a novel about communication and partnership, the most colorful patterns are established through the words of the characters themselves, predominantly in dialogue but also in internal monologues that are clearly transcriptions of characters' thoughts rather than fanciful amplifications offered by the narrator on their behalf. Interestingly, most of the slang, allusions, and stock expressions associated with the extroverted, ambitious Glencora are delivered in dialogue (and echoed by the narrator in internal monologue or in the narrative itself). With the introverted duke we find more patterns in the internal monologues; his brooding repetitions are frequently offered by the narrator, but they are imbued unmistakably with Palliser's own rhythms. Lopez's slang and manipulative allusions (distorted echoes of the duchess's) are given as often directly by Lopez as they are by the narrator. Whether he speaks or not, his dark energy is usually conveyed. Frequently the narrator echoes the character so effectively that it is impossible to tell which is

The Prime Minister 145

speaking. But, overall, the narrator in *The Prime Minister* reflects more often than he initiates.

The perfect resonance between the narrator and the characters[5] helps to establish and reinforce the connections among the numerous characters and stories of this large novel. In addition to reviving patterns of language with familiar characters from the earlier political novels, and sharing specific allusions or expressions with one or two characters, and echoing between the dialogue and commentary a certain quality of expression, both the narrator and characters of *The Prime Minister* use the same expression and image to characterize their uneasy, uncertain partnerships.

The cliché "getting into a boat together" occurs six times in this novel, five times in dialogue and once in the narrator's interpretation of dialogue or monologue. Like the persistent image of the moth and the candle flame that unites *The Small House at Allington*[6] the boat expression here sums up and marks the novel's many shaky coalitions. There is no trust, no instinctive bonding of kindred ideas, in any of the faltering "marriages" of the novel: not between Palliser and his men, Palliser and his position, Palliser and his wife, Lopez and Parker, Lopez and Emily, nor the duchess and her position. The expression is used by Mr. Roby of Palliser (XXXVIII), by Lopez about Parker (XL), twice by Lopez (or the narrator interpreting Lopez) about Emily (XLIV, LIV), by Parker about Lopez (XLV), and finally by Palliser about Mr. Monk (LXXVIII). The danger of leaving one boat for another midjourney or the initial danger of entering the same boat from the shore characterizes the anxiety and eventual distrust that so many of the novel's people suffer. Poor choice of mate dooms many of *The Prime Minister*'s partnerships to misery and dissolution.

Distrust, uneasiness, and downright suspicion are evident in many of the novel's partnerships or coalitions—as the boat image suggests—and yet *The Prime Minister* is not an altogether gloomy book. The characters' repeated failures (in communication, choice of partner, plan of action) are purposely relieved by the narrator's light irony or by the duchess's sturdy matter-of-factness.

The narrator and characters together revive the (comic) atmosphere of the politics of the earlier Phineas novels. In *Phineas Redux* the reader is constantly reminded that there is really no difference between the two parties—men from both parties are equally capable of helping the country muddle through an endless flow of bishoprics, lieutenancies, garters, and bills. In *The Prime Minister* several characters confirm the earlier lesson. Mrs. Finn tells Barrington Erle that she is sorry Phineas still becomes so involved with party movements, "'For there never really is anything special to be done. . .'" (XI). Frank Gresham (from the Barsetshire series) tells a young Conservative aspirant: "'One man in these days is so like another . . . that it requires good eyes to see the shades of the colours'" (XXXIV). The old duke of St. Bungay, carefully promoted throughout the whole novel as a "Warwick" (LXVI), a "Nestor of the occasion" (LXXVI), the young Duke's Mentor (LXIV, LXXX), remarks on the dispensability of individuality: "'. . . I find that though Smith be a very good Minister, the best perhaps to be had at the time, when he breaks down Jones does nearly as well'" (XLI). And that most sagacious if somewhat vituperative critic, the duchess herself, says of the two parties: "'The country goes on its own way, either for better or for worse, whichever of them are in'" (VI). We recognize in the duchess's words the mature Phineas's: "'I remember when I used to think that members of the Cabinet were almost gods, and now they seem to be no bigger than the shoeblacks,—only less picturesque'" (XXXVII). In *Phineas Redux*, Parliament is spoken of in terms of games—word games and even chess (XIII). In *The Prime Minister* the duchess revives the analogy when characterizing changes of ministry: "'You Ministers go on shuffling the old cards till they are so worn out and dirty that one can hardly tell the pips on them'" (XXI). The duchess's tone sets the tenor, throughout the novel, for the political satire, and it is illuminating to recognize something of Phineas's idealism and disillusionment in her anger over parliamentary ways.

In *Phineas Redux* one phrase, "Men, not measures," is supposed to encapsulate the treachery of the times. Even the worthy members of Parliament eventually support this distorted and self-seeking maxim. Indeed, the subtle suggestion is that this principle is the root of the entire English party system. The reader, by the end of the novel, is, ironically, even encouraged to feel that as long as good men lead the parties, the philosophy will not do the country great harm. Here in *The Prime Minister*, when measures are virtually nonexistent and when parties are forced to work together, the phrase takes on new meaning. Mrs. Finn discusses old Lord Brock: "'He loved his country dearly, and wished her to be, as he believed her to be, first among nations. But he had no belief in perpetuating her greatness by any grand improvements. Let things take their way naturally,—with a slight direction hither or thither as things might require. That was his method of ruling. He believed in men rather than measures. As long as he had loyalty around him, he could be personally happy, and quite confident as to the country'" (XI). The catch phrase that began as a shibboleth in *Phineas Redux*, and then became an acceptable motto when an honest man recognizes its dangers, is here glorified by astute Marie Finn as the only comfortable rule that can ensure a leader's control and popularity. Trollope has not changed his view of politics, and he is not "advocating a do-nothing policy as a practical guide for all politicians,"[7] but he is urging his readers to decide how much accommodation there can be between integrity and political acumen. In this novel, the country's need for genial, trusting inactivity underscores the duke's unsuitability for the job of prime minister, for there is no one in the whole of Parliament who is less genial and more active than he. The revival of the phrase "Men, not measures" from *Phineas Redux* focuses the analysis of Palliser and the questions about government.

These reminders of *Phineas Redux* are of twofold importance: they reestablish the atmosphere of political satire, and they encourage comparison of the duke and Phineas Finn. In *Phineas Redux*, overly sensitive reactions to the editor Slide's venomous articles suggest Phineas's need to be hardened by experience.

At the time a friend advises Phineas, "'You have encountered a chimney sweeper, and of course you get some of the soot'" (XXVIII). Phineas is too immature to believe the analogy and far too sensitive to try to shield himself from Slide's attacks. The experiences of his trial and his marriage to Madame Max strengthen him, and in *The Prime Minister* Slide's renewed venom has a different effect. In this second novel, the mature Phineas gives Lord Chiltern this advice concerning Slide's new articles: "'Leave a chimney-sweep alone when you see him, Chiltern. Should he run against you, then remember that it is one of the necessary penalties of clean linen that it is apt to be soiled'" (LXII). The deliberate repetition of the analogy perfectly reveals the extent of Phineas's change. We measure Phineas by his response to Slide's "thunderbolts" and know that Phineas has come to a private reinterpretation of Mrs. Browning's "A Musical Instrument."

In *The Prime Minister* Trollope uses the same two devices— the newspaper and the poem—to make a somewhat different suggestion about Plantagenet Palliser. On the same page that gives Quintus Slide's first letter to the duke, we also find this exchange between the old duke of St. Bungay and the young duke of Omnium:

"I doubt whether such a life [living alone with his wife and children], even for a month, even for a week, is compatible with your duties. You would hardly find it possible. Could you do without your private secretaries? Would you know enough of what is going on, if you did not discuss matters with others? A man cannot be both private and public at the same time."

"And therefore one has to be chopped up, like 'a reed out of the river', as the poet said, 'and yet not give sweet music afterwards' " (XVIII).

Phineas's and Palliser's reactions to their "Musical Instrument" experiences and Slide's attacks show the differences between the men and the novels. Phineas's recovery is of most importance in *Phineas Redux,* and he shows himself briefly in *The Prime Minister* as a new, whole, useful man. Trollope emphasizes Phineas's "poetic" triumph in his words to Chiltern: "'I have long

The Prime Minister 149

been conversant with Mr. Quintus Slide, and have quite made up my mind that I will never play upon his pipe'" LXII). In *The Prime Minister*, Palliser's breakdown is of chief importance, and it is necessary that we see his inability to ignore Slide's attacks as symptomatic of his unfitness as a parliamentary leader. Mrs. Browning's poem suggests that Palliser, like Phineas, will eventually recover, but it is deliberate on Trollope's part that Palliser's recovery is reserved almost completely for the last novel of the series, *The Duke's Children*. In other words, Palliser's identification with the poem is meant to alert the reader to the quality of his suffering more than to the implied recovery. The more alive we are to Palliser's failings, the more critical we become of the system that threatens to destroy him.

Even though *Phineas Redux* is partially revived in the characters and concerns of *The Prime Minister*, the focus of the second novel makes it distinctly different from the milder *Phineas Redux*. Palliser's morbid fancies, the torpor of political life, and the vulgarity of politicians make *The Prime Minister* at times almost bitter. Trollope had just completed his great satire, *The Way We Live Now*, before finishing *The Prime Minister*, and perhaps some of its spirit inspired the darker parts of *The Prime Minister*. The fact remains, however, that though this is a stronger book, politically speaking, than *Phineas Redux*, and though its focus is more closely fixed on politics, it finds power in broad irony rather than in direct criticism. The central unifying elements of the novel are themselves ironic: we may learn about the nature of politics and politicians through the prime minister's wife rather than the prime minister. The entire book, Palliser and Lopez-Wharton sections alike, seems to take cues from the hardheaded duchess of Omnium. It is through Glencora's irreverent adaptations of Shakespeare, proverb, and slang (themselves echoes of *Phineas Redux* and echoed in the other patterns of this novel) that we interpret her husband and his government.

Glencora is realistic and immediate; Palliser is idealistic and removed. So, too, in the story, the duchess is a flesh-and-blood woman, whereas the duke is occasionally too sensitive to be either an attractive or an approachable man. Throughout *The Prime Minister* most readers listen to Glencora's comments and sympathize with her ambitions and difficulties. Her freewheeling but practical ways offer relief from Palliser's starch and governmental and societal buckram. Their inevitable failures in communication are repeated by other similarly mismatched partners.

Glencora's energetic language is a perfect complement to the narrator's irony. Since the days of *Can You Forgive Her?* she has distinguished herself for linguistic verve. In the old days she indulged in puns (she wanted to find the way to the kurds), pitted her strength against Madame Max's, or occasionally shocked her husband (as, for example, calling one of his associates "a baboon with red bristles" in *Can You Forgive Her?* [XLIX]), but in *The Prime Minister* Trollope gives her free rein, and her language is both more entertaining and more influential than that of any other Trollope heroine; she indulges in colorful ". . . irony rather than argument to support her cause and to vindicate her ways" (VI).

When Palliser becomes Prime Minister, Glencora determines to take on the entire country—she confides this audacity to Mrs. Finn—"'I should like to put the Queen down'" (VI)—and even after her failure with her husband and her own strategies, she declares "'. . . a state of pugnacity seems to me the greatest bliss which we can reach here on earth'" (LXXVII). According to her the stately politicians have been going to Windsor "'. . . like buckets in a well for the last three weeks'" (VI). When she fears Palliser may refuse to head the coalition, she complains "'my basket of crockery has been kicked over and every thing smashed'" (VI). When Palliser laments the shortage of good men for the new cabinet, she demands shrewdly if impatiently: "'Why shouldn't there be as good fish in the sea as ever were caught out of it?'" (VII). Ironically this very expression is repeated toward the end of the novel when two old politicians discuss the imminent collapse of the Palliser Coalition: "'We shall not want a Prime Minister as long as there are as good fish in the sea as have been caught out of it'" (LXXIII). Her lively irony establishes a standard for vigor and rough truths.

The tension between Palliser and his wife—the tension that has seldom relaxed since the first days of their marriage—is increased by her excitement over the prospect of her husband's position as prime minister. This early scene demonstrates the narrator's deft intermixing of commentary and character voice and serves as an example of the quality of exchange between the mismatched husband and wife:

> When therefore she asked him what they were going to make him, it was as though some sarcastic housekeeper in a great establishment should ask the butler,—some butler too prone to yield in such matters,—whether the master had appointed him lately to the cleaning of shoes or the carrying of coals. . . . Now, at this moment, he had, as she knew, come direct from the house of Mr. Gresham, and she asked her question in her usual spirit. "And what are they going to make you now? . . . They have told you that they can do without you," she said, breaking out almost into a passion. "I knew how it would be. Men are always valued by others as they value themselves."
> "I wish it were so," he replied. "I should sleep easier to-night."
> "What is it, Plantagenet?" she exclaimed, jumping up from her chair.
> "I never cared for your ridicule hitherto, Cora; but now I feel that I want your sympathy."
> "If you are going to do anything,—to do really anything, you shall have it, Oh, how you shall have it!"
> "I have received her Majesty's orders to go down to Windsor at once. I must start within half-an-hour."
> "You are going to be Prime Minister!" she exclaimed. As she spoke she threw her arms up, and then rushed into his embrace. Never since their first union had she been so demonstrative either of love or admiration. "Oh, Plantagenet," she said, "if I can only do anything I will slave for you." As he put his arm round her waist he already felt the pleasantness of her altered way to him. She had never worshipped him yet, and therefore her worship when it did come had all the delight to him which it ordinarily has to the newly married hero (VI).

Trollope is a master of intimate dialogue. As usual the duchess's fervor overrides caution or sensitivity, and as usual Palliser expresses himself with self-conscious restraint. Throughout their marriage he speaks to her with similar formality, standing while he uses ponderous words or phrases such as "hitherto" or "But this I know"; she, as typically, springs from a chair, hurls herself into his arms, and swears devotion, having only seconds before taunted him with sarcasm. We see, further, that though she is unfair to her (as yet) unambitious husband, she does understand the usual rules of politics and society better than he does. When she says, "Men are always valued by others as they value themselves," she is giving voice to the flawed perception that allows a Lopez to invade the Liberal upper class and the established, landed Conservatives.

The Duke can never find the pleasant, soft phrases of easy comradeship for his colleagues, either, and it is the duchess who keeps the coalition alive by "'telling tarradiddles by the yard'" (XI) and by adapting Aesop as the narrator tells us: "She was always making up the party,—meaning the coalition,—doing something to strengthen the buttresses, writing little letters to little people, who, little as they were, might become big by amalgamation. 'One has always to be binding one's fagot,' she said to Mrs. Finn, having read her Aesop not altogether in vain." She regrets that she is "'not a god, . . . or a Pitt, or an Italian with a long name beginning with M.'" (XXVII), and is at one point disheartened enough to declare ". . . she would retire into private life and milk cows, that she would shake hands with no more parliamentary cads and 'caddesses,'—a word which her Grace condescended to coin for her own use" (XXXVII). But Glencora is seldom seriously discouraged. When her husband, now prime minister, upbraids her for meddling in politics, swearing he will not have his wife's name bandied about by the press, she dismisses him with "'That's high-foluting, Plantagenet'" (LI). She recognizes and declares Sir Timothy Beeswax a "'sounding cymbal of brass'" (LXIII) and even teases the venerable duke of St. Bungay with a street expression, "'If I were not very serious . . . I should make an allusion to the —— Marines" (LXIII). Despite (or perhaps because of) her occasional vulgarity, the duchess is right about politics. She acknowledges the end of the duke's ministry with her usual shrewd playfulness: "'When Mr. Rattler won't come to the Prime Minister's house, you may depend that something is going to happen. It is like pigs carrying straws in their mouths. Mr. Rattler is my pig'" (LXVIII).

Glencora is thick-skinned and she rightly describes her husband as poetic: "'Though in manner he is as dry as a stick, though all his pursuits are opposite to the very idea of romance, though he passes his days and nights in thinking how he may take a halfpenny in the pound off the taxes of the people without robbing the revenue, there is a dash of chivalry about him worthy of the old poets'" (LVI). Trollope reinforces this comment on Palliser's poetic spirit by using Mrs. Browning's lyric "A Musical Instrument," as we have mentioned earlier.

It is the duchess on whom we usually rely for interpretations of Palliser's changing behavior and moods. She explains, "'He is always Cincinnatus, going back to his peaches and his ploughs. But I fear he is beginning to feel that the salt would be gone out of his life if he ceased to be the first man in the kingdom'" (LXIII). He grows imperious, even tyrannical, and his colleagues are afraid of him. She says, "'He has got to be like a bear with a sore head . . .'" (LXIII). Her assessment is bolstered by Palliser's unwittingly repeating her image when he explains to her his feelings of torment: "'When they used to bait a bear tied to a stake, every one around would cheer the dogs and help to torment the helpless animal. It is much the same now, only they have a man instead of a bear for their pleasure'" (LXVI).

The duchess's insight and irony take many forms in the novel. As we have seen, she uses slang and colorful expressions (to her husband over Lopez she demands, "'Do you want to make me roll in the gutter because I mistook him for a gentleman?'" [XLII]), and she refers to fables or history to punctuate her lively words. But perhaps the most interesting and illuminating pattern of language the duchess creates is found in her six references to Shakespeare—*Macbeth, Lear, Coriolanus,* and *Othello* (these six allusions, as a pattern, are interesting to compare with the six uses of the cliché "getting into a boat together"). Beneath her semiserious references to Shakespeare's tragic men we find much of the real sense of *The Prime Minister*. The first reference appears in the first chapter of the novel in which the duke and duchess are (re)introduced to the reader (VI), and the last is made in the last of the novel (LXXX) when the Palliser Coalition has been laid to rest. Following Glencora's references, we can trace Palliser's turmoil and his ministry's decline.

The first reference, from *Macbeth*, shows Glencora's ambition and underscores the tension between her and her husband. The narrator interprets the duchess's thoughts but we recognize the rhythm as the duchess's own:

... she felt in regard to him somewhat as did Lady Macbeth towards her lord.
"What thou would'st highly,
That would'st thou holily."
She knew him to be full of scruples, unable to bend when aught was to be got by bending, unwilling to domineer when men might be brought to subjection only by domination. The first duty never could be taught to him. To win support by smiles when his heart was bitter within him would never be within the power of her husband. He could never be brought to buy an enemy by political gifts,—would never be prone to silence his keenest opponent by making him his right hand supporter (VI).

The duchess's thoughts are really a paraphrase of Shakespeare's lines (I.v.12–23) beginning "Yet do I fear thy nature." The differences between Lady Macbeth's and the duchess's situations are obvious, but the spirit behind the words is what is important. Glencora knows herself to be pushy, possibly unscrupulous; she also realizes that her own lord will become jealous of power once he has experienced it.

The implications of the duchess's thoughts are serious, but when she speaks them aloud she makes light of them with customary flippancy as she does with the second reference to Shakespeare. Here she complains to Mrs. Finn, and echoes her own earlier thought, about Palliser's indifference to the benefits of entertaining: "'... I begin to find myself filled to the full with political ambition. I feel myself to be a Lady Macbeth,

The Prime Minister   155

prepared for the murder of any Duncan or any Daubeny who may stand in my lord's way. In the meantime, like Lady Macbeth herself, we must attend to the banqueting. Her lord appeared and misbehaved himself; my lord won't show himself at all,—which I think is worse'" (XI). Despite its off-handedness, the remark makes an impression, and the story of Palliser's breakdown is enriched by the undertone (though ironic) of tragedy.

When Palliser accuses her of vulgarity, another reference, the third, comes to her mind (the narrator again transcribes her thoughts): "When a man wants to be Prime Minister he has to submit to vulgarity, and must give up his ambition if the task be too disagreeable to him. The Duchess thought that that had been understood, at any rate ever since the days of Coriolanus" (XIX). Inspired by so famous though questionable a precedent, she cannot sympathize with fastidiousness. To her it is sheer folly and weakness that a political leader will refuse to be warned by Coriolanus about what can happen if the tribunes band together. She prefers to bind her fagots in a more pleasing way. With *Macbeth, Coriolanus,* and "A Musical Instrument" to consider as subtle comments on the duke's nature and position, the reader wonders what will become of Palliser's reluctant ambition.

The duchess's reference to *Lear,* her fourth Shakespearean allusion, then suggests the extent of Palliser's suffering. She scolds him for giving up the Silverbridge seat, but the reader, fully accustomed to probe her comparisons, sees more: "'What am I to say? It seems to me that any more suicidal thing than throwing away the borough never was done. Who will thank you? What additional support will you get? How will it increase your power? It's like King Lear throwing off his clothes in the storm because his daughters turned him out'" (XXXII). She exposes her own callousness in rejecting the magnificence of Lear's renunciation, but she also betrays her own fears for her husband's stability. Some time later, when Palliser is writhing under the editor Slide's "lashes," the same strokes that nearly maddened Phineas in *Phineas Redux,* the comparison takes on greater significance. And when we observe the duke in his study, we see another Josiah Crawley, driven by an obsession to be right, close to madness: "He knew that he had been Quixotic, and he would sit in his chair repeating the word to himself aloud, till he himself began to fear that he would do it in company" (LXVI).

Genuine fears for the duke's mind are short-lived. The common sense and the matter-of-factness in Glencora's spirit imbue the novel so effectively with "sanity" that we suspect his suffering will be as efficiently (if not as quickly) cured as Emily "Niobe" Lopez's. Glencora gives him some sympathy when he says he will miss his work as prime minister: "'Yes;—Othello's occupation will be gone,—for awhile; for awhile.' Then she came up to him and put both her hands on his breast. 'But yet, Othello, I shall not be all unhappy'" (LXXII). Her tenderness here recalls her use of the same expression, with the same tone, in *Phineas Redux*. There Palliser has just become duke of Omnium, and so has lost his seat in the House of Commons: "'He'll never sit on the Treasury Bench again.' 'No;—poor dear. He's an Othello now with a vengeance, for his occupation is gone'" (XXVI). Here in *The Prime Minister*, Palliser is most in need of compassion and she gives it to him, but his crisis is past and the reader is hopeful for his new occupation. At the end of the novel we find the Othello allusion again, and this time it is part of the Duke's sad reflections on his perceived inability to join the new ministry, thinking as he does of himself as Caesar (the pattern uppermost with him at this time). The duchess uses Othello to show her sympathy for her husband; Palliser evidently picks up the reference from her but broods over what he believes to be his own tragedy. The new former prime minister, left by himself, laments that "Othello's occupation was, in truth, altogether gone, and there was no reason by which he could justify to himself the step down in the world which the old Duke had proposed to him" (LXXVIII). Thus do we hear Palliser's thoughts echo Glencora's words and turn her irony into his own dark strain.

At the end of the novel in her usual half-bantering, half-serious tone, she again refers to *Macbeth*. This time, however, she puts the whole of the duke's career, and indeed the whole of *The Prime Minister,* into perspective when she says to Marie Finn:

". . . when he became Prime Minister, I gave myself up to it altogether. I shall never forget what I felt when he came to me and told me that perhaps it might be so;—but told me also that he would escape from it if it were possible. I was the Lady Macbeth of the occasion all over;— whereas he was so scrupulous, so burdened with conscience! As for me I would have taken it by any means. Then it was that the old Duke played the part of the three witches to a nicety. Well, there hasn't been any absolute murder, and I haven't quite gone mad" (LXXX).

Her conscious irreverence for tragedy epitomizes the narrator's technique throughout the book. She sees, as Mrs. Finn, and the duke of St. Bungay, and Barrington Erle, and the restored Phineas Finn also see, that nothing dire need come to pass in anyone's ministry. The duchess of Omnium, with all her slang and color, may be an unlikely, but nevertheless effective, personification of Trollope's "middle of the road" philosophy of life.[8] As such she is a staunch supporter of the English party system, and an advocate of "men, not measures." The serious implications of the original identification with *Macbeth* now appear to have been frustrated by her sturdiness.

Trollope shows Palliser's changes through several patterns of language that are purposely interwoven with the duchess's and with the narrator's. We measure him by his own masochistic allegiance to Slide's newspaper as well as against the fresh vigor of his wife's speeches. We feel his kinship to Macbeth and Lear and gauge his anguish through his identification with Mrs. Browning's poem. In the word *Quixotic* we apprehend another dimension of his internal conflict. Glencora has said that though he is as dry as a stick he has a dash of chivalry about him and even "the romance of the old poets." Mrs. Finn says that he is a "Don Quixote" (LXII) in his desire to do good. Palliser is really the misguided, anachronistic knight of chivalrous idealism. He has something in common with the younger Phineas Finn—he wants to be useful and to promote measures rather than men. But even he is corrupted by power and is

158   Patterns of Repetition in Trollope

overtaxed by the pressures of government, and so the Don Quixote ideals degenerate into politically quixotic behavior. The poet in his nature is nearly destroyed by politics.

Neither Palliser's recovery nor the realization of his ideals is demonstrated in *The Prime Minister.* Instead, we are given glimpses of his still troubled thoughts. At the end, even as at the beginning, he is a difficult man to approach. He has spent his hours among too many dry articles to be comfortable with his colleagues. He is something of a political Josiah Crawley, inspired by government documents as thoroughly as Crawley is by the classics: "He had been a scholar, and after a certain fitful fashion he had maintained his scholarship, but the literature to which he had been really attached had been that of blue books and newspapers" (LXXII). He does take some inspiration from his scholarship as his words to the old duke about taking part in the new government suggest: "'Caesar could hardly have led a legion under Pompey'" (LXXII). Almost immediately he regrets the pretension of the speech, knowing that "A man may indeed measure small things by great, but the measurer should be careful to declare his own littleness when he illustrates his position by that of the topping ones of the earth" (LXXII). The words resound in his mind as loudly as did the earlier word *quixotic,* and the repetition makes us realize that the words haunt him because they characterize his reluctant thoughts about himself. They echo through the last chapters of the novel and appear on the very last page: "He had long since made up his mind that after all that had passed he could not return to office as a subordinate. That feeling as to the impropriety of Caesar descending to serve under others which he had been foolish enough to express, had been strong with him from the very commencement of his Ministry" (LXXVIII). Again: "Whether Caesar might or might not at some future time condescend to command a legion, he could not do so when the purple had been but that moment stripped from his shoulders" (LXXVIII). And finally: "He told himself now, after his own secret fashion, that he must do penance for these words by the humiliation of a direct contradiction of them. He must declare that Caesar would at some future time be prepared to serve under Pompey" (LXXX). The deliberate repetition demonstrates the turnings of his mind and perhaps the size of his ego; the full recovery is left for *The Duke's Children*.

Glencora is the more acceptable politician of the two because Palliser is so rigidly scrupulous. In fact, her strength is a source of criticism of the government since her energy is thoroughly partisan even if it is genial. Her ironic uses of Shakespeare intimate the faulty quality of political insight; she recognizes some truths in the tragedies while dismissing their ennobling poetry. Trollope's main purpose in writing *The Prime Minister* was to explore the effects of politics on a sensitive, judicious man. He revives the atmosphere of *Phineas Redux* and releases Glencora's tongue to give spice and direction to his analysis of Plantagenet Palliser. In *An Autobiography* he describes his intentions with his prime minister:

> He should have rank, and intellect, and parliamentary habits, by which to bind him to the service of the country; and he should also have unblemished, unextinguishable, inexhaustible love of country. That virtue I attribute to our statesmen generally. They who are without it are, I think, mean indeed. This man should have it as the ruling principle of his life; and it should so rule him that all other things should be made to give way to it. But he should be scrupulous, and, as being scrupulous, weak. When called to the highest place in the councils of his Sovereign, he should feel with true modesty his own insufficiency; but not the less should the greed of power grow upon him when he had once allowed himself to taste and to enjoy it (xx).

The touching fact about Palliser is that he knows what is happening to him. He admires his wife's freedom, even encourages her to act and speak as she pleases, but he knows that he cannot be like her. In his stiff, formal way he applauds her energy, at first, and says of himself: "'. . . I have put myself into a groove, and ground myself into a mould, and clipped and pared and pinched myself all round,—very ineffectually as I fear,—to fit myself for this thing'" . . . (VII). It is almost as though he has willed himself to become a "musical instrument" and then cannot bear the strains he himself delivers. He has no saving sense of humor to help him keep the government ills in perspective.

The duke of St. Bungay quotes old Lord Brock to him, saying it was "'more difficult to find a good coachman than a good Secretary of State.'" Palliser reflects that Lord Brock was unfit to lead his country because he "ventured to make so poor a joke on so solemn a subject" (VII). Although he admires his wife's energy, he becomes suspicious of it, fearing not only that his rank and wealth are more important than his own personal powers, but also that she may be running the country despite him: "She and she only would have the spirit and the money and the sort of cleverness required. In such a state of things he of course, as her husband, must be the nominal Prime Minister" (XVIII). It is thus the narrator stresses the hopelessness of Palliser's governmental and marital coalitions.

Afraid of his wife's power, yet diffident about his own, Palliser puts his trust into the wrong "word." The popular press becomes his Mentor, and, without his awareness, the cruelty of Slide's pen begins to dominate his thoughts. When he first takes office, he decides he must be fit for the job because the press tells him so: "But when the newspapers told him that he was the only man for the occasion, how could he be justified in crediting himself in preference to them?" (VIII). His fascination with the press begins because he is modest, but it grows as he becomes jealous of power and fearful of his own jealousy. He tries to separate himself from his wife's influence, snapping at her once, "'I wish you wouldn't put slang phrases into my mouth, Cora'" (XXI). And in his suspicion and jealousy he defends himself, to himself, with one of Trollope's favorite expressions—"Ruat caelum, fiat justitia." The use of this phrase alone, to readers familiar with it in *The Last Chronicle of Barset* and *He Knew He Was Right,* suggests the depth of Palliser's misery and the extent of his self-righteousness. The narrator's comment on the internal monologue deflates Palliser's identification: "And in his heart he suspected her of a design of managing the Government in her own way, with her own particular friend, Mrs. Finn, for her Prime Minister. If he could in no other way put an end to such evils as these, he must put an end to his own political life. Ruat caelum, fiat justitia. Now 'justitia' to him was not compatible with feminine interference in his own special work" (XXXII). The quoted expression suggests that Palliser thinks of himself as a beleaguered statesman of the ancient world. (Later, we remember, Palliser even identifies with Caesar, and the narrator, ironically, prepares us for Palliser's repeated references to Caesar with three references of his own to the country's rejection of Palliser as the inevitable disquiet against Aristides[9] [LXIII, LXVI, LXVIII]). Here the narrator's transcription shows Palliser's using the grand "ruat caelum" to disguise fear of Glencora's power and ambition. The narrator reflects Palliser's suspicion and petulance in the phrase "feminine interference in his own special work." In these marvelously compressed words the aloof statesman shows himself as angry, insecure, and jealous.

Though he works to exclude his wife's influence, he falls prey to the *People's Banner*, which is "gall and wormwood" (XXXVIII) to him. Its words torment him far more than his wife's ever could. The old duke of St. Bungay discovers the root of the prime minister's unhappiness:

At that very moment the "People's Banner" had been put out of sight at the bottom of a heap of other newspapers behind the Prime Minister's chair, and his present misery had been produced by Mr. Quintus Slide. . . . "There seems to have come a lethargy upon the country," said the poor victim. Then the Duke of St. Bungay knew that his friend had read that pernicious article in the "People's Banner," for the Duke had also read it and remembered that phrase of a "lethargy on the country," and understood at once how the poison had rankled (XLI).

The young duke's morbid fancies replace his wife's healthy, meddlesome slang with the poison of Slide's newspaper.

Palliser's goodness emerges whenever he can forget the cares of office and remember his political ideals. He is then a mouthpiece for Trollope's ideals and satire,[10] as he proposes the impractical theory of equality. The satire in *Phineas Redux* and *The Prime Minister* is based on the assertion that there is little difference between parties and leaders. The vacant mottoes of *Phineas Redux* and the restlessness in *The Prime Minister* indicate that parties are the same and compete similarly for (empty) power and place. There is little difference between Conservatives and Liberals. (On another level, the universal rejection of Lopez suggests that social as well as political standards are the same for both Conservatives and Liberals.) Palliser believes that both parties should work together toward a golden millennium when equality will be possible. He sees the parties as necessary to each other and justifies supporting superficial differences if only to reinforce fundamental similarities. This insistence that parties share high principles and basic virtues is a wonderfully positive reversal of the belief, almost universally expressed elsewhere, that the parties are similar in corruption and self-seeking: "'The idea that political virtue is all on one side is both mischievous and absurd. We allow ourselves to talk in that way because indignation, scorn, and sometimes, I fear, vituperation, are the fuel with which the necessary heat of debate is maintained'" (LXVIII). He adds, "'Equality would be a heaven, if we could attain it'" (LXVIII). And then, in a mixture of Conservative and Liberal ideals he declares: "'Equality is a dream. But sometimes one likes to dream,—especially as there is no danger that Matching will fly from me in a dream. I doubt whether I could bear the test that has been attempted in other countries'" (LXVIII). Palliser's ideals, though perhaps naive for an experienced statesman, provide part of the message of Trollope's political writing. The perfect politician is one who can encourage his country carefully but steadily to progress, trying as much as he can to resist the alluring colors of partisan strategy. All statesmen may not be able to acknowledge the similarities of their pursuits, but governments and parties become corrupt when they begin to believe the petty differences are really of great importance. Personal ambition then forces party members to glorify factions because only through factions can they attain personal success. Palliser is a great man, and even when he is most strongly tempted by his new love for power, he can still revel in the "cloudlands" of political idealism. Even in adversity he is able to dream about the greatness of a sound government, and we see in this ability a promise that his poetic nature will return. The suggestion in the novel is that any threat of *Lear* is quelled by Glencora's playful *Macbeth*; similarly, obsessive Quixoticism is banished by the promised restoration of "A Musical Instrument." In fact, Glencora's determined prosaicness supports Palliser's theory of amelioration. Sturdiness and progress, Trollope (like his own Septimus Harding) suggests, can complement each other.

Despite the consistencies and subtleties of the Palliser story, *The Prime Minister* was a failure with its first audiences. Modern critics have turned to it with more favor, and many claim that Trollope's "failure" is a significant success.[11] Robert Polhemus shows that the novel is constructed to suggest the instability of all kinds of coalitions.[12] Arthur Mizener maintains that *The Prime Minister* is one of Trollope's richest works for purposeful parallels of situation and character.[13] The patterns and parallels work themselves out in a network of allusions and repetitions. The language bolsters political commentary and sharpens insight into character, but also adds subtlety and indirectness to the quality of the whole. To readers accustomed to Disraeli's political novels, or even Trollope's own Phineas books, this indirectness was probably irritating.

The Palliser story in *The Prime Minister* is most important, but the Lopez-Wharton story occupies more than half of the chapters of the novel and much of our attention. Here, too, but for an entirely different reason, we take many of our cues from the duchess. The most important linguistic reinforcement of the duchess's view of her husband and politics comes, ironically, through the villain Ferdinand Lopez.[14] Glencora's slang and Shakespeare find curious, distorted reflections in Lopez's literary allusions. With the Pallisers we discover evidence of Shakespeare, Mrs. Browning, Cervantes, and Aesop; with Lopez's story we see Byron, Goethe, Dante, Molière, Shakespeare, and the Bible. In the Palliser story, literature, however ironically, expresses true feeling; in the Lopez world it is often used as a blind or as a weapon.

Everything Lopez touches is false, and yet we hear in his language elements of the duchess's. Lopez is a "thorough linguist" (IV), but he depends heavily on slang—he and the duchess even use the same expression, "'tell that to the marines'", once, but the fact that he uses it in a street brawl (XXXIV), and she in intimate conversation with an old friend (LXIII), is crucial. Lopez's slang is devoid of the playful energy of the duchess's— he is cruel, and his language shows the crudity of his thoughts. She is often sharp, but her language shows concern and impatience, not malice. After Lopez's interview with Abel Wharton, the narrator sums up Lopez's thoughts about the difficulty of winning (certainly not deserving) Emily thus: "He had not thought that the cherry would fall easily into his mouth" (III). His words are often aggressive or combative. He tells Everett roundly that he has seen him "'as drunk as Cloe'" (XXII), and when writing to Everett's father to tell him that Everett has been attacked he uses the pugilistic expression Chiltern used in *Phineas Redux* about Phineas and his trial: "'knocked out of time'" (XXII). The narrator tells us that Lopez wonders how he can "win her [Emily] to help him in his cheating" (XXIV), and the man himself brags to his unhappy bride, when her father sends them money, that the old man has "answered to the whip'" (XXVI). He instructs Emily to "'get round" her father" (XXXIX) and observes cheerfully when the old man refuses to give him more money, "'He can't take it with him'" (XXXV). He wants Emily to see her father, as he does, as a "cow capable of being milked" (XXXV). At the outset of the novel he refuses to have anything to do with Parliament, telling Everett that "'it is a comfort to me that I need not put my finger into that pie'" (II), and when he finds that a parliamentary career could enhance his business prospects he enters into it with characteristically deceptive and unbecoming flippancy: "'There are ever so many ways, you know, of killing a cat'" (XXXI). He is furious over his defeat and sickens Emily by forced lightheartedness: "'It is no good groaning over spilt milk'" (XXXV). When he fails in politics and is apparently failing in business, he renews his attack on Mr. Wharton. He cheats him, tries to keep Mr. Wharton and Everett apart, lives in his house, and boasts to Emily that the old man is "'coming round to cotton to me'" (XXXIX).

Emily is gradually forced to see what Lopez is; his language exposes him even when his actions are still mysterious to her. Frustrated by her refusal to gull her father for him, Lopez swears at Emily. When he leaves her, Emily considers her husband's language: "The whole man too was so different from what she had thought him to be. Before their marriage no word as to money had ever reached her ears from his lips. He had talked to her of books,—and especially of poetry. Shakespeare and Molière, Dante, and Goethe had been or had seemed to be dear to him. . . . Now she was awake; her dream was over; and the natural language of the man was still ringing in her ears!" (XLIV). One would like to have read some of Lopez's analyses of literature.

One expression Lopez uses twice seems to sum up his general philosophy of life. He excuses his attempt to run for Parliament—he has no money for the contest—by telling Emily, "'Nothing venture nothing have'" (XXIX). Much later when he has lost Emily, his high-society friends, and his grip on Mr. Wharton, he tries to persuade Lizzie Eustace to invest in Bios (and, failing that, to run away with him to Guatemala) with "'Nothing venture nothing have'" (LIV). The encounter with Lizzie brings Lopez's tactics into high relief. She is more than his match in the art of deception, but he tries to use her love of romance to ensnare her. They both agree that "all is fair in love and war" (LIV); his first ploy, then, is to describe Guatemala in the most romantic of terms. He calls it "a country so golden, so green, so gorgeous, and so grand" (LIV). Somehow (the double-edged irony here is a nice touch), Lopez realizes that Lizzie's greatest weakness is for Byron, and so he quotes from the "Bride of Abydos": "'Lizzie Eustace, will you go with me, to that land of the sun,

> Where the rage of the vulture, the love of the turtle,
> Now melt into sorrow, now madden to crime?'" (LIV).

But Lizzie, who can act like a "Cleopatra" (LIV), refuses to waste her handsome income on Lopez's brand of romance.

Lopez tries to con other people with his smooth references to literature. He tries to deflect Mr. Wharton's investigation of his income by pat reference to the *Merchant of Venice:* "'You have asked for a schedule of my affairs, and I have found it quite impossible to give it. As it was with the merchants whom Shakespeare and the other dramatists described,—so it is with me. My caravels are out at sea, and will not always come home in time'" (XLVI). With the *Merchant of Venice* still fresh in his mind he threatens Sexty Parker: "'. . . you'd better get somebody else to be jolly with. To tell you the truth, Sexty, I suit you better at business than at this sort of thing. I'm like Shylock, you know.' 'I don't know about Shylock, but I'm blessed if I think you suit me very well at anything. I'm putting up with a deal of ill-usage, and when I try to be happy with you, you won't drink, and you tell me about Shylock. He was a Jew, wasn't he?' 'That is the general idea'" (XLVI).[15] It is interesting that Lopez brags of his Jewishness to Parker when he has staunchly denied it to Wharton. Wharton suspects his dark looks from the first, thinking of Lopez as a "son of Judah" (III). The narrator uses words from *Othello* to express Wharton's disgust over Lopez's dark, un-English complexion: "He thought as did Brabantio, that it could not be that without magic his daughter who had shunned—

> 'The wealthy curled darlings of our nation,
> Would ever have, to incur a general mock,
> Run from her guardage to the sooty bosom
> Of such a thing as'—

this distasteful Portuguese" (XIII). It is unclear in the novel whether these words are supposed to reflect Wharton's thoughts directly, or whether they are the narrator's fanciful amplification of them, but in either case, they reinforce the superficial use of Shakespeare in the Lopez story and emphasize the more meaningful allusions in the Palliser section. Everything relating to Lopez smacks of artfulness.

Trollope prepares us for Wharton's use of *Othello* and shows Lopez's shrewd use of literature early in the novel shortly after Wharton and Lopez are introduced. Lopez thinks he can dupe Mr. Wharton because he discovers that the crusty old barrister has a penchant for novel reading. Trollope tells us that in his chambers in Stone Buildings Mr. Wharton reads all kinds of books—"poetry and novels and even fairy tales." The reader is at once alerted to Wharton's gentle nature, and Lopez sees the opportunity to exploit his future father-in-law:

> His quick eye at once discovered the book which Mr. Wharton half hid away, and saw upon it Mr. Mudie's suspicious ticket. Barristers certainly never get their law books from Mudie, and Lopez at once knew that his hoped-for father-in-law had been reading a novel. He had not suspected such weakness, but argued well from it for the business he had in hand. There must be a soft spot to be found about the heart of an old lawyer who spent his mornings in such occupation (III).

Lopez's calculation is partially correct: even though Wharton despises him initially, he gives way to Emily and after the marriage tries to like his son-in-law. The trouble with Lopez is that he cannot pursue his little victories—he wins the duchess, but quarrels with her; he invades Manchester Square, but alienates his father-in-law. He has keen, almost instinctive, insight into his victims' natures and chooses the proper linguistic devices to attack them, but he lacks the depth to sustain his campaigns. Wharton, though temporarily blinded, returns to the tenor of his original assessment: he says sarcastically that Lopez may be an "admirable Crichton" for all he knows (III), but thinks him a "nasty foreigner"; compares Fletcher and Lopez as "Hyperion to Satyr" (XIII); and generally looks upon him as an "interloper" (XV). The reader knows that though there is much of xenophobia in Wharton's initial aversion, there is also instinctive recognition.

Throughout the Lopez-Wharton story there are numerous expressions and references that give it internal consistency and suggest its relationship to the Palliser half. Lopez himself with his abuse of Shakespeare and his use of slang seems a dark distortion of the duchess. He threatens the stability of Manchester Square; she flouts the dignity of Carlton Terrace. It is ironic and typical of their peculiar bond that Lopez's suicide fulfills her mocking prophecies of doom. There is never anything truly tragic in her career as prime minister's wife, just as there is nothing magnificent in his proportions as a villain. But in death Lopez almost achieves tragic stature and thus provides a dark complement to Glencora's allusions. The powerfully restrained writing in "Tenway Junction" reminds us of similar scenes in *Anna Karenina* (VII, XXXI) and *Dombey and Son* (LV)—neither Tolstoy nor Dickens displays greater mastery than Trollope as he reflects Lopez's quiet desperation. Because of Lopez's death, and the strength of Trollope's descriptions, we may interpret anew the allusions to tragedy throughout; we find that Glencora's (and the narrator's) healthy energy reconciles ambition and failure.

The tone of the novel is set by Glencora and by the narrator (of whose spirit she often seems an incarnation); the narrator and minor characters repeat expressions and kinds of expressions that also serve to unify the investigations of coalitions and partnerships for which the duke and duchess serve as prototypes. Little echoes as well as large ones remind us to compare characters and their quality of partnership or coalition or communication. For example, we are prepared for and reminded of the ironic treatment of Palliser's identification with "ruat caelum" (XXXII) through the use of Latin tags by Abel Wharton (XV), by John Fletcher (XXXIII), by the narrator (XXV), and by the duke of St. Bungay (LXXVI). Similarly, three references to Spartan restraint and the boy's gnawed innards subtly align three different comments on hypocrisy or self-indulgence. First, the narrator uses the allusion with Lopez to mock his inability to speak of family (I); second, John Fletcher admonishes the despairing Arthur (Lopez's defeated rival) by urging him to adopt Spartan restraint (LVI); third, the narrator comments jocularly on the dissolution of the Palliser Coalition and the members' apparent unconcern over their loss of seats and offices (LXXIII). As with the six uses of "getting into a boat together" or Glencora's six allusions to Shakespeare, so these minor echoes from the narrator and characters reveal the incredibly complex interconnections and parallels among people and situations only apparently unrelated and dissimilar.

The insistent echoes and parallels encourage us repeatedly

to compare the way the dozens of characters in the novel respond to their various failures in coalition, partnership, or communication. We focus most sympathetically on the duke and duchess, whose marriage serves as an emblem of other social and political mismatches. Their language patterns and internal rhythms are sometimes disastrously incompatible; Trollope uses them to investigate simultaneously the intricacies of private and public politics.

When we imagine the duke and duchess as competing public politicians, as well as husband and wife, we recognize their misalliance as one of the splendid ironies of the novel. If they could only have communicated properly, they together could have made the perfect politician. Through her impatient language and in her cheerful puncturing of pomposity we welcome the pulse of the times, but her unashamed "men, not measures" is potentially dangerous and self-seeking. On the other hand, Palliser is personally unapproachable but is also impeccably honest and steadfast. Had they combined talents and efforts rather than competed, had they been able to "get into a boat together" confidently, they could have formed an ideal leader who could think and act with scrupulous honesty and also speak with genial energy. As it is, Trollope uses the frustrated duke and duchess to remind us that the partnerships, systems, and societies we create will always be limited by universal (often comic, frequently ironic) failures in judgment and trust.

6
The Way We Live Now

In the mid 1870s, Trollope had long since completed the Barsetshire novels and had written four of his six political works. With irony and provocative understatement, he had analyzed and gently criticized the manners and people of his times. He then prepared to write a sweeping satire of society, one which would make hard hits at speculation, gambling, false literary practices, the marriage market, political corruption, and religious prejudices. The chief character of this unflinching exposure was to be Lady Carbury, a literary charlatan who hastily penned trash and then connived with editors and reviewers to palm it off for profit on a gullible public.[1] But something happened to Trollope's scheme; Lady Carbury did not remain the chief character,[2] and the narrator's tempering irony reasserts itself even with the unlikely Melmotte. The densely peopled satire turns into comedy halfway through[3] and we find that Trollope makes his points not through expressing unaccustomed vitriol, but by combining the best of the techniques he learned from the Barsetshire, Palliser, and experimental novels.

As in the best of the earlier novels, here in Trollope's masterpiece we also follow the lead of the narrator. In fact, the role of the narrator is the key to the novel's power. The exuberance of the *Barchester Towers* narrator is here found in vehement asides and apostrophes and in the conscious uses of stagecraft; the *Last Chronicle of Barset* narrator, in the interconnections between London and Suffolk; the *He Knew He Was Right* narrator, in the encouraged ironic judgment of all of the characters; the *Phineas Redux* narrator, in the satiric use of characteristic mottoes or slogans. The narrator of *The Way We Live Now* encourages distance and judgment by offering an unrelentingly clear-eyed view of all of the characters and their actions; as usual, the narrator urges us to see that even the worst can be pitied, even the best are comically self-pitying or self-righteous, but the narrator here does not relieve us from our position as judge even at the story's end by suggesting that the many romances and marriages are really healthy assertions of the basic good in life (the kind of lesson *He Knew He Was Right* suggests, perhaps). The most attractive character in the novel is probably Mrs. Hurtle, and even she is too easily duped by Melmotte for us to find her energy or insight heartening. The resulting sustained distance between narrator and characters (and reader) is essential. The narrator does not give easy answers; he does not let us dismiss wholesale or forgive joyously; it is as though he wants to teach us to read life as a kind of text that is thoroughly intelligible only through serious, almost impartial, scrutiny shared with the narrator. We thus identify and sympathize with the narrator and not with the characters we are repeatedly called on to evaluate. The crucial differences between *The Way We Live Now* and the earlier novels are found in the variety of ways the narrator involves us in the characters' mental rhythms and internal monologues and the larger patterns of the novel, themselves echoing and echoed in vast, loose parallels and contrasts.

The Way We Live Now finds expression through an almost bewildering number of parallels and contrasts, some operating with one or two characters or situations, some operating through the full novel. Overall, the novel repeats implicitly and explicitly the question, Is modern London a direct parallel of decadent Rome? The appropriateness of the Roman parallel is intensified by parallels and contrasts between America and England, London and Suffolk, rich and poor, adventurer and genuine lover. At first glance most of the patterns seem to favor the Roman parallel—bigotry, fraud, materialism, and opportunism repeatedly overwhelm feeble gestures toward virtue. But the novel has other patterns to counterbalance the apparent powers of deceit and greed, and these argue against the gloom of Rome: the end of the novel shows a series of reclamations and a number of marriages that promise to lighten Melmotte's shadow. Yet despite the shift from satire to comedy, the novel refuses to answer questions for the reader. The quality of comic marriage and reclamation demands skepticism as certainly as the presence of comedy qualifies any cynicism. The narrator's balance between the comedy and satire forces the reader to evaluate and keeps the question (and novel) open.[4]

No one character is of greatest importance in the satire or comedy, but Trollope uses two characters to give focus to the various criticisms and questions: Lady Carbury and Augustus Melmotte. Lady Carbury's literary chicanery opens and virtually closes the novel; Melmotte seems to occupy the novel's center, yet ironically neither character dominates interest or analysis. The narrator's treatment of Lady Carbury sets the tone for exposure of fraud and Melmotte acts as chief charlatan; both also direct us to their larger spheres (literary and commercial England) and thus invigorate the far-reaching though ironic attacks.

With most of the characters of the satire, whether they are members of fashionable society, speculators, religious adherents, or politicians, we are aware of the inflated image of Augustus Melmotte. Some are related to him in business; some, like Mrs. Hurtle, simply admire him. In the novel, as in the society he epitomizes, Melmotte is often the center of interest. Yet when he dies society carries on as though he had never been, and so, too, the novel continues its seventeen remaining chapters after his death with minimal attention on him. The satire depends on this irony, and the novel as a whole, like a series of Hogarth prints with continued theme but change of scene, finds strength in it. Much of the satire, just as much of its opening and closing, relies on the comic figure of Lady Carbury, and she directs us to Melmotte since she is eager to lead the literary world in courting him; she even urges her own son to pursue Melmotte's daughter. Thus Lady Carbury and Melmotte together, though insubstantial in themselves, are important in the satiric and comic forms of the novel.

Lady Carbury's own literary allusions and references as well as her self-consciously melodramatic language expose her fraud, and other characters in the novel are similarly satirized through allusions and references, either their own or the narrator's, which then remind us of Lady Carbury. Melmotte is exposed through repetitions of expressions and images belonging primarily to the narrator (yet imitative of the rhythms if not the quality of Melmotte's thoughts), and many of the other individuals are revealed through the repetition (their own or the narrator's) of images and expressions apparently peculiar to them but contributing to the novel's large questions and patterns. The narrator is instrumental in blending together and in isolating the voices and rhythms of the novel so that the reader is aware of the multiple parallels and contrasts without losing the individual people and scenes. The reader is always urged to evaluate the constant interplay of large and small in the very patterns of language themselves and particularly with Lady Carbury and with Augustus Melmotte.

Lady Carbury's "Three Editors" opens the novel and sets the tone for the satire by demonstrating her artifice and ingenuity in manipulating language. She discusses her book *Criminal Queens,* which she acknowledges to have "borrowed" from numerous sources. As with Grantly or Crawley, we learn much about her through the characters about whom she has chosen to read (and, in her case, distort). She lists Cleopatra, Julia, Joanna, Anne Boleyne, Catherine, Mary Queen of Scots, and British Caroline (1). Especially to the reader familiar with *The Last Chronicle of Barset,* Lady Carbury's comments on her subjects perfectly reveal her shallow, prosaic mind. Unable to grasp tragedy, she recognizes only the pitiful or the sensational elements of the stories: "'Poor dear old Belisarius! I have done the best I could with Joanna, but I could not bring myself to care for her. In our days she would simply have gone to Broadmore'" (1). When we remember how the scholarly Crawley identifies with Samson, Milton, and Belisarius, we rightly assess Lady Carbury's superficial dismissal of the dishonored general and the oppressed, crazed queen.

One of the editors to whom she writes even acknowledges to himself that she is a "female literary charlatan" (1) but knows she would be useful in falsely praising his book "A New Tale of a Tub" (I) (many of Trollope's readers would have understood the irony of this allusion to Swift's satire on hack writing). She shows her duplicity in writing to Mr. Alf, "'I have no patience with the pretensions of would-be poets who contrive by toadying and underground influences to get their volumes placed on every drawing-room table'" (I), when she really feels, "'To puff and to get one's self puffed have become different branches of a new profession. Alas, me! I wish I might find a class open in which lessons could be taken by such a poor tyro as myself'" (I). The narrator offers her philosophy of life: ". . . her end was to be obtained not by producing good books, but by inducing certain people to say that her books were good" (II). Her faith in her son is as ridiculous and dishonest as her literary hopes: if ". . . Felix be the husband of the richest bride in Europe, and she be the acknowledged author of the cleverest book of the year, what a Paradise of triumph might still be open to her after all her troubles!" (VII). The whole chapter shows us that literary criticism of the time is as corrupt as (Melmotte's) commercial business meetings; not only does Lady Carbury commend some travesty of Swift, but she is herself lied to by editors. Instead of telling the truth about her books, one editor runs the "Juggernaut's car-wheels" (XI) over her, while another (alluding ironically to Pope's satiric "Epistle to Dr Arbuthnot") says "'One doesn't want to break a butterfly on the wheel;— especially a friendly butterfly'" (XI). Lady Carbury's presence in literary society is an eloquent commentary itself on the corruption of the times. The narrator and the characters together suggest that the words of literature and the words of the press are as meaningless as Melmotte's promises. The use of literary allusions in the rest of the novel is a reminder of Lady Carbury and the corruption of current literature.

Toward the end of the novel (actually in the comedy) the satire on her is more explicit, and we see her at the task of writing. The entire chapter "The Wheel of Fortune" (LXXXIX) is the mature Trollope's ironic word on his own trade. Lady Carbury's habits of forced writing and sketchy outlines are the

The Way We Live Now 175

very things for which Trollope himself was criticized. One publisher's advice to her is, in fact, the advice given to Trollope after *The Three Clerks*[5]: "And whatever you do, Lady Carbury, don't be historical. Your historical novel, Lady Carbury, isn't worth a —." The chapter is good reading, offering an ironic glimpse into Trollope's own habits, but most importantly for this novel, it comments on all of society through Lady Carbury: "I do not think that she prided herself much on the literary merit of the tale. But if she could bring the papers to praise it, if she could induce Mudie to circulate it, if she could manage that the air for a month should be so loaded with 'The Wheel of Fortune,' as to make it necessary for the reading world to have read or to have said that it had read the book,—then she would pride herself very much upon her work." Lady Carbury, despite her "puffing," is really more pitiful than evil. The narrator reveals the quality of her mind in this silly adaptation (meant to be a transcription of *her* deep reflections): "A novel, she knew well, was most unlike a rose, which by any other name will smell as sweet." Sillier still is her quotation from Byron's "English Bards and Scotch Reviewers": ". . . she repeated to herself those well-known lines from the satirist,—

> 'Oh, Amos Cottle, for a moment think
> What meagre profits spread [*sic*] from pen and ink.'[6]

But not on that account did she for a moment hesitate as to further attempts" (LXXXIX). She obviously forgets to identify herself with the foolish Cottle, thinking only of the labor and the promise of small profits. Trollope uses Byron here, as he does in many of his novels, to deride the folly of romantic exaggeration. The presence of Byron, as with Mrs. Dobbs Broughton and Lucy Toogood in *The Last Chronicle* or Lizzie Eustace in *The Eustace Diamonds* or Ferdinand Lopez in *The Prime Minister*, always betokens an immature, frivolous, or even deceitful intelligence.[7] There is double irony in Lady Carbury's use of Byron, for she really despises genuine romance, only imagining that she loves it.

Lady Carbury's contempt for romance amplifies the satire on

the marriage market and furthers our insight into the kind of literature she must have duped her public into accepting. Early in our introduction to her we are told: ". . . she had made up her mind to abandon all hope of that sort of love which poets describe and which young people generally experience" (II). She dislikes her daughter Hetta because she cannot fathom her concept of love. The narrator explains: "If there was anything that she could not forgive in life it was romance. And yet she, at any rate, believed that she delighted in romantic poetry!" (LXXXIV). Hetta's determination to accept the impecunious Paul widens the gulf between mother and daughter: "But that which pained her most was the unrealistic, romantic view of life which pervaded all Hetta's thoughts. How was any girl to live in this world who could not be taught the folly of such idle dreams?" (XCI). Of Mr. Broune's love for her Lady Carbury thinks (and the narrator provides us with the transcription): "What an idiot! But what a god! . . . How wonderfully sweet! How infinitely small!" (XXXI). She remarks contemptuously of Roger's pining for Hetta: "'He will go on boodying over it, till he will become an old misanthrope'" (XVI). We recognize in her "boodying" the heartlessness of Madeline Neroni (*Barchester Towers*, XXVII) and the flippancy of Glencora Palliser (*The Prime Minister,* LXXVI), both of whom use this unusual word to deride a feeling they do not share.

This shallow cynic is a supporter of Melmotte because he may be able to make her son's fortune: "Why, with such a preceptor to help him, should not Felix learn to do his gambling on the Exchange, or among the brokers, or in the purlieus of the Bank?" (XII). The same man who called her a "friendly butterfly" tells her she is an "excellent casuist" when she speaks thus of Melmotte (and echoes the world's eager support of the swindler): "'You have to destroy a thousand living creatures every time you drink a glass of water, but you do not think of that when you are athirst. You cannot send a ship to sea without endangering lives. You do send ships to sea though men perish yearly. You tell me this man may perhaps ruin hundreds, but then again he may create a new world in which millions will be rich and happy'" (xxx). Her nature and her thoughts do much to further the novel's parallel between London and Rome. Yet her hopeful attitude to her own manuscript *The Wheel of Fortune* suggests that there is something redeemable in her fascination with words. She admits to herself that it is trash, knows that she will try to gull the public into reading it, but at the moment of giving it to her publishers compares it wistfully in her imagination to the works of Defoe and Fielding: "If 'Robinson Crusoe' had been lost! If 'Tom Jones' had been consumed by flames! And who knows but that this may be another 'Robinson Crusoe,'—better than 'Tom Jones'? 'Will it be safe there?' asked Lady Carbury" (LXXXIX). In her moment of anxiety we see a woman who is not completely unregenerate; she has learned to hope that she is better than she is. Since the novel changes from satire to comedy, it is fitting that Lady Carbury should actually have a "miraculous rebirth" by the end of the book.[8] Lady Carbury's literary circle is a microcosm of the corrupt London society, and then, Lady Carbury herself stops writing.

With Lady Carbury and with Melmotte the narrator uses different methods of revealing thought and encouraging judgment. In "Three Editors" and "The Wheel of Fortune" in particular, but actually throughout the novel wherever she appears, Lady Carbury exposes herself through the quality of her own words. Sometimes these are given in dialogue; often they are given in letters; sometimes the narrator transcribes her thoughts for us—but whether the words come directly from Lady Carbury or are given through the narrator we hear her own language. The narrator, with Lady Carbury, is thus akin to the narrator who presents Crawley or Phineas, Mrs. Dobbs Broughton, Lady Glencora, and especially the far earlier Madeline Neroni. But with Melmotte himself and with Melmotte's death we find that the narrator plays a large, direct, sometimes fanciful (if sinister) part in our interpretation. The independent asides, the stage directing, the disjunction between low intellect or occasion and lofty allusion are techniques used extensively by the comic narrator of *Barchester Towers*; here these formerly comic devices are darkly ironic. Lady Carbury seems to share the rhythms of her own mind; Melmotte's are given to us with the unmistakable bias of the narrator. The difference is that Trollope means Melmotte to be seen as a force, perhaps even menace, rather than a person: in *The Way We Live Now* Melmotte is an image or a disease or a shadow that must be acknowledged and assessed, especially in relation to the Roman analogy.

To appreciate the difference between the narrator's treatment of Lady Carbury and Melmotte, consider two parts of the Melmotte story while keeping in mind the subtle raillery and irony of "The Three Editors" and "The Wheel of Fortune." In the chapter "The Inquest" (LXXXVIII) when we would expect some revelation about Melmotte's words or Melmotte's thoughts, we find, instead, the narrator's turning the discussion of Melmotte's suicide into an attack on the corrupt system that allows a rich man to be found insane and the poor or philosophical man to be held responsible for his shameful crime. Melmotte is still not a person—he is an issue and occasions the vocal narrator's indignation. (Ignoring the sadness of the death is another way, perhaps, of emphasizing Melmotte's isolation.) At another point, the narrator makes the gruesome scene of Melmotte's beating Marie into surreal drama. The narrator, rather than lecturing or finding fault, becomes a grim, reluctant stage director. He has earlier compared Melmotte to Medea, as a financial sorcerer cooking up new fortunes out of old debts. Here, in the midst of a scene of terrific energy, the narrator injects: "'Nec pueros coram populo Medea trucidet.' 'Let not Medea with unnatural rage / Slaughter her mangled infants on the stage.' Nor will I attempt to harrow my readers by a close description of the scene which followed" (LXXVII). There is a strange irony in this selection; the lines themselves intensify the horror of the beating, suggesting the demented frenzy of the betrayed sorceress (now the use of Medea is a horribly distorted echo of the earlier reference), while the injection into the scene distances the reader from Marie's genuine human struggle to survive. In both instances, at the inquest and at the beating, the narrator's peculiar, insistent distancing makes us see Melmotte as a presence or force who violates, even in death, all that is decent and humane.

The narrator encourages little sympathy for the swollen, hollow figure Augustus Melmotte. The images of scavengers and predators are used frequently by the narrator and other characters to describe him. The narrator recounts gossip about Melmotte's past: "People said of him that he had framed and carried out long premeditated and deeply laid schemes for the ruin of those who had trusted him, that he had swallowed up the property of all who had come in contact with him, that he was fed with the blood of widows and children; . . ." (VIII). Felix Carbury thinks of him as "this surfeited sponge of speculation, this crammed commercial cormorant" (XXIII), and the world (the narrator suggests) looks upon his movements as on those of some powerful bird: "It is true that all this came as it were by jumps, so that very often a part of the world did not know on what ledge in the world the great man was perched at that moment" (XXXV). The people of Suffolk recognize him as a vulture: "Suffolk, as a whole, thoroughly believed that Melmotte had picked the very bones of every shareholder in the Franco-Austrian Assurance Company" (LV). In a partly embroidered re-creation of Melmotte's thoughts about himself, Melmotte apparently echoes the images used by others to describe him. This ironic form of echo (the narrator's fanciful interpretation of thoughts that are close to these but would not be given in these words) adds to the picture of Melmotte's villainy by suggesting that the man himself is proud of the abusive terms others use for him. The narrator implies that Melmotte *likes* being feared as a wolf or vulture. When Melmotte thinks of himself he apparently agrees with the rest of society: "Something might be found out. But the task of unravelling it all would not be easy. It is the small vermin and the little birds that are trapped at once. But wolves and vultures can fight hard before they are caught" (LXII). By using the word *vermin* the narrator comments on Melmotte's thoughts while interpreting them. Melmotte might think of himself as savage or unscrupulous, but he is not likely to accept the characterization "vermin." This blurring of distinction between monologue and commentary characterizes the narrator's insistently ironic treatment of the swindler. When Melmotte beats Marie, his wife interferes, and the narrator reminds us again of the predator: "And she tried to drag him from his prey" (LXXVII).

The narrator directs us to see that for its own reasons, the world argues whether Melmotte is a "Satan of speculation" or a "commercial Jove" (XLIV) when it really knows that he is "the most gigantic swindler that had ever lived" (IV) and that he has a "reputation throughout Europe as a gigantic swindler" (VIII). He is referred to as "the horrid, big, rich scoundrel" (XXIII) and is thought of as "The bloated swindler, the vile city ruffian" (XXIII). Madame Melmotte has reason to believe that he is as "powerful as Satan" (LXXVII). Society chooses to ignore, for a time, the evil in him, because he is the "topping Croesus of the day" (II). He is able to create a nearly perfect facade of solidity with the same apparent ease with which he transforms his house. His hall was a "paradise" and the staircase, "fairyland," while "The lobbies were grottoes rich with ferns" (IV). The aristocracy believe in his powers of magic; this early reference to Medea has its sinister echo later in the novel when the magic begins to fail. Here Mr. Longestaffe's thoughts are shared by all his grasping peers:

There are men,—and old men too, who ought to know the world,— who think that if they can only find the proper Medea to boil the cauldron for them, they can have their ruined fortunes so cooked that they shall come out of the pot fresh and new and unembarrassed. These great conjurors are generally sought for in the City; ... No greater Medea than Mr. Melmotte had ever been potent in money matters, and Mr. Longestaffe had been taught to believe that if he could get the necromancer even to look at his affairs everything would be made right for him (XIII).

Melmotte's magic powers, his ability to make artificial paradises, for a while staves off the inevitable collapse. We know that his is "outrageous prosperity" (II); repeatedly we are told that he is a swollen image that must explode. Miles Grendall tells his father, "'There are a good many who say that Melmotte will burst up,'" to which his father replies: "'There are too many in the same boat to let him burst up. It would be the bursting up of half London'" (XLIV). (We recognize from *The Prime Minister* the importance of the cliché of the boat and its implied uneasy partnership. Here the boat is losing buoyancy.) He makes exorbitant demands on his followers so that his "arrogance in the midst of his inflated glory was overcoming him" (XLV). His bloated figure overshadows the City, Parliament, the press, and even religious controversies. As he prepares to entertain the emperor of China, a priest comes to find out whether he is Catholic, and "Even this poor priest's mad visit added to his inflation" (LVI). He overextends himself so conspicuously that many are forced to realize before his suicide that "the great Melmotte bubble was on the very point of bursting" (LXXXII). His closest companion remarks after his death: "'He vas passionate, and did lose his 'ead; and vas blow'd up vid bigness.' Whereupon Croll made an action as though he were a frog swelling himself to the dimensions of an ox. "E bursted himself. . .'" (XCVIII). The characters reinforce the collected impressions of the narrator so that all levels resonate with the same chords.

The narrator exposes Melmotte through repeated exaggerations and deliberate understatement. While we recognize that some thoughts may belong to the fanciful narrator and not to Melmotte himself, the narrator so successfully mimicks Melmotte's general awkwardness and callousness that we hear in the interpreted words, the tenor of Melmotte's mind as well as the narrator's mocking disjunction between quality of thought and quality of expression. For example, while revealing Melmotte's limited intellect, the narrator imitates Melmotte's inflated rhetoric: "He had contemplated great things; but the things which he was achieving were beyond his contemplation" (XXXV). It is the narrator who shows us that people fall for Melmotte's hollow words and create a new religion: "It seemed that there was but one virtue in the world, commercial enterprise,—and that Melmotte was its prophet" (XLIV). This is indeed a dangerous prophet, the narrator suggests, who will account to himself for his duplicity with the words of Scripture (Ecclesiastes 11:1): "He had thrown his bread upon the waters, assisting St. Fabricius with one hand and the Protestant curates with the other, and must leave the results to take care of themselves" (LVI). The probable Jew, here posing as both Protestant and Catholic, later analyzes his own career, by questioning (in words the narrator again chooses for him): "But why had he, so unrighteous himself, not made friends to himself of the Mammon of unrighteousness?" (LXXXI). The identification with the unjust steward[9] (whether his own or not) shows as little remorse as the perversion of charity. The narrator's use of Scripture to characterize Melmotte is doubly ironic. He is probably too ignorant to use the allusions himself, common though they are, but they represent the kind of power he tells himself he is capable of wielding. Further, the narrator's choice of language probably beyond Melmotte is also a mockery of those who listen to Melmotte, willfully deceiving themselves that the mountebank is an oracle.

Melmotte is friendless; his "faithful Achates" (LIX)[10] runs away at the first signs of difficulty, "as though proclaiming the fate of his own house and the consequent running away of the rat" (LXII). The world for a while believes that Melmotte may "pull through" (LXXIV), but the shrewd businessmen know that despite Melmotte's determination to "put his shoulder to the wheel, [so that he] would yet conquer his enemies" (LXIV), he is really a "gone coon" (LXXV). The slang and clichés are appropriate (as they are in *Phineas Redux* and *The Prime Minister* to suggest evil or potentially dangerous politics), for they suggest the way Melmotte himself interprets his position. The awkward repetitions and clumsy clichés suggest what Melmotte's real thoughts are like, and they provide a different kind of disjunction from the lofty and prosaic mixture already mentioned. Here the common expressions betoken Melmotte's pitiable inability to forestall the disaster he has himself set into motion. When he is facing the possibility of detection and arrest, the deepest thought that seems to come to his mind to characterize the projected aftermath of calamity is this: "And he could see too that there was no help for spilt milk" (LXII).

Some of the images and expressions used with Melmotte are almost jocular; they eventually invite a qualified pity for his failure. The narrator uses with him that allusion he also uses in *Barchester Towers* and *He Knew He Was Right,* "It is so hard not to tumble into Scylla when you are avoiding Charybdis" (LXIII), and here he is making light of Melmotte's attempt to seem undisturbed by his "rats'" defection. In the other two novels the allusion is purely playful, but here it has the edge of irony since the narrator uses words beyond Melmotte to create the tone Melmotte is himself trying to assume (but cannot). In his own home Melmotte is a target for family and servants: "He was regarded as the general enemy, against whom the whole household was always making ambushes, always firing guns from behind rocks and trees" (XXV). He tries to win a friend outside by magnifying his powers and troubles: "'But when they [troubles] do come, they are like a storm at sea. It is only the strong ships that can stand the fury of the winds and waves'" (LXXIV). There is irony in his boast, too, since he is unable to weather the final storm.

There is something almost touching in his attempts to put on a brave front against failure. But, again, the images he chooses, the analogies he uses, make his shallowness all but unpitiable. He romanticizes his position (or the narrator does for him): "As the soldier who leads a forlorn hope, or as the diver who goes down for pearls, or as the searcher for wealth on fever-breeding coasts, knows that as his gains may be great, so are his perils, Melmotte had been aware that in his life, as it opened itself out to him, he might come to terrible destruction" (LXII). The people who believe in him, or at least profess to believe in him, also romanticize his crimes. They are willing, like Nidderdale, to forget that the storms may mean family fortunes or the "blood of widows and children." They accord Melmotte position not only as prophet, but as conqueror: "A Napoleon, though he may exterminate tribes in carrying out his projects, cannot be judged by the same law as a young lieutenant who may be punished for cruelty to a few negroes. 'The Mob' thought that a good deal should be overlooked in a Melmotte, and that the philanthropy of his great designs should be allowed to cover a multitude of sins" (LXIX). These words are echoed in Mrs. Hurtle's analogy to Napoleon and in Lady Carbury's comparison of Melmotte's swallowing of thousands to the innocent and necessary swallowing of microbes in water.

It is sufficient condemnation (by Trollope) of Melmotte that his followers think he is inspired by Disraeli. Trollope makes a sly jab at Disraeli by comparing Melmotte to a "political master, whose eloquence has been employed in teaching us that progress can only be expected from those whose declared purpose is to stand still" (LXIX). To the initiated Trollope reader this revives the image of Daubeny the conjuror from *Phineas Redux* and suggests another dimension to Melmotte as magician. Melmotte is more devious than the great political pyrotechnist, but certainly less eloquent. His speeches are generally as clumsy as his thoughts are clichéd, and yet words from Melmotte are the basis of rampant speculation. As Slakey suggests, his very name seems a deliberate combination of the French *mal* and *mot*:[11] "As for many years past we have exchanged paper instead of actual money for our commodities, so now it seemed that, under the new Melmotte regime, an exchange of words was to suffice" (XLV). After all, "... money was the very breath of Melmotte's nostrils, and therefore his breath was taken for money" (XXXV).

One word sums up Melmotte's chief aim, the foundation for all his fortune and ventures: *unanimity*. Melmotte knows that with this he can con the public, and without it, he cannot. There must be universal complicity if his illusions are to work. Melmotte's mesmerizing repetitions are given in a farce complete with comic stage directions. At a board meeting Melmotte intends to quieten the restless Montague with the irresistible force of "unanimity":

"Unanimity is everything in the direction of such an undertaking as this. With unanimity we can do—everything." Mr. Melmotte in the ecstasy of his enthusiasm lifted up both his hands over his head. "With-

out unanimity we can do—nothing." And the two hands fell. "Unanimity should be printed everywhere about a Board-room. It should, indeed, Mr. Montague."
"But suppose the directors are not unanimous."
"They should be unanimous. They should make themselves unanimous. God bless my soul! You don't want to see the thing fall to pieces!" (XL).

At the end of the interview he again advises Montague: "'... do be unanimous. Unanimity is the very soul of these things;—the very soul, Mr. Montague.'" Later at another meeting with Montague he says, "'I hope you'll be unanimous'" (XLV), and when Melmotte tells the Board of Montague's resignation, he says: "'He could not be made to understand that unanimity in such an enterprise as this is essential'" (XLV). Unanimity is the foundation of Melmotte's claim as a "triumphant Merchant Prince" (LXIII). As long as the City and Westminster are unanimous in their support of him, he can dominate commerce and society in London. Dissension of any kind threatens the thin facade of his elaborate schemes. The thoughtless repetition of the word suggests the rhythm of Melmotte's mind as well as the nature of the society so easily and willingly duped. For Melmotte's repeated "unanimity" to work, his hearers must be eager to imagine eloquent argument magically packed into the single word.

Throughout the novel, the narrator and the other characters deride Melmotte, even when they apparently support him. In death (but not after, as "The Inquest" shows) he achieves something of the grandeur his own arrogance and boastfulness have denied him in the course of the narrative. Even his drunken display in Parliament is touching when we realize that he is trying to brave out his final public appearance. The narrator comments wryly and not cruelly, "It was thus that Augustus Melmotte wrapped his toga around him before his death!" (LXXXIII), and again "He might have wrapped his toga around him better perhaps had he remained at home..." (LXXXIII). The image of the fallen tribune makes his suicide, like Merdle's in *Little Dorrit*, seem almost heroic. After all, it has been society's willing echo of "unanimity" that has given Melmotte the power to feed on widows and children.

Melmotte is used to satirize English corruption, but his powers reach beyond England. The company that makes him most conspicuous in London is American, and the project is led by a man who serves as a transatlantic counterpart for Melmotte. Hamilton K. Fisker, possibly modeled on the real James Fisk of Erie Railway fame,[12] serves the satire in several ways. Fisker's crudity and shrewdness contrast with the elegance and obtuseness of the men Melmotte controls in England. He is a slick salesman who shows that Melmotte's theories of commerce are universal. Fisker is at first repulsive, and yet the Englishmen who condemn him are as guilty as he is of the dishonesties of speculation. In contrast with Melmotte, Fisker is "gorgeous and florid" (IX), and his speech to Melmotte's men is "fluent, fast, and florid" (X). Melmotte lectures Paul Montague on unanimity and the delicate quality of speculation: "'Gentlemen who don't know the nature of credit, how strong it is,—as the air,—to buoy you up; how slight it is,—as a mere vapour,—when roughly touched, can do an amount of mischief of which they themselves don't in the least understand the extent!'" (XL). Ironically we hear many of the reputedly fast-talking Fisker's words through the narrator rather than through dialogue. The narrator translates for us Fisker's ideas on the buoyancy of commerce: "The object of Fisker, Montague, and Montague was not to make a railway to Vera Cruz, but to float a company" (IX). Fisker knows that in being introduced to Melmotte he has "'struck 'ile'" (XXII) because he sees in the Englishman one who matches his unscrupulous energy: "According to his theory of life, nine hundred and ninety-nine men were obscure because of their scruples, whilst the thousandth man predominated and cropped up into the splendour of commercial wealth because he was free from such bondage" (XCII). This approbation of freedom makes the press acclaim Melmotte a Napoleon and is echoed in the respect of two other adventurers, Mrs. Hurtle and Lady Carbury. Fisker, like Mrs. Hurtle, despises the squeamishness of many of the London speculators. He tells Montague

"'. . . you've never above half spirit enough for a big thing. You nibble at it instead of swallowing it whole,—and then, of course, folks see that you're only nibbling'" (XCII). Fisker's propensities are more like the voracious predator Melmotte's than the fastidious "nibbler" Montague's, and for this reason Fisker is instrumental in forwarding Melmotte's already swelling career: "He had never read a book. He had never written a line worth reading. He had never said a prayer. He cared nothing for humanity. He had sprung out of some Californian gully, was perhaps ignorant of his own father and mother, and had tumbled up in the world on the strength of his own audacity. But, such as he was, he had sufficed to give the necessary impetus for rolling Augustus Melmotte onwards into almost unprecedented commercial greatness" (XXXV). Fisker gauges Melmotte's popularity by the corrupt standards of commercialism, and when he hears evil of the financier remarks knowingly, twirling his cigar: "'There is always a want of charity . . . when a man is successful'" (IX).

Melmotte is a palpable threat to English morality, encouraging and exploiting vice, but Fisker, who is evidently capable of as much evil, is treated as a comic figure. He exposes the young English aristocrats' self-righteousness and stupidity. The reader is alerted to Fisker's function in the novel by an allusion to Bret Harte's poem "Plain Language from Truthful James,"[13] used in the narrator's rendering of Nidderdale's very vague but nevertheless comically xenophobic thoughts:

> Nidderdale, who did not understand much about the races of mankind, had his doubts whether the American gentleman might not be a "Heathen Chinee," such as he had read of in poetry. . . . Mr. Fisker made an allusion to poker as a desirable pastime, but Lord Nidderdale, remembering his poetry, shook his head. "Oh, bother," he said, "let's have some game that Christians play." Mr. Fisker declared himself ready for any game,—irrespective of religious prejudices (X).

Fisker is too sharp to carry twenty-four packs in his sleeves as Ah Sin does, but he manages to carry away the winnings, and we laugh at the Englishman who prides himself on shrewdly avoiding poker but is not smart enough to refuse to play. We know Trollope will not make a serious villain out of a character he connects with a comic figure from poetry; indeed, Hamilton Fisker turns out to have a good heart underneath his gambler's coolness and faintly resembles another Harte character, John Oakhurst from "The Outcasts of Poker Flats." Like Mrs. Hurtle, Fisker eventually seems to be one of the more likable characters in the novel.[14] Nidderdale, who has been suspicious of him, and has lost to him, remarks with telling innocence: "'He's not half a bad fellow, but he's not a bit like an Englishman'" (x). Hamilton Fisker despite his vulgarity turns the joke on the polished Englishman's complacent chauvinism. (The comic allusion to the popular American Western writer is itself a subtle reminder, perhaps, of Lady Carbury's preoccupations with market and audience.)

Young gambling men like Lord Nidderdale, Dolly Longestaffe, and Felix Carbury are easy marks for Melmotte and Fisker because they often must speculate in two other markets—stocks, if they can afford them, and marriage. They represent the numerous bored, energyless young men who marry fortunes in order to continue their pleasures. Men like Nidderdale and Longestaffe are characterized by slang and thoughtless expressions. Nidderdale's confusion over "The Heathen Chinee" is indicative of his general deficiencies. He asks Felix whether he ever reads the Bible, and then tells Felix his philosophy of life with a touching but pathetic sincerity: "'I often think I shouldn't have been the first to pick up a stone and pitch it at that woman. Live and let live;—that's my motto'" (xxii).[15] Nidderdale regards the closing down of his club with equal gravity: "'If one wants to keep one's self straight, one has to work hard at it, one way or the other. I suppose it all comes from the fall of Adam'" (xcvi). Nidderdale's companion answers him with an irony Nidderdale cannot understand: "'If Solomon, Solon, and the Archbishop of Canterbury were rolled into one, they couldn't have spoken with more wisdom'" (xcvi). Nidderdale's shallow good nature enables him to regard Melmotte calmly without fear but also without moral repugnance: "'He's a wretched old reprobate, and I don't doubt but he'd skin you and me if he could make money of our carcases. But as he can't skin me, I'll have a shy at him'" (XXII). Lord Nidderdale's "speculation" is to marry Melmotte's daughter, and his easy conscience allows him to tell her comfortably, "'I was awfully spoony on you . . .'" (XXXV) and then, on the morning after she has tried to elope with Felix Carbury, to sing this song unconcernedly to Marie's father:

> "Cheer up, Sam;
> Don't let your spirits go down,
> There's many a girl that I know well,
> Is waiting for you in the town" (LIII).

When Marie is again on the marriage market, his thoughts are interpreted with a form of cliché echoed again in this novel and frequently used by Trollope to characterize arrogance or complacency: "He had expected that the plum would fall into his mouth. He would now stretch out his hand to pick it" (LVII). There is something even more dangerous, the book suggests, in Nidderdale's languor than there is in Melmotte's evil. In fact the reader feels that Melmotte's rise is but a symptom of the widespread presence of Nidderdale's kind of amorality. Dolly Longestaffe does not even have sufficient energy to pursue a lady of fortune, and his words are less inspiring and less good-natured than Nidderdale's. He, too, has dealings with Melmotte even though "'he's the biggest rogue out, you know'" (XXVIII). He tells his friends that he has discovered as "plain as a pikestaff " (LXXV) that Melmotte is a thief, but he still finds it a "horrid bore" (LXXXI) to have to drive around in hot London cabs to recover his twenty-five thousand pounds. Together with Fisker and Melmotte men such as Nidderdale and Dolly constitute a humorous yet harsh criticism of the times. They are all shallow, and whether they are cunning or indifferent, they collectively suggest the sinister reverberations of "unanimity."

Felix Carbury is a more fully revealed character than Nidderdale or Dolly, and he brings into focus more areas of the satire than they do. The pattern of language associated with him is more complex and is really a combination of the techniques used with his mother and with Melmotte—allusions and repetitions. With Melmotte, Lady Carbury, and Sir Felix we find similar reinforcements for the satiric parallels between London and Rome. We remember that before his death Melmotte "wraps his toga round him" like a rejected tribune. We find that Felix supports the philosophy of "carpe diem" (III), and the narrator makes biting criticism of Felix's selfish villainy by linking him—even facetiously—with the high-minded Roman martyr: "The death of Cato would hardly have for him persuasive charms" (LII). The narrator, in a manner reminiscent of the fanciful narrator of *Barchester Towers*, makes fun of Felix's quandary over Marie with words from *Julius Caesar* (IV.iii.218–19) (which also call to mind the London-Rome parallel): ". . . this idea of starting to New York with Melmotte's daughter immediately after he had written to Melmotte renouncing the girl, frightened him. 'There is a tide in the affairs of men, / Which taken at the flood leads on to fortune.' Sir Felix did not know these lines, but the lesson taught by them came home to him at this moment. Now was the tide in his affairs at which he might make himself, or utterly mar himself " (XLI). Here the narrator enjoys several jokes with the reader at Sir Felix's expense. Not only does Felix not know the lines, but he is utterly incapable of feeling inspired to do the brave or daring thing. The sense of the words that comes home to him, in his hangover stupor, is that he will be drowned indeed by his flood of misfortunes. The coward decides to stay home, ignore the bothersome tide, and sneak out that night for the consolation he believes he deserves. The sniveling cur of London could not be further from the mighty Caesar, and the narrator's fanciful quotation makes us wonder whether perhaps modern London is not worse even than ancient Rome. At the end of the novel when Felix does leave England, the narrator again interprets ironically: "He had, according to his own account, completely run through London life and found that it was all barren.

    'In life I've rung all changes through,
        Run every pleasure down,
    'Midst each excess of folly too,
        And lived with half the town.'

The Way We Live Now 191

Sir Felix did not exactly quote the old song, probably having never heard the words. But that was the burden of his present story" (xcvi). Felix's inarticulate villainy is amply exposed by the narrator's ironic quotations. The suggestion is that in his moments of crisis, the real rhythm of Felix's thoughts is not even worth mimicking.

Felix, like Melmotte, suggests the depravity of the times. The system of credit (familiar to all the London speculators) is explained: "'I do with as little as most fellows. I pay for nothing that I can help. I even get my hair cut on credit, and as long as it was possible I had a brougham, to save cabs'" (III). He, like the Great Financier, is overly conscious of money: "It is hard even to make love in these days without something in your purse" (III). He does not care whom he has to hurt in order to get what he wants. When Roger Carbury complains of his heartlessness Lady Carbury answers (with words that remind us of the predator Melmotte), "'You say that Felix is seeking for his—prey, and that he is to be brought here to be near—his prey'" (xv). Felix, like Nidderdale, and exactly like Ferdinand Lopez, expects immediate success with the woman he woos, and the narrator again uses a form of the insulting cliché about ripe fruit's dropping into the hand or mouth: "He paused as though he supposed that she would drop into his mouth like a cherry" (xvII). And his admiration of Marie's misguided energy betrays his cowardly villainy: "She had been able at an early age, amidst the circumstances of a very secluded life, to throw off from her altogether those scruples of honesty, those bugbears of the world, which are apt to prevent great enterprises in the minds of men" (xxix). He frequently gets as "drunk as Cloe" (LIII), thinks love talk is all "trash and twaddle" (XVII) (echoing his mother's disgust with romance), and believes that Melmotte is an "old screw" (XXIX) because he does not want Marie to marry him. It is easy for Melmotte to take advantage of him, for Felix recognizes that he is going into "deep waters" (XXIX) and likes the danger without understanding it (the narrator has fun with the "deep water" notion later with the mocking allusion to the flood of time from *Julius Caesar*). Even his suspicious and narrow mind accepts Melmotte: "As to danger;—who could think of danger in reference to money intrusted to the hands of Augustus Melmotte?" (XXXVII). Melmotte thinks of Felix as a "Lothario" (XXV), and Felix thinks of himself as a "gallant, careless, sparkling Lothario" (LXX) when he is trying to ruin Ruby Ruggles. All in all Felix is really personally more objectionable than Fisker or Melmotte, for he is spineless as well as arrogant. The narrator tells us at the beginning of the novel: "Whether Sir Felix be rich or poor, the world, evil-hearted as it is, will never think him a fine fellow" (IV). Sir Felix's vanity, like Sim Tappertit's in *Barnaby Rudge*, is punished, and the narrator uses the image of the bedaubed cock (that Crawley uses with a very different self-conscious abasement in *The Last Chronicle of Barset*) to suggest Felix's utter degradation: "The plasters were not removed from his face, so that he was still subject to that loss of self-assertion with which we are told that hitherto dominant cocks become afflicted when they have been daubed with mud" (LXXXII). The narrator encourages the reader's satisfaction over Felix's thrashing, while also inviting consideration of the dunghill on which he has been trained to crow.

Felix is a forceful part of the satire, not only because he furthers the parallel of London and Rome, or because he embodies many of the evils of speculation and fortune hunting, but because he offers a link between London and Suffolk. He is supposed to be Roger Carbury's heir and would inherit the Suffolk home of Carbury Manor. There is no better way to suggest the iniquities of the times than to imagine that Felix Carbury could invade permanently the rural simplicity of Suffolk with his degenerate London habits.

Felix admires Marie because he thinks she is unscrupulous, but she is really more highly principled than most of the characters in the novel. She, at least, does what she does for Felix out of love, whereas he knows that "Romance was not the game which he was playing" (XXIV). Even though she lets herself stand in the marriage market and eventually drives a bargain with Fisker, Marie is spirited and in the main, honest. The language associated with her belongs to misguided romance rather than to harsh satire. She is romantic and has fed her imagination with ideas of love, and the narrator uses the cliché "building castles in the air" to characterize her hopeless visions: "When alone,—and she was much alone,—she would build castles in the air, which were bright with art and love, rather than with gems and gold. The books she read, poor though they generally were, left something bright on her imagination" (XVII). She chooses a poor recipient for her affections: "Sir Felix was her idol, and she abandoned herself to its worship. But she desired that her idol should be flesh and blood, and not of wood" (XXV). Later she finds her mistake and the narrator echoes her own earlier thoughts with the word *idol*: ". . . her gold idol was made of the basest clay. . . . but even the clay had turned away from her and had refused her love!" (LXXXII). Her father says of her: "A silly little romantic baggage! She's been reading novels till she has learned to think she couldn't settle down quietly till she had run off with somebody" (LIII). And at the end the narrator uses *idol* a third time and summarizes: ". . . she had learned from novels that it would be right that she should be in love, and she had chosen Sir Felix as her idol" (XCVIII). Despite her romantic longings, Marie is usually clear-sighted. She knows Felix's weaknesses and was never ". . . so far gone in silliness as to suppose that he was a staff upon which any one might lean" (LXXXVI). Marie never mistakes the idol for a staff. She is friendly with Nidderdale, because she recognizes his good nature, even though he is "not at all an Adonis such as her imagination had painted" (LVII). She tells him frankly after her father's death, "'I have been an impostor'" (LXXXVI). Marie was brought up to be used by her father, as a "chattel for his own advantage" (LXXVII), but she knows how to assert her romantic and prosaic sides and adopts as her watchword against her father "'He may cut me into pieces'" (LXXXVI).

It is surprising that she has as much energy and as many scruples as she does, considering as the narrator explains for us the ". . . unevenness of her life, vacillating between knocks and knick-knacks, with a blow one day and a jewel the next, as the condition of things which was natural to her" (XCII). When she is first in London, and even after she has lived there for more than a year, she is willing to sacrifice herself by making a marriage that is advantageous to her father. She faces her situation after his death: "She herself, as well as all others, had known that she was to be married for her money, and now that bubble had been burst" (LXXXV). Marie puts aside romance altogether and decides to engage herself to the energetic Fisker. Her new businesslike spirit as well as her honesty are expressed in her words to him: "'I'm not going to marry a pig in a poke'" (XCVIII). The contrast between the vigorous Marie (sounding here like the admirably energetic and plain-dealing duchess of Omnium) and the spineless Felix is complete, and yet both offer commentary on speculation and false romance. At least the final statement on Marie is hopeful—she learns to take nothing at face value. R. D. McMaster explains Trollope's sympathy toward Marie thus: "Though not a feminist, he sees how Marie is moulded both by exploitation and by learning to resist exploitation and assert her own desires and her own will."[16] The pattern of language with her reveals a gradual awakening from a false romance necessary to ward off her father's cruelty to an energetic shrewdness that makes her able to defend herself against the Fiskers of the world. (There is always, of course, the vexed question with Trollope—why does he suggest that she *must* marry someone?)

Georgiana Longestaffe, another character used to satirize the marriage market, is also used to expose anti-Semitism. Georgey, like Marie, had once believed in romance and had once had her castle in the air, but (the narrator reuses the cliché slightly differently with the proud woman) ". . . Georgiana was beginning to allow her aspirations to descend. It was in that very season that she moved her castle in the air from the Upper to the Lower House" (XXXII). Georgey's aspirations "descend" all the way to the Jew Ezekiel Brehgert. The Longestaffes are horrified by his open Jewishness, although they let their daughter stay in Melmotte's house, knowing Madame Melmotte to be Jewish and suspecting that Melmotte himself is. Georgey's mother's selfish, bigoted reaction to Brehgert reminds us of Nidderdale's similar confusion of Scripture and prejudices: "'It seems to me that it can't be possible. It's unnatural. It's worse than your wife's sister. I'm sure there's something in the Bible against it. You never would read your Bible, or you wouldn't be going to do this.... An accursed race;—think of that, Georgiana;—expelled from Paradise'" (LXXVIII). Mr. Longestaffe's thoughts are similarly summarized in an unreflecting adaptation (that we see in *Barchester Towers, He Knew He Was Right*, and later again in this novel): "He told himself that he could not touch pitch and not be defiled!" (LXXXVIII). The real prejudice of the times is evident in Lady Monogram's lecture to Georgey on the necessities of selectivity. She warns that Jews and "other new people" must be avoided: "'But if they were suddenly to turn out wonderful men, and go everywhere, no doubt I should be glad to have them here. That's the way we live, and you are as well used to it as I am'" (LX). Lady Monogram's heartless social cunning is emblematic of the times, as her echo of the novel's title suggests.[17]

The Longestaffe shallowness is instrumental in criticizing both London and Suffolk life, for they reside in both places. They offer a contrast to Roger Carbury, a near neighbor, even though his own prejudices are themselves revealed in the narrator's irony. The strongest contrast to the aristocratic Longestaffes and their use of the marriage market is found in the rural Suffolk lovers, John Crumb and Ruby Ruggles. Ruby's career is a comic parallel of both Marie Melmotte's and Georgey Longestaffe's and is an expression of the solidity of Suffolk.

Ruby is like Georgey Longestaffe in that she wants to marry money and position, but she is more like Marie Melmotte because she associates wealth and position with romantic love. The narrator echoes Ruby's reflections with the castle building cliché and thus aligns the three variously hopeful young women who have apparently resorted to the same dreams and the same language. Like the other two, Ruby "... builds castles in the air, and wonders, and longs" (XVIII). She is one of those to whom the "young squire is an Apollo" (XVIII), and she wonders "Why should she ... marry ... John Crumb, before she had seen something of the beauties of the things of which she had read in the books which came in her way?" (XVIII). With her Trollope uses that image so familiar in *The Small House* and *The Last Chronicle*: "She thought, as the moths seem to think, that she might fly into the flame and not burn her wings" (XVIII). When she is with Felix she thinks, "This was a realisation of those delights of life of which she had read in the thrice-thumbed old novels which she had gotten from the little circulating library at Bungay" (XVIII). She is in danger, after she goes to London to be with Felix, of renouncing the safety and comfort of Suffolk forever: "Surely a lease of Paradise with the one, though but for one short year, would be well purchased at the price of a life with the other!" (XXXIII). After Crumb beats Felix, Ruby realizes the truth of her position and returns to Suffolk to marry Crumb. At the jovial, down-to-earth celebrations we are reminded of the pleasantries of *Barchester Towers* (and the Quiverful family) with the baker's Scriptural allusion (Psalms 127:5): "... he hoped that before long there would be any number of young Crumbs for the Bungay birds to pick up. 'Appy is the man as 'as his quiver full of 'em. ..." (XCIV). (The Suffolk baker's cheerful allusion to Psalms is echoed ironically shortly afterward in the title of the chapter concerning Felix's fate. The words "Where 'the Wild Asses Quench their Thirst'" [XCVI], also taken from Psalms [104:11], are part of a description of a world that is a paradise of plenty. Ruby settles for the homely comforts of Suffolk plenty, and Felix, her would-be ravisher, is sent from the corrupt watering hole of his club The Beargarden [the name of which itself suggests the shameful, political bear baiting that Palliser suffers in *The Prime Minister*] to the undetermined watering places of a world that is sure to be anything but paradise to one so selfish and shallow.) Ruby's return to Suffolk after her brief troubles in London, and her willingness to abandon, like Marie, false romance for respectable security, suggest that the degeneracy of the age is not complete. (Again, as with Marie, we notice that Ruby's possible unhappiness and her shamefully bleak alternatives are not Trollope's points.[18])

The Suffolk squire, Roger Carbury, tells himself that the corruption of the age is complete. Roger's staunch Conservatism acts as a foil for Melmotte's self-aggrandizement, just as his love for Hetta Carbury provides a complete contrast to the many false romances and marriage speculations. The solid squire assesses Melmotte immediately: "'I have heard of the great French swindler who has come over here, and who is buying his way into society'" (VII). He tells others, "'I look upon him as dirt in the gutter'" (XV) and thinks (as does Mr. Longestaffe) to himself, "The old-fashioned idea that touching of pitch will defile still prevailed with him" (VIII). In fact Melmotte comes to represent to him all that is evil in society; he sees him as a ". . . hollow vulgar fraud from beginning to end,—too insignificant for you and me to talk of, were it not that his position is a sign of the degeneracy of the age'" (LV).

Roger's debates with the bishop of Elmham over Melmotte and the times frequently involve the London-Rome parallel, which we have heard echoed throughout the novel in other patterns of language and in questions of conduct and standards. In keeping with the novel's balancing of satire and comedy, their argument is unresolved. In this exchange, the bishop carries the moment, and the narrator reinforces his victory, but, then, many of the activities and developments in the rest of the novel confirm Roger's skepticism if not his pessimism. The bishop begins:

"Taking society as a whole, the big and the little, the rich and the poor, I think that it grows better from year to year, and not worse. I think, too, that they who grumble at the times, as Horace did, and declare that each age is worse than its forerunner, look only at the small things beneath their eyes, and ignore the course of the world at large."

"But Roman freedom and Roman manners were going to the dogs when Horace wrote."

"But Christ was about to be born, and men were already being made fit by wider intelligence for Christ's teaching. And as for freedom, has not freedom grown, almost every year, from that to this?"

"In Rome they were worshipping just such men as this Melmotte. Do you remember the man who sat upon the seats of the knights and scoured the Via Sacra with his toga, though he had been scourged from pillar to post for his villainies? I always think of that man when I hear Melmotte's name mentioned. Hoc, hoc, tribuno militum! Is this man to be Conservative member for Westminster?" (LV).

The reader may be left to puzzle over the extent of the corruption in society, but here the narrator follows up the bishop's hopeful words with this shrewd assessment of Roger's bitterness: "The Bishop was not hopelessly in love with a young lady, and was therefore less inclined to take a melancholy view of things in general than Roger Carbury" (LV). (*Is* the narrator suggesting that all who share Roger's kind of pessimism are also responding to some private pain rather than to larger, perhaps promising, impersonal truths?)

Roger's genuine, hopeless love for Hetta offers a contrast to Marie's, Georgey's, and even Ruby's romantic imaginings: "The man had no poetry about him. He did not even care for romance" (VIII). But although Roger's love may be mature and sincere, it can also be wrongheaded. He begins to glory in his misery and becomes at first self-righteous and then pathetically self-abnegating. Roger's uses of Scripture and cliché characterize his thoughts. When he doubts the worth of his best friend (also his rival), the narrator conveys Roger's adaptation of Matthew 7:26: "What but a sham could be a man who consented to pretend to sit as one of a Board of Directors to manage an enormous enterprise with such colleagues as Lord Alfred Grendall and Sir Felix Carbury, under the absolute control of such a one as Mr. Augustus Melmotte? Was not this building a house upon the sand with a vengeance?" (XIV). He then transfers his fear of Melmotte and Paul to Hetta herself, and the narrator interprets: "Would not the touch of pitch at last defile her?" (XIV). Many of Roger's thoughts are also summarized in old if not easy expressions. He complains to Hetta (borrowing lines we remember Madeline Neroni's singing to Mr. Slope in *Barchester Towers*): "'It used to be the way—to be off with your old love before you are on with the new; . . .'" (LXXII). Of Paul he says to her: "'He owed it to me not to take the cup of water from my lips'" (LXXII). He perverts the spirit of Luke 6:29 to justify to himself his resistance to the rampant corruption and thievery around him: "If you pardon all the evil done to you, you encourage others to do you evil! If you give your cloak to him who steals your coat, how long will it be before your shirt and trousers will go also?" (VIII). Toward the end of *The Way We Live Now,* when he is conquered by his better nature, he is more temperate in his words, but even here he refuses to be responsible for or responsive to those not of his own way of thinking: "As to giving his coat to the thief who had taken his cloak,—he told himself that were he and others to be guided by that precept honest industry would go naked in order that vice and idleness might be comfortably clothed" (C). The bishop of Elmham steps in again at the end to restrain Roger from any mistaken excess of wrongly conceived Christian charity. Roger declares that he will settle his property on Hetta's child, and the wise bishop (how conspicuously thoughtful and well-read he is next to the supposedly literary Lady Carbury!) uses *Lear* to warn him: "'There are not, perhaps, many fathers who have Regans and Gonerils for their daughters;—but there are very many who may take a lesson from the folly of the old king. "Thou hadst little wit in thy bald crown," the fool said to him, "when thou gav'st thy golden one away." The world, I take it, thinks that the fool was right'" (C). Roger is thus forced to reconcile himself to his lot without the luxury of turning to poetic sacrifices that are, really, out of harmony with his prosaic and sturdy soul. Perverse Scripture and self-pitying clichés are thus righted by appropriate Shakespearean analogy.

Paul and Hetta, for whom Roger sacrifices so much, are the palest people in the book, but their story, like Grace Crawley's and Major Grantly's in *The Last Chronicle,* does offer some insight into different parts of the satire. Montague's position brings into question speculation, the nature of romance, and the English response to Americans. Hetta is an insipid creature whose only claims to the reader's sympathy are that she opposes her mother and reads Dante (XXXIX). The narrator makes Paul more interesting by using a few playful allusions and comments. The narrator alludes to Thomas Haliburton's novel when he says that Paul left his money in California with his uncle, ". . . accepting with much dissatisfaction an assurance from his uncle that an income amounting to ten per cent upon his capital should be remitted to him with the regularity of clockwork. The clock alluded to must have been one of Sam Slick's. It had gone very badly" (VI). The fanciful narrator (evidently bent on enlivening Paul's predictably dull words) describes, with an adaptation of Hamlet's "fool me to the top of my bent" and a reference to the proverbial sword of Damocles, Paul's relationship with Mrs. Hurtle: "Paul was flattered to the top of his bent; and, though the sword was hanging over his head, though he knew that the sword must fall,—must partly fall that very night,—still he enjoyed it" (XXVII). The narrator pretends that Paul forms an unconscious echo of the bitter words Roger uses to Hetta regarding him: "He was off with one love, and now he thought that he might be on with the other" (LXVI). There are no provocative disjunctions between intellect and allusion to explore with Paul or Hetta; the narrator clearly embroiders Paul's language because otherwise it would bore us entirely (perhaps the narrator's imagined need to entertain is as much a comment on the reader as on Paul). Paul's and Hetta's general dullness remind us of Trollope's own assessment of the novel: "The interest of the story lies among the wicked and foolish people,—with Melmotte and his daughter, with Dolly and his family, with the American woman, Mrs. Hurtle, and with John Crumb and the girl of his heart. But Roger Carbury, Paul Montague, and Henrietta Carbury are uninteresting" (XX).

Through Mrs. Hurtle the narrator comments on anti-American feeling (complementing remarks already made on Fisker) and criticizes English insularity and xenophobia. With her Roger Carbury shows his prejudice, as the narrator relates: "It may, perhaps, be confessed that he was prejudiced against all Americans, looking upon Washington much as he did upon Jack Cade or Wat Tyler; and he pictured to himself all American women as being loud, masculine, and atheistical" (LXXXVII).

If Mrs. Hurtle were another Wallachia Petrie, Roger might have reason to complain, but she is, as the narrator is careful to show, a wild, but generous woman "voluptuous without the aid of artifice."[19] The narrator himself says: "I think Mrs. Pipkin was right, and that Mrs. Hurtle, with all her faults, was a good-natured woman" (XCVII). Mrs. Hurtle's admiration of Melmotte indicates the dangerous part of her nature—her enthusiasm is reckless. She echoes the novel's other reference to Napoleon when she praises Melmotte: "'They tell me that he holds the world of commerce in his right hand. What power;—what grandeur!'" And, she continues, "'Such a man rises above honesty . . . as a great general rises above humanity when he sacrifices an army to conquer a nation. Such greatness is incompatible with small scruples. A pigmy man is stopped by a little ditch, but a giant stalks over the rivers. . . . Of course such a man will be abused. People have said that Napoleon was a coward, and Washington a traitor'" (XXVI). Her anticipation of Roger's words of condemnation (fearing that all Americans are traitors like Washington) is amusing, but her zeal is frightening. Since Melmotte can fool someone as sharp-sighted as Mrs. Hurtle, his image is powerful indeed. The underlying suggestion is that Melmotte appeals to the savagery in Mrs. Hurtle just as he appeals to the unscrupulousness in the polished Londoners. When she is angry, it is "as a lioness who had lost her cub" (XXVII); fellow travelers think of her as "a queer card" who has "a bit of the wild cat in her breeding" (XXXVIII). The image is repeated in Paul's thoughts—"If he meant to reject the lady finally on the score of her being a wild cat, he must tell her so"—and he acknowledges that ". . . he had submitted to be loved by a wild cat" (XXXVIII). Later, when again trying to break away from her he contemplates his difficulties: "But having his own subject before him, with all its dangers, the wild-cat's claws, and possible fate of the gentleman in Oregon, he could not talk freely on the subjects which she introduced. . ." (XLII). She urges Paul to stay with Melmotte, saying that English society is becoming effete but that "Civilization was becoming effete, or at any rate men were, in the time of the great painters; but

Savonarola and Galileo were individuals" (XLII). She tells most about herself in her identification with Medea, for we are reminded of the narrator's using both the bloodthirsty and the magical Medea with Melmotte: "'Medea did not weep when she was introduced to Creusa.' 'Women are not all Medeas,' he replied. 'There's a dash of the savage princess about most of them'" (XXVII). The narrator later adds: "She was a witch of a woman, and, as like most witches she could be terrible, so like most witches she could charm" (XLII).

Occasionally Mrs. Hurtle is too violent even for the sympathetic reader; she reacts to Paul's words at Lowestoffe: "Then she gave way to a flood of tears, and at last lay rolling upon the floor" (XLVII). We are reminded of Lady Laura in *Phineas Redux*, "crouching" in her agony when she hears of Phineas's imprisonment, and are chilled equally by the exaggerations. Similarly, too, we are reconciled to Mrs. Hurtle just as we are to Lady Laura, through her farewell to her lover: "'Paul, I have loved you, and do love you,—oh, with my very heart of hearts.' So speaking she threw herself into his arms and covered his face with kisses. 'For one moment you shall not banish me. For one short minute I will be here. Oh, Paul, my love;—my love!'" (XCVII). For both women, one with the "volcanic" nature, the other with the spirit of the "wild cat," the narrator encourages admiration. Mrs. Hurtle's thoughts of Paul are as energetic though not as literary as Lady Laura's in "'I Hate Her'": ". . . should she succumb and be trodden on like a worm?" Was Paul to have a "good time" and "roam away like a bee, while she was so dreadfully scorched, so mutilated and punished!" (LI). Her reactions are often savage, yet we sympathize with her apparent helplessness before the resolute but colorless Paul: "A pistol or a horsewhip, a violent seizing by the neck, with sharp taunts and bitter-ringing words, would have made the fitting revenge" (XC). She is contemptuous even in her love for him: "How weak he was . . . how swathed and swaddled by scruples and prejudices" (XCVII). And yet the final image she uses to herself is not harsh: "He could look about for a fresh flower and boldly seek his honey; whereas she could only sit and mourn for the sweets of which she had been rifled" (XCVII). Mrs. Hurtle is an interesting character because the narrator keeps the images of rifled flower and wild cat consistent with her dual role of romantic and adventurer. Her genuine energy and real heart are foils for English complacency and heartlessness.

Throughout *The Way We Live Now,* with the characters and with the general narrative, the narrator is a master at balancing comedy and satire through ingenious repetitions, echoes, and parallels. Look at the way the narrator's elaborate, apparently gratuitous, remark on the jilt actually connects and echoes numerous related patterns of the novel. In this aside (but one of many) the narrator repeats the title of the novel and then quotes from Milton and Virgil to satirize the unscrupulous grasping of the marriage market: "There is no duty more certain or fixed in the world than that which calls upon a brother to defend his sister from ill-usage; but, at the same time, in the way we live now, no duty is more difficult, and we may say generally more indistinct." He continues the discussion with a favorite quotation from "Lycidas": "It is her purpose again to —'trick her beams, and with new-spangled ore / Flame in the forehead of the morning sky.'" This resilient and heartless female, the narrator assures us, will be able to use "Uno avulso non deficit alter"[20] as her motto (LXX). The imagined brother's unwillingness to do anything about the misconduct toward his sister is typical of the apathy and irresponsibility of the society the narrator has exposed throughout. The use of the title (also mouthed by Lady Monogram about the mistreatment of Jews) suggests that the phrase itself has become a kind of verbal shrug of the shoulders, a glib formula that accounts for and excuses all manner of evil. The ready phrase is also a reminder of Melmotte's repeated "unanimity." The lines from "Lycidas" offer a touch of false elegance to the actual callous opportunism. The quotation is an ironic reminder of the young woman's desperate scrounging artfully concealed as romance. The fanciful allusion is also a reminder of other times (as with Felix, Melmotte, and Paul) when the narrator embroiders a plain or sordid thought with literature. And finally, the adaptation of

Virgil's Latin recalls simultaneously several elements in the novel: Roger Carbury's use of Horace to condemn the times, a corrupt editor's use of a Latin motto to disguise his puffing and lying or to obscure the facts in a case (X, XXX), and, of course, the novel's extended question about the appropriateness of the parallel between London and Rome. The entire aside has sinister significance if we recognize in the conveniently baffled brother and the heartless, scheming sister an articulate, willful degeneracy, but the aside also has light charm if we see it as part of the ironic narrator's playful exaggerations. The narrator's intricate, perhaps ambiguous, repetitions suggest the interrelatedness of the characters and the moral complexity of their situations.

Other briefer comments from the narrator may sound even more playful than this one on the jilt, and yet similarly echo the novel's serious concerns. For example, when Georgey Longestaffe argues with Lady Monogram over Brehgert and the Melmotte party, Sir Damask thinks, "'They may fight it out between them now like the Kilkenny cats'" (LXV). (The allusion to the popular limerick is comic, but it may also serve as a reminder of the narrator's gruesome use of Medea when we recall how the two rival cats ripped each other to shreds. The husband's apparent lightness sounds like the callousness we expect from scoundrels such as Felix or Dolly.) Similarly, when word of Melmotte's possible ruin spreads, the narrator summarizes the public's heartless glee thus: "It was only hoped that the fraud might be great and horrible enough" (LXII). At another time, Mr. Squercum, Dolly Longestaffe's outspoken lawyer, is summarized by the narrator in a rapid string of clichés that reflects the lazy aristocrat's perfunctory, bored acknowledgment of his lawyer's vulgar tenacity: ". . . Squercum was a pest and a musquito, a running sore and a skeleton in the cupboard" (LVIII). At Melmotte's dinner for the emperor, the narrator calls the numerous vacancies "Banquo's seats" (LIX)—and the image of them haunts Melmotte all evening (and warns him to begin thinking of suicide). Throughout the novel, whether using Lady Pomona to expose anti-Semitism, or Father

Barham's annoying repetitions of "sow the seed or plough the ground" (XVI twice; XIX) to suggest anti-Catholicism, the narrator keeps the reader amused but critical.

The Way We Live Now is Trollope's masterpiece. He uses understatement and overstatement, irony and satire, to make the reader assess the evils of the time and the people who live with them. The powerful images and repeated phrases, many of them offered by the narrator, show that no one is exempt from the influence of the tainted "word." A characteristic, Trollopian blend of comedy and criticism encourages us to laugh at the characters' motto "gold, and grandeur, pomatum, powder and pride" (XXXII) while also reflecting on our own sympathy for the gun-toting Mrs. Hurtle. After all, the novel suggests, readers eager primarily for dash, color, and passion will spawn the literary Lady Carburys of life.

In *The Way We Live Now* there is no sentimental figure like Septimus Harding or intriguing woman like Madame Goesler on whom the reader focuses attention. No single pattern of repetitions or allusions controls the novel; no single character absorbs warmest sympathy or harshest criticism.[21] Instead Trollope's most powerful novel makes a full sweep of English society, offering the internal rhythms and external portraits of singularly unlovable people. Trollope's apparent attack is really a coolheaded, evenhanded treatment of society's fevered pursuit of wealth, status, amusement, and (most ironically) security. This society has enduring fascination perhaps because readers appreciate in the echoic interplay of London and Suffolk, and England and America, people whose self-deceptions are repeated, even yet, in *the way we live now*.

Conclusion

In an article identifying one of Trollope's frequently used quotations, N. John Hall remarks: "Anthony Trollope was not a man who hesitated to repeat his favourite themes, situations, formulas. He got good mileage out of certain pet lines of poetry...."[1] Certainly Trollope loved to repeat some phrases and images: a lover as a Lothario; the moth as attracted to the flame of a candle; the world as one's oyster; getting into a boat together; "The lovely Thais sits beside thee, / Take the goods the gods provide thee"; "It's good to be merry and wise, / It's good to be honest and true"; reaching for the top brick of the chimney. In the best novels Trollope deliberately uses these apparently jaded expressions: through parallels and echoes he transforms the commonplace into the emblematic. He uses (paradoxically) favorite allusions and common expressions to invigorate and to illuminate.

The most allusive, entertaining, repetitive, and prominent character in the fiction as a whole is Trollope's own narrator. He is responsible for most of the allusions and word games in *Barchester Towers,* and though his playful speaking role diminishes in the later novels, it is still he who summarizes and interprets many of the characters' thoughts with allusions and stock expressions. As the chapters of this study show, Trollope uses the narrator to blur the borders between transcribed internal monologue and re-created, summarized internal monologue. The most effective repetitions occur when the narrator echoes words the character himself or herself has actually spoken or when the narrator uses expressions we can easily imagine the characters' using. Though he actively directs the reader's responses, the narrator-character often seems merely to reinforce what the characters have actually said (or shown about) themselves. Trollope's control of tonal register enables him to sustain the separate voices of the characters and the

Conclusion 207

narrator while making a whole novel resonate with multiple-level repetitions. He masters pitch, volume, and echo.

Trollope created meaningful repetitions within single novels (as the preceding chapters show) and from one novel to another. Shared allusions or references often suggest important parallels. Some of these allusions and repetitions are comic; some are serious. For example, Trollope's references to Byron are almost always playful. He cites Byron when he wants to ridicule self-indulgent sentimentality, misanthropy, and romantic excess.[2] We know just how Trollope means for us to respond to Ayala Dormer (*Ayala's Angel*); Lucy Toogood, Mrs. Dobbs Broughton, and Conway Dalrymple (all in *The Last Chronicle of Barset*); Lady Carbury (*The Way We Live Now*); Lizzie Eustace (*The Eustace Diamonds, Phineas Redux, The Prime Minister*); and Ferdinand Lopez (*The Prime Minister*) when Byron is alluded to or quoted by them. Each person is different, but the use of Byron encourages us to see their similar misguidedness. Allusion to Byron becomes a continuing joke to the initiated Trollope reader.

Some favorite expressions may be comic in one place and ominously ironic in another. When Trollope refers to Charybdis and Scylla in *Barchester Towers* and *He Knew He Was Right*, we laugh; in *The Way We Live Now* we recognize that in using the reference, the narrator is imitating the jauntiness Melmotte himself assumes shortly before he commits suicide. Similarly, Trollope refers to Medea in bouncing, mock-heroic passages of *Barchester Towers* and *He Knew He Was Right* and with chilling detachment to suggest how Melmotte beats his daughter in *The Way We Live Now*. The comic parts of *Barchester Towers* and the Heavitree sections of *He Knew He Was Right* provide revealing contrast for the incisive, somber irony of *The Way We Live Now*.

Even a commonplace Latin tag such as "Ruat caelum, fiat justitia" is invigorated both by its immediate context and surrounding patterns and by the (initiated) reader's remembrance of its importance with other troubled characters. At their crucial moments, three of Trollope's most careful psychological "studies" summarize their thoughts with the tag. Crawley, Trevelyan, and Palliser show themselves in crises to be similarly stubborn, powerful, self-conscious, and misguided, and the Latin tag reminds us to compare them—as Trollope had obviously done in his own mind.

Both the Bible and Shakespeare are used in all of the novels of this study—suggesting parallels in the writing and the writer over a twenty-year period. It is delightful to find, for example, the colorful Madeline Neroni in *Barchester Towers* in 1857 and the equally colorful and more fully explored duchess of Omnium in *The Prime Minister* in 1876 each quoting Shakespeare with telling appropriateness. Trollope encourages us to see that the shrewd vamp and the frustrated prime minister's wife are indeed sisters under their skins.

The repetitions within novels and from one novel to another are legion. They are not all artistic or subtle or revealing, but in the best novels, Trollope uses them superbly. The Latin tags, Biblical echoes, common expressions, and numerous literary allusions prompt the reader's assessment of individuals, themes, whole novels, series, and even groups of supposedly unrelated novels. The variety of ways in which Trollope used works of literature and common images and phrases proves that he was not, as Clark suggested, merely "spontaneously reminded of his reading as he wrote."[3] Instead, as he puzzled out the details of internal monologues and scenes,[4] he relied on many of his favorite allusions and expressions to define and symbolize the characters' similar thoughts and difficulties. Trollope did not have George Eliot's sensitive intellect, or Thackeray's graceful balance, or Dickens's intensity, but he mastered a combination of rhythmic and structural repetitions that makes his characters engaging and his conversational voice irresistible.

Notes

INTRODUCTION

1. *Fiction and Repetition: Seven English Novels* (Cambridge: Harvard University Press, 1982), p. 2.
2. For a discussion of each of these novelists, see Michael Wheeler, *The Art of Allusion in Victorian Fiction* (London: The Macmillan Press Ltd., 1979).
3. Herman Meyer, *The Poetics of Quotation in the European Novel*, trans. Theodore and Yetta Ziolkowski (Princeton, N.J.: Princeton University Press, 1968).
4. Studies of Trollope's library (the catalogue of which is in the Forster Collection of the Victoria and Albert Museum): Lance O. Tingay, "Trollope's Library," *N&Q*, 195 (October 1950), 476–78; Andrew Wright, "Anthony Trollope as a Reader" in *Two English Novelists: Aphra Behn and Anthony Trollope* (University of California: William Andrews Clark Memorial Library, 1975), pp. 45–68; Richard H. Grossman and Andrew Wright, "Anthony Trollope's Libraries," *Nineteenth-Century Fiction*, 31 (1976), 48–64.
5. N. John Hall, "An Unpublished Trollope Manuscript on a Proposed History of World Literature," *Nineteenth-Century Fiction*, 29 (1974), 206–10; Bodleian MS. Don. C. 10*, p. 96.
6. N. John Hall, "Trollope's Commonplace Book, 1835–40," *Nineteenth-Century Fiction*, 31 (1976), 15–25.
7. N. John Hall, "Trollope Reading Aloud: An Unpublished Record," *N&Q*, 220 (March 1975), 117–18.
8. The Folger Shakespeare Library in Washington, D.C., has these volumes. See Elizabeth R. Epperly, *Anthony Trollope's Notes on the Old Drama* (ELS monograph series, University of Victoria, 1988).
9. For Trollope's uses of Dickens, see Ernest Boll, "The Infusions of Dickens in Trollope," *Trollopian*, 1 (September 1946), 11–24; for a catalogue of Trollope's uses of Shakespeare, see William Coyle, "Trollope and the Bi-Columned Shakespeare," *Nineteenth-Century Fiction*, 6 (1951), 33–46.
10. *The Language and Style of Anthony Trollope* (London: André Deutsch, 1975), pp. 143–45.
11. See Robert Tracy, "*Lana Medicata Fuco*: Trollope's Classicism" in *Trollope Centenary Essays*, ed. John Halperin (New York: St. Martin's Press, 1982), pp. 1–23.
12. Carmela Perri, "On Alluding," *Poetics* 7 (1978), 301.
13. "The Poetics of Literary Allusion," *PTL: A Journal for Descriptive Poetics and Theory of Literature* 1 (1976), 107. For an ingenious, but to me unconvincing, definition of allusion as separate from reference, see J. H. Coombs, "Allusion Defined and Explained," *Poetics* 13 (1984), 475–88.

14. Wheeler, *The Art of Allusion*, p. 11.
15. Ben-Porat, "The Poetics of Literary Allusion," p. 114.
16. By "tags" I mean both familiar Latin quotations (which could also be called clichés) and repeated, identifying expressions such as Grantly's "good heavens!"
17. "*The Last Chronicle of Barset*: Trollope's Comic Techniques" in *The Classic British Novel*, ed. Howard M. Harper, Jr., and Charles Edge (Athens, University of Georgia Press, 1972), pp. 126–27.
18. Roland Barthes, "Texte /Theorie du/" in *Encyclopedia Universalis*, vol. xv (Paris: 1973) quoted by Michel Gresset in *Intertextuality in Faulkner*, ed. by Michel Gresset and Noel Polk (University: Mississippi University Press, 1985), p. 4.
19. Ben-Porat, "The Poetics of Literary Allusion," 127.
20. *Trollope: A Commentary* (1945; rpt. London: Oxford University Press, 1961), p. 375.
21. "Anthony Trollope, or The Man with No Style at All," *Victorian Newsletter*, 35 (1969), 11.
22. *Trollope's Palliser Novels: Theme and Pattern* (London: Macmillan, 1978), pp. 3–19.
23. Perri, "On Alluding," 305.
24. I adopt three of Eric Partridge's four categories in my use of the term *cliché*: "1. Idioms that have become clichés, 2. Other hackneyed phrases, 3. Stock phrases and familiar quotations from foreign languages." *A Dictionary of Clichés* (London: Routledge & Kegan Paul Ltd., 1966), p. 4.
25. This is what C. P. Snow calls the "psychological stream": "The Psychological Stream," in *On the Novel: A Present for Walter Allen on His 60th Birthday from His Friends and Colleagues*, ed. B. S. Benedikz (London: Dent, 1971), pp. 15–16; and what W. J. Overton calls "mental rhythms": "Trollope: An Interior View," *Modern Language Review*, 71 (July 1976), 489.
26. "Trollope's *Orley Farm*: Artistry Manqué," in *From Jane Austen to Joseph Conrad*, eds. Robert C. Rathburn and Martin Steinmann, Jr. (Minneapolis: University of Minnesota Press, 1958), p. 155.
27. See Marlene Springer, *Hardy's Use of Allusion* (Lawrence: University Press of Kansas, 1983), especially pp. 1–17.
28. See this excellent study: Jean M. Wyatt, "*Mrs. Dalloway*: Literary Allusion as Structural Metaphor," *PMLA* 88 (1973), 440–51.
29. *Literary Quotation and Allusion* (Port Washington, N.Y.: Kennikat Press, 1933), p. 9.
30. Clark, *The Language and Style of Anthony Trollope*, p. 142.
31. "Afterword to the Second Edition" (London: Routledge & Kegan Paul, 1984), 273.

CHAPTER 1

1. Helen Garlinghouse King has edited these seven letters and they appear in "Trollope's Letters to the *Examiner*," *Princeton University Library Chronicle*, 26 (1965), 71–101.

Notes 211

2. This is the play that thrifty Trollope later used as the basis for *Can You Forgive Her?*
3. There may be a case for *The Kellys* as a typical Trollope novel; see Robert A. Donovan, "Trollope's Prentice Work," *Modern Philology*, 53 (1956), 179.
4. See Ralph Arnold's entertaining book *The Whiston Matter* (London: Rupert Hart-Davis, 1961).
5. See *An Autobiography*, V; Lionel Stevenson, "Dickens and the Origin of *The Warden*," *Trollopian*, II (1947), 83–90; G. F. A. Best, "The Road to Hiram's Hospital," *Victorian Studies*, 5 (1961), 135–50.
6. The divisions are described in M. S. Bankert, "Newman in the Shadow of Barchester Towers," *Renascence*, 20 (1968), 153–61.
7. R. W. Daniel, Afterword to Signet Edition of *Barchester Towers*, 1963, p. 530.
8. Murray Kreiger's perceptive discussion of *Barchester Towers* argues that no one poses a real threat to the values of Barsetshire—not the Proudies nor Slope nor the Stanhopes. "Barchester Towers" in *The Classic Vision: The Retreat from Extremity in Modern Literature* (Baltimore: The Johns Hopkins University Press, 1971), pp. 243–52.
9. See N. John Hall, "Anthony Trollope: Honest and True," *N&Q* 217 (November 1972), 416–17.
10. For a discussion of the dramatic elements of this scene and of the influence of drama on Trollope's novels in general, see Geoffrey Harvey, *The Art of Anthony Trollope* (New York: St. Martin's Press, 1980).
11. I. Ekeblad, "Anthony Trollope's Copy of the 1647 Beaumont and Fletcher Folio," *N&Q* CCIV (1959), 153–54.
12. John W. Clark notes in *The Language and Style of Anthony Trollope*, p. 143, that Trollope "must have consciously and designedly conceived the idea of filling—indeed, over-filling—a novel with literary references...."
13. Trollope read Beaumont and Fletcher's play *Bonduca* on 29 January 1851 (Ekeblad, "Anthony Trollope's Copy," 154) and was fond enough of it to reread it and comment on it on 9 June 1874. See Elizabeth R. Epperly, *Anthony Trollope's Notes on the Old Drama*, pp. 44, 136.
14. R. W. Daniel's comments are typical: "The inexperienced hand shows itself also in the irrelevancies of the eight chapters, XXXV–XLII, taken up with the Ullathorne fete, and in the imperfect connection between the love interest and the struggle that is the dominant concern of the novel." Afterword, p. 532.
15. For a discussion of this reversal of the usual comic technique of the triumph of the young over the old, see James R. Kincaid, *The Novels of Anthony Trollope* (Oxford: Clarendon Press, 1977), pp. 101–103.
16. For an interesting study of Trollope and Thackeray, see R. H. Super, "Trollope's *Vanity Fair*," *Journal of Narrative Technique*, 9 (Winter 1979), 12–20.
17. The lines are also found in Thomas Tusser's *Five Hundred Points of Good Husbandry*, which Trollope had in his library.

Notes

18. I am grateful to my colleague Annette Staveley for this point.

19. Lionel Stevenson, "The Rationale of Victorian Fiction," *Nineteenth-Century Fiction*, 27 (1973), 398–99.

20. Philemon, verse 17.

21. For a discussion of the highly allusive quality of *Tristram Shandy* itself, see: Meyer, *The Poetics of Quotation in the European Novel*, pp. 72–93.

22. Clark, *The Language and Style of Anthony Trollope*, p. 170, believes that Trollope would have to have looked up the chapter to quote it so accurately and to discuss it so thoroughly. This helps us to believe that Trollope had the companion chapter fresh in his mind also when he quoted from II Timothy. Trollope's readers may also have remembered the misogynist Joe Scott in Charlotte Brontë's *Shirley* (xviii), who quoted I Timothy to silence Shirley and Caroline.

23. Gamaliel, a Pharisee, was St. Paul's tutor. Acts 22:3.

24. For an interesting suggestion about the inspiration for Madeline, see Anthony Laude, "*Barchester Towers*: A New Source?" *N&Q* 23 (February 1976), 59–61.

25. The *OED* cites only two works in its definition of the archaic *boody*—*Rachel Ray* and *Barchester Towers*. Anthony Laude identifies it as French (from *bouder*, to sulk) and says that it is "pure Thackeray": "*Barchester Towers*: A New Source?" *N&Q* 23 (February 1976), 60.

26. Robert Bernard Martin, *Enter Rumour: Four Early Victorian Scandals* (London: Faber and Faber, 1962), pp. 83–134.

27. Chapter LXVII.

28. "*Barchester Towers* and the Nature of Conservative Comedy," *Journal of English Literary History*, 37 (1970), 612.

29. Chapter LXVII.

30. Perhaps from Shakespeare's *The Rape of Lucrece*.

31. For an excellent discussion of Harding's importance and quiet centrality, see Kincaid, *The Novels of Anthony Trollope*, pp. 103–13.

32. "Janet's Repentance," chapter xix.

33. Queen Victoria recommended it to the Princess Royal, who remarked on it: "I like Barchester Towers very much, it makes one laugh till one cries it is so very true. . . ." Victoria, Queen of Great Britain and Ireland, *Dearest Child*, ed. Roger Fulford (London: Evans Brothers, 1964), p. 151.

CHAPTER 2

1. The last was *The Two Heroines of Plumplington*, which was to have appeared in the Christmas number of *Good Words* in 1882. Trollope died on 6 December 1882, and the story (until the 1950s) was printed only in pirated editions in New York. (London: André Deutsch, 1953).

2. "The best novel I ever wrote was The Last Chronicle of Barset." *Letters*, p. 613. Trollope immediately recognized the quality of the book. In 1869 he tried (unsuccessfully) to dramatize it under the title *Did He Steal It?*

Notes 213

3. For "honesty" see Jerome Thale, "The Problem of Structure in Trollope," *Nineteenth-Century Fiction*, 15 (1960), 147–57.

4. In *On the Novel*, pp. 15–16.

5. In "*The Last Chronicle of Barset*: Trollope's Comic Techniques," 127.

6. With the exception of the Greek Testament, Trollope had all of these books in his library in 1874. He began his *Commentaries of Caesar* in 1870 and his *Life of Cicero* in 1877.

7. Peter Fairclough, in his notes to the Penguin edition, p. 865, tells us that this was a popular traditional ballad existing in several versions.

8. *The Tragedies of Aeschylus*, trans. R. Potter (Oxford: A. J. Valpy, 1808), p. 109.

9. Proverbs 31:10–12, 18–19.

10. *The Poetical Works of John Milton*, ed. Henry John Todd (London: 1801), IV, 364.

11. *The Mirror in the Roadway* (London: Hamish Hamilton, 1957), p. 180.

12. For an interesting assessment of Toogood's clichés and of Crawley's response, see Norman Page, "Trollope's Conversational Mode," *English Studies in Africa* 15 (1972), 34–35.

13. Intro. to *The Last Chronicle of Barset* (London: Pan Books, 1967), p. 17.

14. Trollope thought this such an important part of the story that he makes it the feature line in his own play *Did He Steal It?* and ends with Hoggett's saying, "It's dogged as done it all."

15. *The Works of Lord Byron: With His Letters and Journals, and His Life*, ed. Thomas Moore (London: John Murray, 1832), X, 241–42.

16. Unsigned notice, *Athenaeum*, 3 August 1867, Smalley, p. 302.

17. The *OED* defines "Brummagem" as a corruption of *Birmingham*. It can mean either lower-class or counterfeit.

18. Juliet McMaster, *Trollope's Palliser Novels: Theme and Pattern* (London: Macmillan, 1978), pp. 3–19.

19. *Twelfth Night* (II.v.168).

20. "Out of this nettle danger we pluck this flower safety" (II.iii.9–10).

21. Trollope even received letters begging him to let Lily and Johnny get married. *An Autobiography*, x.

22. Introduction to *The Last Chronicle of Barset* (Hammondsworth: The Penguin English Library, 1967), p. 16.

23. Mrs. Dale is understandably surprised by Lily's use of the word. According to the *OED* it had just come into existence in 1861 with the American Civil War and had become anglicized in 1864. When Trollope was writing the novel in 1866 the word still would have been considered "fast." Lily makes it particularly daring because she uses it in reference to Major Grantly—thus making a double play on the military term.

24. For Trollope's own scathing satire of Lily and particularly on her initials "O.M." see the little story "Never, Never—Never, Never," first published in Susan Hale's magazine in Boston called *Sheets for the Cradle* in 1875. Privately printed by Lance O. Tingay in 1952.

25. Matthew 7:16: "Ye shall know them by their fruits. Do men gather grapes of thorns, or figs of thistles?"
26. Trollope visited the United States at the beginning of the war in 1861. In 1862 he published his journal, *North America*, giving his views on the future of America.
27. "Trollope: An Interior View," *Modern Language Review*, 71 (July 1976), 489.
28. P. T. Marsh, *The Victorian Church in Decline* (London: Routledge & Kegan Paul, 1969), p. 11.
29. *As You Like It* (II.vii.158).
30. From *Ten Thousand a Year* and *Pickwick Papers*.
31. From Canning's "Friend of Humanity."

CHAPTER 3

1. For appreciations of the experimental nature of this novel and/or for the power of the portrait of Trevelyan, see especially T. H. S. Escott, *Anthony Trollope: His Work, Associates, and Literary Originals* (London: John Lane, 1913), pp. 292–93; Sadleir, *Trollope: A Commentary*, 1945; rpt. (London: Oxford University Press, 1961), pp. 393–94; Hugh Walpole, *Anthony Trollope* (London: Macmillan and Company, 1928), p. 138; A. O. J. Cockshut, *Anthony Trollope: A Critical Study* (London: Collins, 1955), p. 197; Polhemus, *The Changing World of Anthony Trollope* (Berkeley and Los Angeles: University of California Press, 1968), p. 163; Ruth apRoberts, *Trollope: Artist and Moralist* (London: Chatto & Windus, 1971), p. 103; Peter K. Garrett, *The Victorian Multiplot Novel* (New Haven and London: Yale University Press, 1980), pp. 180–221; Simon Gatrell, "Jealousy, Mastery, Love and Madness: A Brief Reading of *He Knew He Was Right*," in *Anthony Trollope*, ed. Tony Bareham (New York: Barnes & Noble, 1980), pp. 95–99.
2. "The man is made to be unfortunate enough, and the evil which he does is apparent. So far I did not fail, but the sympathy has not been created yet" (*An Autobiography*, XVII).
3. Christopher Herbert, "*He Knew He Was Right*, Mrs. Lynn Linton, and the Duplicities of Victorian Marriage," *Texas Studies in Literature and Language*, 25 (1983), 448–69.
4. Jane Nardin, "Tragedy, Farce, and Comedy in Trollope's *He Knew He Was Right*," *Genre*, 15 (Fall 1982), 303–13.
5. King Cophetua is referred to by Shakespeare in *Romeo and Juliet* (II.i.13) and was popularized by Tennyson in "The Beggar Maid."
6. William Coyle sees the casting of Bozzle as Iago as a weakening of the novel. "Trollope and the Bi-Columned Shakespeare," *Nineteenth-Century Fiction*, 6 (1951), 44.
7. Walpole, *Anthony Trollope*, p. 10.
8. An echo of Daniel 3:6,11,19.
9. *Hamlet* (II.ii.211).
10. In light of research on manic speech, Trollope's understanding of the "flight of ideas" and the "push of speech" is truly impressive.

Notes 215

See Marshall Durbin and Ronald L. Martin, "Speech in Mania: Syntactic Aspects," *Brain and Language*, 4 (April 1977), 208–18.

11. John W. Clark, *The Language and Style of Anthony Trollope* (London: André Deutsch, 1975), p. 183. This is the description of Polyphemus in *Aeneid* (iii). It is interesting to compare Gibson's "relationship" to Polyphemus with Crawley's.

12. II Kings 19:26: "... they were as grass of the field. . ."; Job 5:7: "Yet man is born unto trouble, as the sparks fly upward"; Matthew 6:30: "... the grass of the field, which today is, and tomorrow is cast into the oven. . ."; Aphra Behn's "Faith, sir, we are here today, and gone tomorrow" from *The Lucky Chance*, IV.

13. Gibson could have met this (now proverbial) line in either Euripides' *Fragments* or a Latin translation.

14. Trollope included Colenso in his series of articles *Clergymen of the Church of England* (x), "The Clergyman Who Subscribes for Colenso."

15. Thomas Brown, *Works* (London: 1719), IV, 113:

I do not love you Dr. Fell,
By why I cannot tell;
But this I know full well,
I do not love you, Dr. Fell.

16. Ruth apRoberts says of this "glancing reference," "... Trollope invokes the theme and center of the novel, ringed round with the many variations of the subsidiary stories." "Emily and Nora and Dorothy and Priscilla and Jemima and Carry" in *The Victorian Experience: The Novelists*, ed. Richard A. Levine (Athens, Ohio: Ohio University Press, 1976), p. 118.

17. It is such remarks that fuel the perennial debate over Trollope's quality of sympathy with women.

18. "Come Down, O Maid": "Come down, O Maid, from yonder mountain height. / . . . And come, for Love is of the valley, come, / For Love is of the valley, come thou down."

19. Lines 19–24 of "Allen-a-Dale" from *Rokeby*.

20. For some evidence of Trollope's friendly contact with the Brownings, see Michael Sadleir, *Trollope: A Commentary*, 1945; rpt. (London: Oxford University Press, 1961), pp. 194–96, and chapter IV, n. 20, in this study.

21. I Corinthians 13:1–2: "Though I speak with the tongues of men and angels, and have not charity, I am become as a sounding brass, or a tinkling cymbal. And though I have the gift of prophecy, and understand all mysteries, and all knowledge; and though I have all faith, so that I could remove mountains, and have not charity, I am nothing."

22. Trollope finished the first Phineas novel in May 1867, wrote *Linda Tressel* and *The Golden Lion of Granpere*, and started to work on *He Knew He Was Right* in November. Sadleir, *Trollope: A Commentary*, p. 409. Bodleian MS Don. C. 9, p. 191.

23. James R. Kincaid says, "the various plots give different answers to the same question." *The Novels of Anthony Trollope* (Oxford: Clarendon Press, 1977), p. 31.

24. Trollope alludes to Thackeray and his *Snob Papers* in chapter XCII: "From all which, and in accordance with the teaching which we got,—alas, now many years ago,—from a great master on the subject, we must conclude that poor, dear Mrs. Spalding was a snob."

25. "Tragedy, Farce, and Comedy," 310.

CHAPTER 4

1. *Phineas Redux* was begun on 23 October 1870 and completed on 1 April 1871, but was not published until 1873 in *The Graphic*. The book form appeared in 1874. Bodleian MS. Don. C. 9, pp. 268–69.

2. Notes by John C. Whale for the World's Classics edition (1983), II, 366, say the reference is to Horace, *Epistles*, I.viii.12. "When at Rome I love Tivoli, when there I prefer Rome."

3. Job 39:25.

4. Notes to the Oxford University Press edition (1973), p. 363, give this: "'Measures, not men': the cant of *Not men, but measures*, a sort of charm by which many people get loose from every honourable engagement. Burke, *Present Discontents*."

5. From Virgil's *Aeneid*, VI.96: "The first step to safety will appear where it is least expected, from a Grecian town." Whale's notes, II, 370.

6. Practically everyone who has written on the Palliser novels has written about the originals for Trollope's characters. I follow this same argument: J. R. Dinwiddy, "Who's Who in Trollope's Political Novels,' *Nineteenth-Century Fiction*, 22 (1967), 31–46.

7. Michael Sadleir, *Trollope: A Commentary*, 1945; rpt. (London: Oxford University Press, 1961), pp. 302–304.

8. Many of Trollope's speeches are given in Arthur Pollard, *Trollope's Political Novels* (Hull: University of Hull, 1968).

9. Book II, chapter VI.

10. One concerning the Reform Bill, given in Edinburgh on 29 October 1867, is a good example. *Times*, 30 October 1867, p. 5.

11. Pollard, *Trollope's Political Novels*, p. 7.

12. One can see the increasing importance of Disestablishment of the Irish Church in the Speeches from the Throne for the fall and winter sessions of 1866 and 1867. Hansard, *Journal of the House of Commons*, vols. 121, 12–13; 122, 5–6; 123, 4–5.

13. One wonders whether the name *Von Moltke* (Count Helmuth, 1800–1891) had become a byword for more-than-zealous cleverness. George Henry Lewes uses it in 1875 ("O Moltke of Edinburgh!") to exclaim over the low sum offered for the Australian reprints of *Middlemarch* and *Daniel Deronda*. *The George Eliot Letters*, ed. Gordon Haight (London: Oxford University Press, 1956), VI, 197.

14. Hebrews 7:11.

15. This is the last stanza of Horace's "The Apotheosis of Romulus"

in Theodore Martin's translation (which Trollope had in his library), *The Odes Epodes and Satires of Horace* (Edinburgh: Blackwood and Sons, 1870), p. 124.

16. For an interesting discussion of Trollope's attitude to the House see Morris Edmund Speare, *The Political Novel: Its Development in England and in America* (New York: Russell and Russell, 1966), pp. 185–220.

17. *Cornhill*, II (July 1860), 84–85.

18. *Letters*, p. 115.

19. E. B. Browning's letter to Isa Blagden appears in T. A. Trollope's autobiography *What I Remember* (London: Richard Bentley and Son, 1887), II, 177.

20. Trollope met the Brownings in 1857 when he made his first trip to Florence to visit his brother and mother. (Sadleir, *Trollope: A Commentary*, p. 194). Sadleir calls the A. Trollope-Browning contact a "rather combative acquaintanceship" (p. 196) even though he admits that of this first trip, "no details survive of his adventures" (p. 195). On the contrary, it seems to me that the initial encounters must have been pleasant, for Mrs. Browning records in glowing terms Trollope's two visits to her when he was again in Florence in 1860 (after she had replied to his criticism of her poem). *Letters of the Brownings to George Barrett*, ed. Paul Landis and Ronald E. Freeman (Urbana: University of Illinois Press, 1958), pp. 244, 247–48.

21. Chapman's notes, p. 364.

22. *Trollope's Palliser Novels: Theme and Pattern* (London: Macmillan, 1978), p. 72.

23. *Gyas* is probably a mistake for *Gyes*. Gyas was a companion to Aeneas, but Gyes was one of the Hundred-Handed Giants. *Lempriere's Classical Dictionary*.

24. From Horace's *Satires*, II.iv.36: "the subtle theory of flavours." Notes in World's Classics edition (1983), II, 370.

25. From Scott's *The Bride of Lammermoor*.

26. "Being in Love in *Phineas Finn/Phineas Redux*: Desire, Devotion, Consolation," *Nineteenth-Century Fiction*, 37 (December 1982), 393.

27. John C. Whale's notes (II, 378) also say that the Moabitish woman could have been suggested by the discovery of the Moabite Stone in 1868.

28. R. W. Chapman, Introduction to *Phineas Redux* (World's Classics edition, 1970), p. vi.

29. Chapman's notes, p. 363, gives Marris's translation of Horace's *Odes* (III.xi):

> Like some young filly that careers
> About the meadows free, and fears
> The touch of man, she recks not of
> A mate—as yet o'er-young for love

30. For two unsympathetic views of Madame Max, see Charles Blinderman, "The Servility of Independence: The Dark Lady in Trol-

lope," in *Images of Women in Fiction: Feminist Perspectives,* edited by Susan Cornillon (Bowling Green, Ohio: Bowling Green University Popular Press, 1971), pp. 56–67; and the particularly virulent Rebecca West, "A Nineteenth-Century Bureaucrat," in *The Court and the Castle: Some Treatments of a Recurrent Theme* (New Haven: Yale University Press, 1957), pp. 133–64; for a positive assessment, see Elizabeth R. Epperly, "From the Borderlands of Decency: Madame Max Goesler," *Victorians Institute Journal,* 15 (1987), 25–35.

CHAPTER 5

1. See particularly: Unsigned notice, *Spectator,* 22 July 1876, Smalley, p. 422; Unsigned notice, *Saturday Review,* 14 October 1876, Smalley, p. 426.
2. See *An Autobiography,* xx.
3. *Letters,* p. 693.
4. See L. S. Amery, Introduction to *The Prime Minister* (World's Classics Series, 1970), pp. xi–xii.
5. A recent article also discusses the importance of the blending of the narrator's commentary and internal discourse. See Patricia A. Vernon, "The Poor Fictionist's Conscience: Point of View in the Palliser Novels," *Victorian Newsletter* (Spring 1987), 16–20.
6. Juliet McMaster, *Trollope's Palliser Novels: Theme and Pattern* (London: Macmillan, 1978), pp. 3–19.
7. James R. Kincaid warns us against this mistake, *The Novels of Anthony Trollope* (Oxford: Clarendon Press, 1977), p. 217.
8. See C. J. Vincent, "Trollope: A Victorian Augustan," *Queen's Quarterly,* 52 (1945), 415–28.
9. See Juliet McMaster, *Trollope's Palliser Novels,* pp. 118–19, for a comment on the importance of this allusion.
10. Two articles are still helpful in understanding Trollope's political opinions: Asa Briggs, "Trollope, Bagehot, and the English Constitution," *Cambridge Journal,* 5 (1952), 327–38; W. L. Burn, "Anthony Trollope's Politics," *Nineteenth Century,* 143 (1948), 161–71.
11. See Helmut Klinger, "Varieties of Failure: The Significance of Trollope's 'The Prime Minister,'" *English Miscellany,* 23 (1972), 167–83.
12. Robert Polhemus, *The Changing World of Anthony Trollope* (Berkeley and Los Angeles: University of California Press, 1968), p. 198.
13. "Anthony Trollope: The Palliser Novels," in Robert C. Rathburn and Martin Steinmann, Jr., Eds., *From Jane Austen to Joseph Conrad* (Minneapolis: University of Minnesota Press, 1958), p. 163.
14. Juliet McMaster demonstrates that important parallels in the novel are found between Palliser and Emily and between Glencora and Lopez. *Trollope's Palliser Novels,* p. 228. My argument emphasizes the prominence of Glencora rather than Palliser.
15. Geoffrey Harvey argues convincingly that Trollope took Lopez's name from Fletcher's *Women Pleased. The Art of Anthony Trollope* (New York: St. Martin's Press, 1980), pp. 33–34. Nevertheless, my own

reading of Trollope's marginalia for this play shows that Trollope recorded the date for reading *Women Pleased* as "23 Oct. 1874" rather than as "23 March 1874" as Harvey says. (Folger Shakespeare Library Pr/2421/D8/1843 As. Col./ vol. VII, 94.) The later date does not invalidate Harvey's argument, for he says elsewhere that Trollope could have read the plays at other times not recorded, but it does suggest that the play may have shaped the writing of the novel rather than in some way immediately inspiring it. For Trollope's marginal notes on the old drama, see Elizabeth R. Epperly, *Anthony Trollope's Notes on the Old Drama* (ELS monograph series, University of Victoria, 1988). Perhaps Lopez's name also recalls Queen Elizabeth I's surgeon Roderigo Lopez, who may have served as prototype for Shylock. *DNB*, XII (1882; Rpt. 1921–22), 132–34.

CHAPTER 6

1. Bodleian MS. Don. C. 10, pp. 15–21. For an analysis of the working diary, see John A. Sutherland, "Trollope at Work on *The Way We Live Now*," *Nineteenth-Century Fiction*, 37 (December 1982), 472–93.

2. The working diaries show that originally Trollope intended Lady Carbury as the "chief character" of the novel, but half-way through he took time to reread the manuscript and make adjustments (since Melmotte had taken over the center from Lady Carbury). Interestingly, after revising the plans, Trollope wrote most quickly. For six weeks he kept up the incredible daily pace of twelve, twelve, twelve, twelve, sixteen pages, writing for five days each week. Bodleian MS. Don. C. 10, p. 20.

3. James R. Kincaid, *The Novels of Anthony Trollope* (Oxford: Clarendon Press, 1977), p. 165.

4. For an interesting discussion of closure, see Marianna Torgovnick, "Closure and Victorian Novel, 1986," *The Victorian Newsletter* (Spring 1987), 4–6.

5. *An Autobiography*, VI.

6. George Gordon, Lord Byron, *The Works of Lord Byron: With His Letters and Journals and His life*, 14 vols., ed. Thomas Moore (London: John Murray, 1832), VII, 248.

7. For a good study of Trollope and Byron, see Donald D. Stone, "Trollope, Byron, and the Conventionalities" in *The Worlds of Victorian Fiction*, ed. Jerome H. Buckley (Cambridge, Mass.: Harvard University Press, 1975), pp. 179–203.

8. Kincaid, *The Novels of Anthony Trollope*, p. 165.

9. Luke 16:9.

10. Achates was faithful friend to Aeneas.

11. Roger L. Slakey, "Melmotte's Death: A Prism of Meaning in 'The Way We Live Now,'" *Journal of English Literary History* 34 (1967), 248–59.

12. P. D. Edwards, Unpublished Doctoral Thesis (University of London, 1961), p. 364.

13. The first stanza of the famous poem begins:

Which I wish to remark,
And my language is plain,
That for ways that are dark
And for tricks that are vain,
The heathen Chinee is peculiar,
Which the same I would rise to explain.

The Complete Works of Bret Harte (London: Chatto & Windus, 1911), I, 131.

14. It is interesting to note that shortly after introducing Fisker, Trollope paused in writing the novel to compose the Christmas story *Harry Heathcote of Gangoil*. The story is about the Australian bush, and its straightforward pace and rough-and-tumble characters make it resemble Bret Harte's own Westerns.

15. John 8:7.

16. "Women in *The Way We Live Now*," *English Studies in Canada*, VII (Spring 1981), 71.

17. Ruth apRoberts says that Trollope may have taken the title of his novel from Cicero's *Sic Vivitur*. *Trollope: Artist and Moralist* (London: Chatto & Windus, 1971), p. 167.

18. For a sympathetic reading of Ruby's dilemma, see J. D. Coates, "Moral Patterns in 'The Way We Live Now,'" *Durham University Journal*, 71 (1978), 60.

19. R. D. McMaster, "Women in *The Way We Live Now*," *English Studies in Canada*, VII (Spring 1981), 72.

20. From Virgil, "On the removal of one, another is not wanting." Sutherland, "Trollope at Work," II, 492.

21. Kincaid, *The Novels of Anthony Trollope*, p. 164, calls the novel "Trollope's rendition of *Vanity Fair* thirty years afterwards."

CONCLUSION

1. "Anthony Trollope: Honest and True," *N&Q*, 217 (November 1972), 416.

2. For Trollope's early, hostile editing of his mother's rhapsodic verses on Byron, see N. John Hall's edition of *Salmagundi: Byron, Allegra, and The Trollope Family* (Pennsylvania: Beta Phi Mu, 1975).

3. *The Language and Style of Anthony Trollope* (London: André Deutsch, 1975), p. 142.

4. Anthony Trollope, "A Walk in a Wood," *Good Words*, 20 (1879), 595–600.

Works Cited

For contemporary reviews see Donald A. Smalley, *Trollope: The Critical Heritage* (London: Routledge & Kegan Paul, 1969), and David Skilton, *Trollope and His Contemporaries: A Study in the Theory and Conventions of Mid-Victorian Fiction* (London: Longman, 1972). For a useful working bibliography, see James R. Kincaid, *The Novels of Anthony Trollope* (Oxford: Clarendon Press, 1977).

Under "Trollope" I have listed only the novels and works I have quoted from or referred to directly in the text; I give the original publication date and then the other editions I have consulted. I have included here only those works of literature (by authors other than Trollope) from which I have quoted directly. I have not included standard reference works.

Aeschylus. *The Tragedies of Aeschylus*. Trans. R. Potter. Oxford: A. J. Valpy, 1808.
apRoberts, Ruth. "Anthony Trollope, or The Man with No Style at All." *Victorian Newsletter*, 35 (1969), 10–13.
——. "Emily and Nora and Dorothy and Priscilla and Jemima and Carry." *The Victorian Experience: The Novelists*. Ed. Richard A. Levine. Athens, Ohio: Ohio University Press, 1976, 87–120.
——. *Trollope: Artist and Moralist*. London: Chatto & Windus, 1971.
Arnold, Ralph Crispian Marshall. *The Whiston Matter: The Reverend Robert Whiston versus the Dean and Chapter of Rochester*. London: Rupert Hart-Davis, 1961.
Bankert, M. S. "Newman in the Shadow of Barchester Towers." *Renascence*, 20 (1968), 153–61.
Ben-Porat, Ziva. "The Poetics of Literary Allusion." *PTL: A Journal for Descriptive Poetics and Theory of Literature*, 1 (1976), 105–28.
Best, G. F. A. "The Road to Hiram's Hospital." *Victorian Studies*, 5 (1961), 135–50.
Blinderman, Charles. "The Servility of Independence: The Dark Lady in Trollope." *Images of Women in Fiction: Feminist Perspectives*. Ed. Susan Cornillon. Bowling Green, Ohio: Bowling Green Popular Press, 1971, pp. 56–67.
Bodleian MS. Don. C. 9, 10, 10*.
Boll, Ernest. "The Infusions of Dickens in Trollope." *Trollopian*, 1 (1946), 11–24.
Briggs, Asa. "Trollope, Bagehot, and the English Constitution." *Cambridge Journal*, 5 (1952), 327–38.
Brown, Thomas. *Works*. London: 1719.
Browning, Elizabeth Barrett. "A Musical Instrument." *Cornhill*, II (July 1860), 84–85.

Browning, Robert and Elizabeth Barrett. *Letters of the Brownings to George Barrett.* Ed. Paul Landis and Ronald E. Freeman. Urbana: University of Illinois Press, 1958.
Burn, W. L. "Anthony Trollope's Politics." *Nineteenth Century,* 143 (1948), 161–71.
Byron, George Gordon, Lord. *The Works of Lord Byron: With His Letters and Journals and His Life.* Ed. Thomas Moore. 14 vols. London: John Murray, 1832.
Clark, John W. *The Language and Style of Anthony Trollope.* London: André Deutsch, 1975.
Coates, J. D. "Moral Patterns in 'The Way We Live Now.'" *Durham University Journal,* 71 (1978), 55–65.
Cockshut, A. O. J. *Anthony Trollope: A Critical Study.* London: Collins, 1955.
Coombs, J. H. "Allusion Defined and Explained." *Poetics,* 13 (1984), 475–88.
Coyle, William. "Trollope and the Bi-Columned Shakespeare." *Nineteenth-Century Fiction,* 6 (1951), 33–46.
Dinwiddy, J. R. "Who's Who in Trollope's Political Novels." *Nineteenth-Century Fiction,* 22 (1967), 31–46.
Disraeli, Benjamin, Earl of Beaconsfield. *Coningsby: or The New Generation.* Vol. VIII. Bradenham Edition. London: Peter Davis, 1927.
Donovan, Robert A. "Trollope's Prentice Work." *Modern Philology,* 53 (1956), 179–86.
Durbin, Marshall and Ronald L. Martin. "Speech in Mania: Syntactic Aspects." *Brain and Language,* 4 (April 1977), 208–18.
Edwards, P. D. Unpublished Doctoral Thesis. University of London, 1961.
Ekeblad, I. "Anthony Trollope's Copy of the 1647 Beaumont and Fletcher Folio." *Notes and Queries,* 204 (1959), 153–54.
Eliot, George. *The George Eliot Letters.* Ed. Gordon Haight. London: Oxford University Press, 1956.
———. *Scenes of Clerical Life.* 2 vols. Edinburgh: William Blackwood, 1895.
Epperly, Elizabeth R. *Anthony Trollope's Notes on the Old Drama.* University of Victoria ELS monograph series, 1988.
———. "From the Borderlands of Decency: Madame Max Goesler." *Victorians Institute Journal,* 15 (1987), 25–35.
Escott, T. H. S. *Anthony Trollope: His Work, Associates, and Literary Originals.* London: John Lane, 1913.
Garrett, Peter K. *The Victorian Multiplot Novel.* New Haven and London: Yale University Press, 1980.
Gatrell, Simon. "Jealousy, Mastery, Love and Madness: A Brief Reading of *He Knew He Was Right.*" In *Anthony Trollope.* Ed. Tony Bareham. New York: Barnes & Noble, 1980, pp. 95–99.
Gresset, Michel and Noel Polk, Eds. *Intertextuality in Faulkner.* University: Mississippi University Press, 1985.
Grossman, Richard and Andrew Wright. "Anthony Trollope's Libraries." *Nineteenth-Century Fiction,* 31 (1976), 48–64.

Hall, N. John. "Anthony Trollope: Honest and True." *Notes and Queries*, 217 (November 1972), 416–17.
———, Ed. *Salmagundi: Byron, Allegra, and the Trollope Family*. Pittsburgh: Beta Phi Mu, 1975.
———. "Trollope Reading Aloud: An Unpublished Record." *Notes and Queries*, 220 (March 1975), 117–18.
———. "Trollope's Commonplace Book, 1835–40." *Nineteenth-Century Fiction*, 31 (1976), 15–25.
———. "An Unpublished Trollope Manuscript on a Proposed History of World Literature." *Nineteenth-Century Fiction*, 29 (1974), 206–10.
Halperin, John, Ed. *Trollope Centenary Essays*. New York: St. Martin's Press, 1982.
Hansard, Henry. *Journals of the House of Commons*. Vols. 121–23. 1866–68.
Harte, Bret. *The Complete Works of Bret Harte*. 9 vols. London: Chatto & Windus, 1911.
Harvey, Geoffrey. *The Art of Anthony Trollope*. New York: St. Martin's Press, 1980.
Herbert, Christopher. "*He Knew He Was Right*, Mrs. Lynn Linton and the Duplicities of Victorian Marriage." *Texas Studies in Literature and Language*, 25 (1983), 448–69.
Horace. *The Odes Epodes and Satires of Horace*. Trans. Theodore Martin. Edinburgh: Blackwood and Sons, 1870.
Kellett, E. E. *Literary Quotation and Allusion*. Port Washington, N.Y.: Kennikat Press, 1933.
Kincaid, James R. "*Barchester Towers* and the Nature of Conservative Comedy." *Journal of English Literary History*, 37 (1970), 595–612.
———. *The Novels of Anthony Trollope*. Oxford: Clarendon Press, 1977.
King, Helen Garlinghouse. "Trollope's Letters to the *Examiner*." *Princeton University Library Chronicle*, 26 (1965), 71–101.
Klinger, Helmut. "Varieties of Failure: The Significance of Trollope's 'The Prime Minister.'" *English Miscellany*, 23 (1972), 167–83.
Kreiger, Murray. *The Classic Vision: The Retreat from Extremity in Modern Literature*. Baltimore: The Johns Hopkins University Press, 1971.
Laude, Anthony. "*Barchester Towers*: A New Source?" *Notes and Queries*, 23 (February 1976), 59–61.
Lodge, David. *The Language of Fiction*. 2nd ed. London: Routledge & Kegan Paul, 1984.
Marsh, P. T. *The Victorian Church in Decline*. London: Routledge & Kegan Paul, 1969.
Martin, Robert Bernard. *Enter Rumour: Four Early Victorian Scandals*. London: Faber and Faber, 1962.
McMaster, Juliet. *Trollope's Palliser Novels: Theme and Pattern*. London: Macmillan, 1978.
McMaster, R. D. "Women in *The Way We Live Now*." *English Studies in Canada*, VII (Spring 1981), 68–80.
Meyer, Herman. *The Poetics of Quotation in the European Novel*. Trans. Theodore and Yetta Ziolkowski. Princeton, N.J.: Princeton University Press, 1968.

Miller, J. Hillis. *Fiction and Repetition: Seven English Novels.* Cambridge, Mass.: Harvard University Press, 1982.
Milton, John. *The Poetical Works of John Milton.* Ed. Henry Todd. 7 vols. London: 1801.
Nardin, Jane. "Tragedy, Farce, and Comedy in Trollope's *He Knew He Was Right.*" *Genre,* 15 (Fall 1982), 303–13.
O'Connor, Frank. *The Mirror in the Roadway.* London: Hamish Hamilton, 1957.
Overton, W. J. "Trollope: An Interior View." *Modern Language Review,* 71 (July 1976), 489–99.
Page, Norman. "Trollope's Conversational Mode." *English Studies in Africa,* 15 (1972), 33–37.
Partridge, Eric. *A Dictionary of Clichés.* London: Routledge & Kegan Paul, 1966.
Perkins, David, Ed. *English Romantic Writers.* New York: Harcourt, Brace & World, Inc., 1967.
Perri, Carmela. "On Alluding." *Poetics,* 7 (1978), 289–307.
Polhemus, Robert M. "Being in Love in *Phineas Finn/Phineas Redux*: Desire, Devotion, Consolation." *Nineteenth-Century Fiction,* 37 (December 1982), 383–95.
———. *The Changing World of Anthony Trollope.* Berkeley and Los Angeles: University of California Press, 1968.
Pollard, Arthur. *Trollope's Political Novels.* Hull: University of Hull, 1968.
Rathburn, Robert C. and Martin Steinmann, Jr., Eds. *From Jane Austen to Joseph Conrad.* Minneapolis: University of Minnesota Press, 1958.
Sadleir, Michael. *Trollope: A Commentary.* 1945; rpt. London: Oxford University Press, 1961.
Shakespeare, William. *Shakespeare: The Complete Works.* Ed. G. B. Harrison. New York: Harcourt, Brace & World, 1968.
Slakey, Roger L. "Melmotte's Death: A Prism of Meaning in 'The Way We Live Now.'" *Journal of English Literary History,* 34 (1967), 248–59.
Snow, C. P. "Trollope: The Psychological Stream." In *On the Novel: A Present for Walter Allen on His 60th Birthday from His Friends and Colleagues.* Ed. B. S. Benedikz. London: Dent, 1971, pp. 3–16.
Speare, Morris Edmund. *The Political Novel: Its Development in England and in America.* New York: Russell and Russell, 1966.
Springer, Marlene. *Hardy's Use of Allusion.* Lawrence: University Press of Kansas, 1983.
Stevenson, Lionel. "Dickens and the Origin of *The Warden.*" *Trollopian,* II (1947), 83–90.
———. "The Rationale of Victorian Fiction." *Nineteenth-Century Fiction,* 27 (1973), 391–404.
Stone, Donald D. "Trollope, Byron, and the Conventionalities." In *The Worlds of Victorian Fiction.* Ed. Jerome H. Buckley. Cambridge, Mass.: Harvard University Press, 1975, pp. 179–203.
Super, R. H. "Trollope's *Vanity Fair.*" *Journal of Narrative Technique,* 9 (Winter 1979), 12–20.

Works Cited   225

Sutherland, John A. "Trollope at Work on *The Way We Live Now.*" *Nineteenth-Century Fiction*, 37 (December 1982), 472–93.
Tennyson, Alfred, Lord. *Tennyson's Poetry.* Ed. Robert W. Hill, Jr. A Norton Critical Edition. New York: W. W. Norton & Company, 1971.
Thackeray, William Makepeace. *Vanity Fair: A Novel Without a Hero.* Eds. Geoffrey and Kathleen Tillotson. London: Methuen, 1963.
Thale, Jerome. "The Problem of Structure in Trollope." *Nineteenth-Century Fiction*, 15 (1960), 147–57.
[Reform Bill]. *Times.* 30 October 1867, p. 5.
Tingay, Lance O. "Trollope's Library." *Notes and Queries*, 195 (October 1950), 476–78.
Torgovnick, Marianna. "Closure and Victorian Novel, 1986." *The Victorian Newsletter* (Spring 1987), 4–6.
Trollope, Anthony. *An Autobiography.* [1883]. Ed. Michael Sadleir and Frederick Page. Oxford Crown Edition, 1950.
———. *Ayala's Angel* [1881]. Intro. Simon Raven. World's Classics, 1975.
———. *Barchester Towers.* [1857]. Ed. Sadleir and Page. 2 vols. Oxford Crown, 1953; Afterw. Robert W. Daniel. Signet Classic, 1963; Intro. James R. Kincaid. World's Classics, 1980; Ed. Robin Gilmore. Penguin, 1982.
———. *Can You Forgive Her?* [1864]. Ed. Sadleir and Page. 2 vols. Oxford Crown, 1948.
———. *Catalogue of His Books.* [1874]. Forster Collection, Victoria and Albert Museum.
———. *Clergymen of the Church of England.* [1866].
———. *The Commentaries of Caesar.* [1870].
———. *Did He Steal It?* [1869].
———. *Doctor Thorne.* [1858]. World's Classics, 1963.
———. *The Duke's Children.* [1880]. Ed. Sadleir and Page. Oxford Crown, 1964.
———. *The Eustace Diamonds.* [1873]. Ed. Sadleir and Page. Oxford Crown, 1950.
———. *Framley Parsonage.* [1861]. London: Zodiac Press, 1955.
———. *The Golden Lion of Granpère.* [1872].
———. *Harry Heathcote of Gangoil: A Tale of Australian Bush Life.* [1874].
———. *He Knew He Was Right.* [1869]. World's Classics, 1963; Dover Edition, 1983.
———. *Is He Popenjoy?* [1878]. World's Classics, 1973.
———. *The Kellys and the O'Kellys.* [1848]. World's Classics, 1951.
———. *The Last Chronicle of Barset.* [1867]. Intro. Walter Allen. Notes by Ara Calder-Marshall. London: Pan Books, 1967; Intro. Bradford Booth. World's Classics, 1967; Ed. Peter Fairclough. Penguin English Library, 1967.
———. *The Letters of Anthony Trollope.* Ed. N. John Hall. 2 vols. Stanford, Calif.: Stanford University Press, 1983.
———. *The Life of Cicero.* [1880].

——. *Linda Tressel.* [1868]. World's Classics, 1951.
——. *The Macdermots of Ballycloran.* [1847]. 6th ed. London: Chapman and Hall, 1928.
——. "Never, Never—Never, Never." [1875]. Privately printed by Lance O. Tingay, 1952.
——. *The Noble Jilt.* [1923].
——. *North America.* [1862]. Penguin Books, 1968.
——. *Orley Farm.* [1862]. World's Classics, 1974.
——. *Phineas Finn: The Irish Member.* [1869]. Ed. Sadleir and Page. 2 vols. Oxford Crown, 1949; Intro. Sir Shane Leslie. World's Classics, 1969.
——. *Phineas Redux.* [1873]. Ed. Sadleir and Page. 2 vols. Oxford Crown, 1951; Intro. R. W. Chapman. World's Classics, 1970; Ed. R. W. Chapman. Oxford University Press, 1973; Ed. John C. Whale, World's Classics, 1983.
——. *The Prime Minister.* [1876]. Ed. Sadleir and Page. 2 vols. Oxford Crown, 1952; Intro. L. S. Amery. World's Classics, 1970.
——. *Rachel Ray.* [1862, dated 1863]. World's Classics, 1951.
——. *Ralph the Heir.* [1871]. World's Classics, 1951.
——. *The Small House at Allington.* [1864]. World's Classics, 1970.
——. *The Three Clerks.* [1858]. Intro. W. Teignmouth Shore. World's Classics, 1959.
——. *The Two Heroines of Plumplington.* [1953], London: André Deutsch, 1953.
——. *La Vendée: An Historical Romance.* [1850].
——. "A Walk in a Wood." *Good Words*, 20 (1879), 595–600.
——. *The Warden.* [1855]. London: Zodiac Press, 1953.
——. *The Way We Live Now.* [1875]. World's Classics, 1962; Ed. John Sutherland. World's Classics, 1982.
Trollope, Thomas A. *What I Remember.* 2 vols. London: Richard Bentley and Son, 1887.
Vernon, Patricia A. "The Poor Fictionist's Conscience: Point of View in the Palliser Novels." *Victorian Newsletter* (Spring 1987), 16–20.
Victoria, Queen of Great Britain and Ireland. *Dearest Child.* Ed. Roger Fulford. London: Evans Brothers, 1964.
Vincent, C. J. "Trollope: A Victorian Augustan." *Queen's Quarterly*, 52 (1945), 415–28.
Walpole, Hugh. *Anthony Trollope.* London: Macmillan and Company, 1928.
West, Rebecca. *The Court and the Castle: Some Treatments of a Recurrent Theme.* New Haven: Yale University Press, 1957.
West, William A. "*The Last Chronicle of Barset*: Trollope's Comic Techniques." In *The Classic British Novel.* Ed. Howard M. Harper, Jr., and Charles Edge. Athens: University of Georgia Press, 1972, pp. 121–42.
Wheeler, Michael. *The Art of Allusion in Victorian Fiction.* London: The Macmillan Press, Ltd., 1979.

Wright, Andrew. "Anthony Trollope as a Reader." In *Two English Novelists: Aphra Behn and Anthony Trollope*. University of California: William Andrews Clark Memorial Library, 1975, pp. 45–68.
Wyatt, Jean. "*Mrs. Dalloway*: Literary Allusion as Structural Metaphor." *PMLA* 88 (1973), 440–51.

Index

À Becket, Thomas, 48, 121
Abraham and Isaac, 64
Achates, 182
Achilles, 29
Adam, 188
Adam Bede, 10
Adams, Parson, 74
Addison, Thomas, 37
Admirable Crichton, 100, 167
Admiralty, Secretary of the, 131
Adonis, 193
Aeneas, 66
Aeschylus, 49, 56
Aesop, 152, 163
Agamemnon, 26
Ah Sin, 187
"Alexander's Feast," 53, 101, 106
Alf, Mr., 174
Allen, Walter, 56
Allen-a-Dale, 102, 103, 109
America, 171, 205
American, 106, 107, 186–188, 200
American, anti-, 200
American Civil War, 72
Americans, 103, 106, 199–201
Ammon, 137
Anacreon, 48
An Autobiography, 1, 77, 159
Anna Karenina, 168
Antigone, 49
Apollo, 69, 85, 100, 195
Apollyon, 133
apRoberts, Ruth, 6
Arabin, Francis, 16, 21, 22, 27, 28, 34, 36, 38–41, 43, 46, 52–54, 56–58, 61
Arabin, Mrs., 67, 70, 79. *See also* Bold, Eleanor
Archer, Isabel, 106
Arden, 23
Argus, 29
Aristides, 161
As You Like It, 23, 68
Athens, 58
Augustan, 38
Aurora Leigh, 4

Ayala's Angel, 62, 207

Baal, 32
Bacchus, 88
Bacon, Sir Francis, 4
Balderstone, Caleb, 133
Banquo, 204
Barchester, 15, 16, 20–23, 25, 28, 29, 33, 36, 38, 42–44, 47, 61, 71, 72, 75, 76, 78, 81
Barchester Towers, 4, 11, 14–17, 19, 22–24, 27, 34, 35, 41, 44–47, 50, 53–55, 57, 64–66, 71, 72, 74–77, 79–81, 83, 93, 97, 98, 101, 109, 122, 135, 170, 176, 177, 183, 190, 195, 196, 198, 206–208
Barham, Father, 204
Barkis, 27
Barnaby Rudge, 192
Barsetshire, 12, 32, 46, 48, 60, 61, 65, 74, 78, 79, 82, 83, 109, 146, 170
Barthes, Roland, 5
Bateman, Lord, 49, 57
Beargarden, 196
Beaumont and Fletcher, 20
Beeswax, Sir Timothy, 152
Behn, Aphra, 94
Belial, 133
Belisarius, 49, 51, 173
Ben-Porat, Ziva, 3
Benthamism, 15
Beverley, 120
Bible, 3, 14, 17, 24, 31, 32, 64, 71, 76, 90, 109, 136, 137, 163, 188, 195, 208
Biblical, 5, 67, 84, 94, 105, 113, 117, 136, 208
Bios, 165
Blagden, Isa, 128
Bold, Eleanor, 15, 16, 21–23, 26–28, 32, 33, 36, 38–42. *See also* Arabin, Mrs.
Bold, Mary, 40
Boleyne, Anne, 173
Boncasen, Isabel, 106

229

230 Index

Bonduca, 20
Bonnivard, 65
Bonteen, Mr., 115, 123, 132
Book of Common Prayer, 97
Booth, Bradford, 8
Bozzle, Inspector, 86, 87, 89
Brabantio, 166
Branksome, Lady of, 38
Brave New World, 122
Brehgert, Ezekiel, 194, 195, 204
"The Bride of Abydos," 165
Broadmore, 173
Brock, Lord, 147, 160
Brocklehurst, Mr., 74
Brontë, Charlotte, 2, 10
Broughton, Dobbs, 63, 66
Broughton family, 63, 65
Broughton, Mrs. Dobbs, 48, 62–66, 68, 77, 175, 177, 207
Broune, Nicholas, 176
Brown, Thomas, 98, 109
Browning, Elizabeth and Robert, 104, 109
Browning, Elizabeth Barrett, 4, 10, 87, 104, 109, 112, 118, 123, 125, 126, 128, 148, 149, 153, 157, 163
Browning, Robert, 118
Brummagem, 65
Bulwer-Lytton, Edward George Earle Lytton, 125
Bungay, 196
Bunyan, John, 31, 41, 88, 109
Burgess, Brooke, 94, 99
Burton, Richard, 37
Byron, George Gordon, Lord, 10, 11, 14, 35, 53, 61–63, 65, 66, 68, 128, 163, 165, 175, 207

Cade, Jack, 200
Caesar, 86, 109, 156, 158, 161, 190
Caesar's Commentaries, 48
Cagliostro, 121
California, 200
Californian, 187
Calvary, 58, 59
Calypso, 138
Canterbury, Archbishop of, 188
Cantrip, Lord, 124
Can You Forgive Her?, 82, 102, 143, 150
Carbury, Hetta, 99, 176, 197–200

Carbury, Lady, 35, 62, 170, 172–178, 184, 186, 188, 190, 191, 199, 205, 207
Carbury, Roger, 98, 176, 191, 192, 195, 197–201, 204
Carbury, Sir Felix, 37, 174, 176, 179, 188–194, 196, 198, 203, 204
Carlton Terrace, 167
Caroline, Queen, 173
Cassandra, 18
Catherine, 173
Cato, 37, 190
Cerberus, 18
Cervantes, Miguel de, 163
Chaffanbrass, 124, 125
Chapman, R. W., 128
Charybdis, 40, 95, 183, 207
Chaucer, Geoffrey, 6
Chiltern, Lady (Violet Effingham), 7, 124, 134
Chiltern, Lord, 112, 124, 134, 148, 164
Chiltern family, 139, 140, 143
China, Emperor of, 181
Christianity, 38
Chrysostom, 48
Church of England, 19
Cicero, 48
Cincinnatus, 153
Circe, 138
Clarence, 88
Clark, John W., 3, 11, 208
Cleopatra, 165, 173
Cloe, 164, 191
Colchis, 29
Colenso, Bishop, 97
Coningsby, 120
Conquest, 37
Conrad, 10, 62
Conservatism, 119, 197, 198
Conservative, 37, 120, 142, 144, 146
Conservatives, 112, 113, 115–118, 120, 122, 152, 162
Constitution, 119
Cooper, James Fenimore, 14
Cophetua, King, 85, 107
Coriolanus, 155
Coriolanus, 153, 155
Cornhill, 126
Corsair, 62
Cottle, Amos, 175
Crawley, Grace, 48, 49, 54, 69–75, 83, 99, 199

Index 231

Crawley, Jane, 49–51, 58, 60
Crawley, Josiah, 10–12, 30, 34, 40, 46–62, 65, 67, 70, 71, 73–81, 83, 84, 87, 90, 91, 94, 99, 114, 125, 136, 143, 156, 158, 173, 177, 192, 207
Crawley, Mrs., 60, 72
Cressid, 35
Creusa, 93, 136, 202
Criminal Queens, 173
Croesus, 180
Croll, Herr, 181
Crosbie, Adolphus, 67, 69, 80
Crumb, John, 195, 196, 200
Crumble, Mrs., 98
Cupid, 64
Cymbeline, 10

Dale family, 46
Dale, Lily, 48, 66–71, 74, 75
Dalrymple, Conway, 62–64, 207
Damocles, 200
Daniel, Robert, 15
Dante, 163, 165, 199
Dartmoor, 89
Daubney, 112, 113, 115–122, 124, 131, 132, 155, 184
Dead Sea, 118
De Arte Poetica, 48
De Courcy, Lady, 21, 34
Defoe, Daniel, 37, 177
De Guest, Lady Julia, 67, 69
Demolines, Lady, 66
Demolines, Madalina, 48, 66–68
Desdemona, 35
Dickens, Charles, 2, 6, 11, 14, 19, 27, 31, 64, 168, 208
Dido, 33, 35
Disraeli, Benjamin, 19, 120, 122, 163, 184
Dodson and Foggs, 80
Dombey and Son, 168
Don Juan, 95, 96
Don Quixote, 29, 157, 158
Dormer, Ayala, 62, 207
Dresden, 134
Druid, 20
Druidess, 38
Dryden, Thomas, 37, 53
Dublin, 113
The Duke's Children, 106, 130, 149, 159
Duncan, 155

Eames, Johnny, 48, 61, 65–70, 74, 75
Ecclesiastes, 71, 98, 182
Effingham, Violet. *See* Chiltern, Lady
Eglinton Tournament, 22, 36
Eisel, 136
Eleusinian mysteries, 37
Eli, 121
Eliot, George, 2, 6, 10, 44, 208
Elizabethan, 38
Elizabethan drama, 3
Elizabeth I, Queen, 36
Elmham, Bishop of, 197–199
Emilius, Rev., 129
"English Bards and Scotch Reviewers," 175
"Epistle to Dr. Arbuthnot," 174
Erie Railway, 186
Erle, Barrington, 113, 114, 124, 135, 139, 146, 157
Ernulfus, 31
Esau, 116
Esil, 135, 137
Esquimaux, 38
Eteocles, 49, 50
Eugene Aram, 125
Euripides, 48, 49
Eustace, Lizzie, 10, 11, 62, 165, 175, 207
The Eustace Diamonds, 141, 175, 207
Evangelicals, 19
The Examiner, 14
Exe, 95
Exeter, 86, 87, 96, 97, 100, 108
Exodus, 50, 57, 71

Fagin, 64
Falstaff, 23, 96
Faustus, 8, 9
Fell, Dr., 98
Fielding, Henry, 14, 17, 25, 37, 76, 177
Finn, Phineas, 6, 7, 10–12, 87, 98, 101, 104, 109, 111–117, 122–126, 128–141, 143, 146–149, 155, 157, 163, 164, 177, 202
Fisk, James, 186
Fisker, Hamilton K., 186–189, 192, 194, 200
Fitzgibbon, Laurence, 115
Fletcher, Arthur, 167, 168
Fletcher family, 144

Index

Fletcher, John, 168
Florence, 96, 100, 101, 103, 108
Florentine, 106
Framley Parsonage, 53, 127
French, 17–19, 24, 28, 34, 49, 140, 184, 197
French, Arabella, 83, 94
French, Camilla, 83, 93, 94, 98
French, Mrs., 98
French sisters, 95

Galileo, 202
Gamaliel, 33
Gamp, Sarah, 27
Gaza, 51, 52
George, Lady, 4
German, 135
Ghosts, 91
Giaour, 62
Gibson, Thomas, 83, 92–99, 103, 105, 108, 109
Gladstone, 133
Glascock, Mr., 87, 88, 100, 103–107
Glencora, Lady. *See* Omnium, Duchess of
Goesler, Madame Max (Mrs. Finn), 7, 112, 130, 132, 133, 135–141, 143, 146–148, 150, 152, 154, 157, 160, 205
Goethe, Wolfgang Von, 14, 39, 163, 165
Goldsmith, Oliver, 14, 40
Gomorrah, 137
Goneril, 199
Grandison, Sir Charles, 37, 67
Grantly, Archdeacon, 18, 20, 23–29, 37–39, 42, 46–49, 54, 71–75, 77, 79, 81, 136, 173
Grantly, Bishop, 49, 79
Grantly family, 42
Grantly, Griselda, 72
Grantly, Major Henry, 48, 69–73, 75, 79, 199
Grantly, Mrs., 28
Greece, 59
Greek, 26, 37, 48–50, 54, 56, 60, 68, 71, 75, 81, 84, 90, 95
Greeks, 51, 117
Greenacre family, 21
Grendall, Lord Alfred, 198
Grendall, Miles, 180
Gresham, 112, 115–119, 130, 131, 151

Gresham family, 46
Gresham, Frank, 146
Grimaldi, 34
Guardian, 37
Guatemala, 165
Gwynne, Dr., 20, 30, 42, 50
Gyas, 131

Hades, 27
Haidee, 35, 63
Haliburton, Thomas, 200
Hall, N. John, 206
Hamelin, 118
Hamlet, 67, 68, 130, 136, 200
Hamlet, 32, 55, 67, 88, 114, 125, 135, 137, 138, 140
Harding, Septimus, 12, 15–17, 21, 24, 25, 27, 28, 30, 36, 40, 42–47, 50, 74, 77–79, 81, 125, 163, 205
Hardy, Thomas, 10
Harte, Bret, 187, 188
"Heathen Chinee," 187, 188
Heavitree, 83, 87, 93, 95, 97, 105, 140
Hebrew, 54
Heep, Uriah, 32
He Knew He Was Right, 4, 11, 12, 40, 59, 82–84, 87, 109, 140, 160, 170, 171, 183, 195, 207
Helen of Troy, 9
Henry IV, Pt. I, 68
Henry IV, Pt. II, 22
Henry V, 134
Herbert, Christopher, 82
Hercules, 22
Hesperides, 22, 64
High and Dry church, 19, 20
High Church, 19
Hiram's Hospital, 14
History of English Prose Fiction, 3
History of World Literature, 3
Hogarth, William, 172
Hoggett, Giles, 59, 60
Hogglestock, 48, 50, 57, 61
Holy Land, 58
Homer, 40
Hood, Robin, 112
Horace, 48, 113, 122, 131, 197, 204
Hurtle, Winifred, 171, 172, 184, 186, 188, 200–203, 205
Hyperion, 167

Iachimo, 10

Iago, 89, 90
Ibsen, Henrik, 91
Ichabod, 115
Idler, 37
Iliad, 15
Imogen, 35, 63
Indians, 38
Ireland, 116
Ireland, Secretary of, 131
Irish, 113
Irish Church, 121
Isaac, 64
Isaiah, 57, 58, 60, 117
Is He Popenjoy?, 4
Israel, 52, 137
Italian, 34, 71, 152
Ivanhoe, 36

Jacob, 67, 68
Jacobean drama, 3, 23
Jael and Sisera, 21, 48, 61, 62, 64, 65, 83
Jane Eyre, 10
Jaques, 23
Jason, 93, 136
Jew (Jewish, Jewishness), 121, 124, 166, 182, 194, 195, 203
Jewess, 135
Jezebel, 34
Joanna, 173
Job, 78, 94, 113
Jocasta, 50
Jove, 131, 132, 180
Juan, 63
Judah, 166
Judas, 97
Juggernaut, 174
Julia, 173
Juliet, 35
Julius Caesar, 190, 191
Juno, 26, 76, 98, 99, 139

Kellett, E. E., 11
The Kellys and the O'Kellys, 14
Kenilworth, 125
Kennedy, Robert, 132, 133, 138, 140
Kilkenny cats, 204
Kincaid, James, 41
Kings II, 94
Kingston Harbour, 114

Laertes, 135–137
Laius, 50

Lambro's Island, 63
The Language of Fiction, 12
Languish, Lydia, 101
The Last Chronicle of Barset, 11, 18, 21, 30, 46–48, 50, 53, 55, 60, 61, 66, 72–74, 81, 83, 84, 86, 101, 109, 114, 117, 125, 160, 170, 173, 175, 192, 196, 199, 207
Latin, 1, 3, 18, 19, 48, 49, 59, 80, 81, 86, 117, 118, 122, 125, 140, 168, 204, 207, 208
Laud, Archbishop, 48
Laura, Lady (Kennedy and Standish), 6, 7, 88, 111, 112, 124, 130–140, 202
La Vendée, 14, 18
Leander, 67
Lear, 4, 84, 87, 89–91, 155, 157
Lear, 63, 89, 91, 104, 109, 153, 155, 163, 199
Lerner, Laurence, 68
Levites, 121
Liberal, 115, 117, 118, 120, 142, 152
Liberals, 112, 113, 115, 116, 120, 122, 123, 162
Little Dorrit, 19, 185
The Lives of the Saints, 10
Lodge, David, 12
London, 12, 34, 46, 48, 61, 65, 113–116, 134, 170, 171, 177, 181, 185, 186, 189–192, 194–196, 204, 205
Londoners, 201
London-Rome, 190, 197
Longestaffe, Dolly, 188, 189, 200, 204
Longestaffe family, 194
Longestaffe, Georgiana, 194, 195, 198, 204
Longestaffe, Mr., 180, 195, 197
Lookaloft family, 21
Lopez, Emily (Wharton), 145, 156, 164, 165, 167
Lopez, Ferdinand, 12, 30, 63, 142, 144, 145, 152, 153, 156, 162–168, 175, 191, 207
Lopez-Wharton, 142, 149, 163, 167
Lothario, 39, 93, 94, 96, 192, 206
"The Lovers' Resolution," 67
Love's Labour's Lost, 22, 37, 64
Low Church, 28
Low, Mr., 125
Lowestoffe, 202
Lucifer, 34, 99

234 Index

Lucretia, 42
Lufton family, 46, 74
Lufton, Lady, 60, 73, 75
Luke, 57, 199
"Lycidas," 32, 54, 135, 203
The Lyrical Ballads, 10

Macbeth, 154, 157
Macbeth, 23, 32, 55, 125, 153–157, 163
Macbeth, Lady, 23, 154, 155, 157
The Macdermots of Ballycloran, 14
MacHugh, Mrs., 98
Malvolio, 67, 68
Mammon, 182
Manchester Square, 167
Mann, Mr., 116
Marlowe, Christopher, 8, 9
Marmaduke, Sir (Rowley), 85, 88, 91, 95
Mary, Queen of Scots, 173
Mason, Lady, 7–9, 17, 125, 136
Mason, Lucius, 9
Matching, 162
Matthew, 94, 105, 198
Maule, Gerard, 139
Maule, Mr., 139, 140
McMaster, Juliet, 6, 130
McMaster, R. D., 194
Medea, 16, 29, 30, 93, 136, 178, 180, 202, 204, 207
Medean, 135, 136, 137
Medora, 62
Melchisedek, 121
Melmotte, Augustus, 12, 63, 170–174, 176–192, 194, 197, 198, 200–204, 207
Melmotte, Madam, 180, 194
Melmotte, Marie, 178, 180, 189–196, 198
Mentor, 40
The Merchant of Venice, 166
Merdle, Mr., 185
Meredith, George, 11
Merry Andrew, 94
Mill, John S., 106, 109
Miller, Daisy, 106
Miller, J. Hillis, 1
Milton, John, 14, 18, 31, 51, 52, 173, 203
Mista, 36
Mizener, Arthur, 163
Moab, 137

Moabitish woman, 135, 137
The Mob, 184
Molière, 163, 165
Monk, Mr., 124, 145
Monogram, Lady, 195, 203, 204
Monogram, Sir Damask, 204
Montague, Paul, 176, 184–187, 198–203
Montaigne, 37
Moore, Tom, 53, 61
Mount Ida, 26
Mowbray Street, 108
Mrs. Dalloway, 10
Mudie, 167
"A Musical Instrument," 10, 11, 109, 112, 118, 123, 126, 128, 132, 137, 140, 141, 148, 153, 155, 159, 163

Napoleon, 183, 184, 186, 201
Nardin, Jane, 83, 110
Neroni, Madeline, 20, 21, 22, 29, 32–35, 37, 40, 41, 64, 176, 177, 198, 208
Nestor, 146
Newman, Mr., 140
"A New Tale of a Tub," 174
New York, 190
Nidderdale, Lord, 183, 187, 188, 189, 191, 193, 195
Nineteen Eighty-four (1984), 122
Niobe, 156
The Noble Jilt, 14
Norman, 18, 36, 37
Numbers, 137

Oakhurst, John, 188
O'Connor, Frank, 52
Odyssey, 48
Oedipus, 49–51
Old Testament, 50
Omnium, Duchess of (Lady Glencora), 29, 35, 68, 138–140, 142–146, 149–157, 159–161, 163, 164, 167–169, 176, 177, 194, 208
Omnium, Duke of (old), 137, 138, 141, 156–158
Omnium, Duke of (Plantagenet Palliser), 7, 12, 82, 86, 109, 119, 128, 138, 142–158, 160–163, 166–169, 208
Onesimus, 28, 42
Ophelia, 35, 136, 140
Oregon, 201

Index 235

Orlando, 95
Orley Farm, 7, 9, 124, 125
Orme, Sir Peregrine, 9
Osborne, Colonel, 85–87, 93, 97, 99
Ossas, 135–137
Othello, 4, 84, 89, 90, 156
Othello, 89–91, 109, 125, 153, 166
"The Outcast of Poker Flats," 188
Outhouse, Mr., 88, 107
Overton, W. J., 73
Oxford, 15, 22, 38, 42
Oxford Movement, 14, 15

Paladin, 95, 98
Palliser, Adelaide, 139, 140
Palliser Coalition, 150, 154, 168
Palliser family, 139, 140
Palliser, Glencora. *See* Omnium, Duchess of
Palliser novels, 109, 142. *See also Phineas Redux* and *The Prime Minister*
Palliser, Plantagenet. *See* Omnium, Duke of
Pan, 127–129
Paris, 26
Parker, Sexty, 145, 166
Parker's Hotel, 108
Parliament (House of Commons), 115, 117, 118, 120, 121, 129–131, 143, 146, 147, 156, 164, 165, 181, 185
Peel, Sir Robert, 37
The People's Banner, 132, 161
Perri, Carmela, 3
Peterborough, Lady, 105
Petrie, Wallachia, 96, 98, 103–107, 109, 201
Petruchio, 31
Pharisee, 116
Philemon, 28, 29
Philistian, 52
Phillip Van Artevelde, 39
Philpotts, Dr., 48
Phineas Finn, 6, 7, 82, 98, 111, 114, 133, 134, 138, 141
Phineas Redux, 11, 38, 43, 59, 88, 93, 104, 111, 112, 120–122, 126, 133, 134, 138, 139, 141–144, 146–149, 155, 156, 159, 161, 164, 170, 182, 202, 207
"The Pied Piper of Hamelin," 118
Pindar, 48, 49
Pipkin, Mrs., 201

Pitt, Sir William, 152
"Plain Language from Truthful James," 187
Plumstead, 39, 71
Polhemus, Robert, 133, 163
Polynices, 50
Polyphemus, 49, 51
Pomona, Lady, 204
Pompey, 158, 159
Pope, Alexander, 38, 76, 174
Portuguese, 166
Potiphar's wife, 64
Prague, 135
Prettymans, the Misses, 80, 81
The Prime Minister, 11, 18, 29, 30, 35, 38, 43, 59, 86, 112, 119, 130, 139, 140, 142–150, 154, 156–159, 161, 163, 175, 176, 181, 182, 207, 208
The Princess, 102
"The Prisoner of Chillon," 63, 65
Proudie, Bishop, 20, 25, 29, 42, 59, 76–78
Proudie, Mrs., 14, 16, 20, 21, 23–26, 29–31, 33, 34, 43, 48–51, 55–57, 66, 72, 75–78, 80, 98
Proudie family, 46, 47, 49, 50, 72, 75, 80
Proudie Reception, 19, 21, 23, 25
Proverbs, 51, 57
Psalms, 57, 196

Quirk, Gammon, and Snaps, 80
Quiverful, Mrs., 16, 30
Quiverful family, 196
Quixotic, 156, 157
Quixoticism, 163

Rabelais, 18, 48
Rachel, 67
Rachel Ray, 55
Ralph the Heir, 4, 120
Rambler, 37
The Rape of the Lock, 37
Rasselas, 10
Rattler, Mr., 115, 153
Reform Bill of 1867, 120
Regan, 199
Richard III, 88
Richards, Mrs., 108
Richmond, 103
The Rivals, 101
Robarts, Mark, 49, 56, 75, 80
Robinson Crusoe, 177

Index

Robson edition, 29
Roby, Mr., 145
Roman, 37, 42, 56, 171, 178, 190, 197
Romans, 57
Rome, 58, 101, 113, 171, 177, 190, 192, 198, 204
Romulus, 139
Rosalind, 23, 68
Rousseau, 128
Rowena, Lady, 36
Rowley, Lady, 85, 102
Rowley, Nora, 83, 92, 96, 99–103, 106–108
Rubens, 33
Rubicon, 101
Ruddles, Gadmire, and Traddles, 117
Ruggles, Ruby, 192, 195, 196, 198
Ruth, 137

Sabbath, 29
Sadleir, Michael, 6
Samson, 49–52, 173
"Samson Agonistes," 10, 51, 52, 60
Satan, 133, 180
Satyr, 167
Saulsby, 137
Savonarola, 202
Saxon, 81
Saxon, Cedric the, 37
Scenes of Clerical Life, 44
Scott, Sir Walter, 14, 17, 22, 36, 38, 102, 103, 109, 125, 134
Scripture, 25, 30, 32, 39, 48, 50, 52, 57, 59, 65, 69, 78, 84, 88, 94, 99, 105, 117, 182, 195, 196, 198, 199
Scylla, 40, 95, 183, 207
Sedley, Amelia, 41
Semitism, anti-, 194, 204
Seven Against Thebes, 10, 49, 81
Shakespeare, William, 3, 4, 14, 22, 23, 31, 35, 37, 63, 67, 87, 90, 94, 109, 134–136, 149, 153–155, 159, 163, 165–168, 208
Shallow, Justice, 140
Sharp, Becky, 10, 34, 41
Shelley, Percy B., 10, 11
Sheridan, Richard, 109
Shittim, 137
Shylock, 166
Siddons, Mrs., 98
Sidonia, 19

Siena, 91
Silverbridge, 155
Sinbad, 18
Skogula, 36
Slakey, Roger, 184
Slick, Sam, 200
Slide, Quintus, 132, 133, 147–149, 155, 157, 160, 161
Slop, Dr., 26, 31, 32
Slope, Obadiah, 18, 20, 21, 23–35, 38–43, 198
The Small House at Allington, 6, 65, 66, 69, 145, 196
Smith, Adam, 139
Snow, C. P., 47
Sodom, 137
Solomon, 188
Solon, 188
Sorrows of Young Werther, 39
Spalding, Caroline, 83, 96, 98, 100, 101, 103, 105–107
Spalding, Jonas, 106
Spalding, Olivia, 106
Spartan, 168
Spectator, 37
Spenser, Edmund, 38
Spooner, Ned, 140
Spooner, Tom, 140
Spooner family, 140
Spooner-Maule story, 140
Squercum, Mr., 204
St. Augustine, 48
St. Bartholomew, 42
St. Bungay, Duke of, 116, 143, 146, 148, 152, 157, 160, 161, 168
St. Ewold's, 28, 36, 39, 65, 79, 81
St. Fabricius, 182
St. Lorenzo, 42
St. Paul, 28, 29, 35, 42, 57, 58, 67, 80
St. Sebastian, 42
Stag and Antlers, 100
Stanbury, Dorothy, 83, 94, 96–100, 105, 107
Stanbury, Hugh, 85, 89, 98–103
Stanbury, Jemima, 95–100, 103
Stanbury, Priscilla, 100
Stanbury story, 86, 95
Stanhope, Bertie, 20, 25, 26, 40
Stanhope, Dr. Vesey, 20
Stanhope family, 19, 40
Steele, Richard, 37

Index   237

Sterne, Lawrence, 14, 17, 26, 27, 31, 32, 40
Stone Buildings, 167
Strand Theatre, 131
Suffolk, 170, 171, 179, 192, 195–197, 205
Sunday, 40, 133
Sunday School, 35
Swift, Jonathan, 37, 174

Tadpole, 120
Talleyrand, 132
The Taming of the Shrew, 31
Tankerville, 117, 131
Taper, 120
Tappertit, Sim, 192
Tarquin, 42
Tatler, 37
Taylor, Jeremy, 99
Taylor, Sir Henry, 3, 14, 39
Tempest, 117
Tempest, Dr., 54, 60, 77
Tennyson, Alfred, Lord, 99, 100, 102, 109
"Tenway Junction," 168
Thackeray, William Makepeace, 2, 10, 11, 14, 17, 22, 41, 109, 208
Thais, 53, 61, 101, 206
Thames, 107
Thebes, 50
Thorne family, 22, 36, 37, 39, 43, 46, 74, 81
Thorne, Monica, 16, 19, 36–38
Thorne, Mrs., 75
Thorne, Wilfred, 22, 34, 36, 37, 64
The Three Clerks, 5, 67, 99, 124, 175
Three-fingered Jack, 131
Thumble, Rev., 49, 54, 56, 76
Tibur, 113
Timon of Athens, 87
Timothy I and II, 32
Tolstoy, Leo, 10, 168
Tom Jones, 177
Toogood, Lucy, 53, 61, 62, 175, 207
Toogood, Mr., 53–58, 60–62, 65, 79, 80
Toogood, Polly, 62
Tory, 37, 120
Tracts, 140
Treasury Bench, 119
Trevelyan, Emily, 85–88, 90–92, 96, 100, 107, 108
Trevelyan, Louey, 88, 91

Trevelyan, Louis, 4, 12, 82–87, 89–97, 101–103, 106–110, 133, 136, 144, 207
Tristram Shandy, 26, 31
Troilus, 35
Trollope, Anthony, 1–7, 9–15, 17–19, 22–25, 31, 32, 34, 35, 38, 41, 43–49, 55, 59–62, 64, 65, 70–73, 77, 80–84, 87–89, 91–94, 99–104, 108, 109, 111, 113, 120–122, 124, 126–128, 130, 133, 137, 141, 142, 144, 147–151, 153, 157, 159–163, 166, 168–170, 172, 174, 175, 178, 184, 188, 189, 194, 196, 197, 200, 205–208
Trollope, Thomas A., 128
Trotwood, Betsey, 97
Tryan, Edgar, 44
Tusser, Thomas, 14
Tyler, Wat, 200

Ullathorne, 18, 38, 40, 41
Ullathorne Sports, 15, 18, 19, 21–23, 26, 27, 33, 34, 36–39, 65, 83, 93
Ulrica, 36
Underwood, Sir Thomas, 4
United States, 104

Vanity Fair, 10, 20, 41
Van Siever, Clara, 62, 64
Vera Cruz, 186
Victoria, Queen, 119, 150
Victorian, 3, 82, 96
Victorians, 17
Virgil, 203, 204
Von Moltke, 121

Walpole, Horace, 116
War and Peace, 10
The Warden, 14, 20, 22, 27, 40, 42, 48
Warwick, 146
Washington, George, 200, 201
The Way We Live Now, 11, 12, 18, 35, 37, 40, 43, 70, 86, 93, 98, 135, 149, 170, 171, 178, 199, 203, 205, 207
Werther, 39
West, William, 4, 47
Western, Squire, 37
Westminster, 116, 198
Wharton, Abel, 164–168

Wharton, Emily. *See* Lopez
Wharton, Everett, 164
Wharton family, 142, 144
Wheeler, Michael, 3
The Wheel of Fortune, 177
Whig, 117, 120
Whiston Matter, 14
Whitehall, 113, 116
Windsor, 150, 151

Wither, George, 3, 67, 68
Wolsey, Cardinal, 48
Woodward girls, 99
Woolf, Virginia, 10

Yankee, 115

Zephaniah, 137
Zernebock, 36